Online Investing

FULLY UPDATED 6TH EDITION

Online Investing

FULLY UPDATED 6TH EDITION

RESEARCH, TRADE AND INVEST ON THE AUSTRALIAN SHARE MARKET

Roger Kinsky

WILEY

This sixth edition first published 2026 by John Wiley & Sons Australia, Ltd

ISBN: 978-1-394-41658-5

NATIONAL LIBRARY OF AUSTRALIA

A catalogue record for this book is available from the National Library of Australia

Registered Office
John Wiley & Sons Australia, Ltd. Level 4, 600 Bourke Street, Melbourne, VIC 3000, Australia

For details of our global editorial offices, customer services, and more information about Wiley products visit us at www.wiley.com.

Wiley also publishes its books in a variety of electronic formats and by print-on-demand. Some content that appears in standard print versions of this book may not be available in other formats.

At the time of writing, CommSec brokerage for Australian share trades is as shown in table 5.1. For international shares and other types of trades, please consult the CommSec site.

Cover design by Wiley

Set in 11/14pt and Liberation Serif by Straive, Chennai, India.

Contents

Acknowledgements

I would like to thank CommSec for permission to reproduce information from its website, which continues to be the most popular share investing website in Australia. I would also like to thank my editor, Kerry Laundon, for her many pertinent comments and suggestions that I'm sure have improved this edition of the book.

Introduction

Share research, trading and investing are ideally suited to the online world. Trading is the process of buying or selling shares, whereas investing is about longer-term share ownership and management. Traders aim to make profits from short-term trading by selling shares at a better price than they paid for them, whereas investors aim to grow their wealth over the longer term.

Traditionally, share research trading and investing were the domain of offline brokers and advisers who provided their clients with information and advice, and arranged the trades. Nowadays this information is readily obtained online, and online investing can be carried out quickly, conveniently and cheaply. Some investors still prefer to use an adviser, but the majority of investors and traders have moved online entirely, which is unsurprising—a huge amount of information and resources are readily available online, much of it at no cost.

This leads to what I call the 'Kinsky Principle':

> ***Never pay for any share information or facilities unless you are sure you can't obtain the information or facility for free.***

That said, if you decide to invest online then you're on your own and need to make decisions without guidance from an adviser. To do this effectively, you need a reasonable level of knowledge and expertise, which is where this book comes in. It provides all the information you need to make sound and profitable investing and trading decisions. In these pages, I have included many tips and suggestions gleaned from my 30-odd years of share investing, and if you follow them you should be able to avoid disaster and tip the balance of probabilities in your favour.

This is the sixth edition of this book, which has been thoroughly updated to keep abreast of changes and developments since the last edition. As the title suggests, the book's primary focus is on investing; also, I concentrate on Australian shares and don't delve in any great depth into overseas investing or trading in some of the more exotic investment instruments, such as currency (forex), options, futures, cryptocurrencies or CFDs (contracts for difference).

I've aimed to make this new edition completely up to date and error free, and my publisher has done a fine job of assisting me in this endeavour. However, perfection is very difficult to achieve, so if you spot any apparent discrepancies, if you have suggestions for improvement or if you'd simply like to offer feedback, please email me at **rkinsky@bigpond.com.** Alternatively, you can contact me via my website: rogerkinskyshares.com.au. I'll be very happy to hear from you and promise to respond promptly. Bear in mind that online content changes constantly, so some of the websites I recommend and the more detailed information I provide may have evolved by the time you access them.

Finally, I wish you every success as an online investor and trust that this book will prove valuable in helping you to achieve your investment goals.

Roger Kinsky

Chapter 1
Online investing basics

In this chapter I explain some basic concepts and terminology associated with online share investing. I also outline why it's a good option to trade shares online, some potential pitfalls and how to avoid them. I'll start from the beginning, so if you have some knowledge and experience with shares and investing you may choose to skim quickly through this chapter.

Using the internet for investing

Investing is one situation where the internet has revolutionised business dealings. Physical share-trading floors are now obsolete. More and more investors are trading online without dealing with an offline broker or financial adviser.

Tip

If you decide to invest online via apps or websites, be aware that hacking is a growth industry. Hackers are becoming increasingly sophisticated in the way they present false information, making it look authentic. You should have security on your device but, even so, hackers can often work around these defences. Be vigilant at all times to ensure that the information you receive is authentic and your share trading and financial accounts are secure. Never scan a QR code (it's the same as clicking an online link) unless you're sure the linked page is safe. The rule is 'if in doubt, leave it out'.

Increasing competition among online investment service providers means they are constantly looking for ways to increase their market share. Fees and charges have been decreasing, while the amount of information and services available has been increasing.

For example, you can now trade online for a cost of only 0.12% of the trade value, with a minimum charge of $5 or so. This makes share investing feasible even for small investors, as you don't need a big cash pool to get started.

Tip

Increasing competition is good news for online investors, and the resulting favourable benefits are likely to continue into the future.

Investing

Investing implies the following two conditions:

- You have an available cash pool. Perhaps you've saved this spare cash from your income, or you may have inherited some assets, received a tax refund or had a financial windfall. In some cases, investing capital is obtained from an investment loan, which for the purpose of investing in shares is known as a margin loan.
- You want this cash to produce a profitable return. That's to say, you want to grow your wealth—to 'put your money to work' as opposed to 'allowing your money to take a holiday'.

Taxation

If you obtain income from investments of any type, you'll most likely need to submit a tax return each year to the Australian Taxation Office (ATO). For an investor, taxation is a very important consideration because your real earnings from any investment are after-tax earnings. For example, if you make 50% profit on your investments and are taxed at a rate of 30%, your real return (after-tax) reduces to 35%.

Tip

I'll discuss ways to minimise tax on your investing profits in later chapters, but for now bear in mind that your real earnings on any investment are your after-tax earnings.

Inflation

Inflation is an increase in the average price of goods and services. This increase is measured using a price index, typically a consumer price index (CPI). Australia has a relatively stable inflation rate, which is usually around 3%. Inflation of 3% means that any cash or assets you hold lose 3% of their value each year due to inflation alone.

Tip

If inflation is running at 3%, you need to achieve the same increase in the value of your assets just to stand still. In order to grow your wealth, you need an after-tax return of better than 3%.

Investment instrument (security)

An investment instrument or security is a general term that applies to any asset or commodity that can be used for the purpose of investing. In this book I'll concentrate on shares, but they are just one type of security. There are many others, including bonds, managed funds, hybrids, derivatives (such as CFDs, forex, options, warrants), fixed-interest securities and rare metals, such as gold.

Tip

Unless you're an experienced investor, I suggest you avoid the more sophisticated instruments.

If you're interested in investing in securities other than shares, the principles I outline in this book should still apply. Just substitute the word 'security' for 'share'.

Capital

Capital is a business term that means wealth. It can be money that's directly available (such as cash in the bank) or the monetary value of assets. The difference between cash and capital is that capital isn't necessarily in the form of directly available cash. In fact, most of the capital in a business isn't in cash but rather in the form of property, stock, machinery, equipment and debtors.

Tip

While a business may have a certain amount of capital (as shown in its books of account), a great deal of this may be tied up in stock or assets that won't necessarily have the same cash value if they're sold.

Businesses, stocks, shares and portfolio

A business is a separate legal entity and must be set up and operated legally. There are various types of business in Australia, including:

- *Sole trader (also known as a sole proprietor):* This is a one-person business; that is, it is owned and operated by one person. It typically applies to a tradesperson, shop owner or entrepreneur exploiting some niche in the market.
- *Partnership:* Here, a number of people jointly own the business. In larger partnerships it's often the case that one or more of the partners may not actually take part in the day-to-day operation of the business.

- *Proprietary company (private company):* A company has a legal identity distinct from the owners and needs to submit a separate tax return and pay tax at the company rate. Proprietary companies are usually relatively small ones and are identified by Pty Ltd after their name. The Pty indicates it is a proprietary company, while the Ltd indicates that the liability of the company is limited—that is, the liability of the business is quite distinct from that of the owners.
- *Public company:* Larger companies are often public ones and owned by many people. These companies issue shares that can be purchased by the general public, and those who own shares become shareholders in the business. Usually, the directors of the company are major shareholders.
- *Trust:* A trust is set up by a trust deed and enables a number of people to share in a business venture. An investment trust issues units rather than shares. There are many types of trust, but the most common investment trust is a property trust.

A public company obtains much of the capital it needs by issuing a number of shares at a certain price. This capital is known as equity capital because the capital is obtained from shareholders (investors) who have equity (or ownership) in the business.

Shares are units of ownership. When you own shares in a company, you effectively become a part-owner of the company, and this gives you the right to participate in the company's management. You have voting rights and can vote at any company meetings that are open to shareholders. Shares are also known as equities, because shareholders have ownership, or equity, in the company and a claim to a share of the company's assets and profits.

The total number of shares issued by a company is known as stock, but this word is also often used to describe the company itself. For example, you can own a number of different stocks (such as Telstra and ANZ Bank), and you can own a different number of shares in each. Your total holding of all the shares you own is known as your portfolio.

Initial public offering (float)

When a company first offers shares that can be taken up by the general public, this is known as an initial public offering (IPO) or 'float'. The float is usually underwritten, which means a broking firm or financial institution undertakes to purchase any shares left over if the offer is under-subscribed. Shares in an IPO can be purchased by an investor by application using a document known as a prospectus that contains all information of relevance to potential investors.

Some floats have proved successful long-term investments (such as Commonwealth Bank and CSL), but many floats are risky for the simple reason that there's no track record of the business operating as a public company.

Tip

I suggest you avoid IPOs unless you have some very reliable information that persuades you the investment is likely to be profitable.

Splits and amalgamations

Sometimes a company will decide to split or amalgamate its shares. A split usually occurs when the share price is high and considered by the directors to be unaffordable for the average investor. For example, a 2:1 split means there are twice as many shares available but each share is half the price (and therefore more affordable).

An amalgamation is the opposite—when the share price is low and in the 'penny dreadful' category. By amalgamating shares, there are less shares available but each share becomes more valuable.

Tip

If you own shares in a company that splits or amalgamates its shares, you don't need to take any action as the change occurs automatically.

Securities exchange

For shares in a public company to be traded by the general public, the company must be listed with a securities exchange and so become a 'listed company'. Before a securities exchange can operate in Australia, it must have a licence granted to it by the Australian Securities and Investments Commission (ASIC). Most Australian companies are listed with Australian exchanges, but a few are listed with overseas exchanges because their business is more relevant to an overseas country. Some shares are listed on both Australian and overseas exchanges, and these can be traded directly by investors overseas and at times when our exchange is closed.

In order to be listed with a securities exchange, a company has to pay fees and comply with listing rules that can be quite stringent and are designed to protect investors. After listing, the company must comply with ongoing rules and may be investigated for possible breaches of rules or behaviour that appears suspect—such as a sudden change in the market price or traded volume of their shares without any obvious reason. Listing rules also stipulate that any new information of relevance to shareholders must be submitted to the exchange by the company and be available to the public before being divulged to privileged parties or released to the press. This rule is designed to eliminate 'insider trading', where a select number of people in the know can profit from information that's not available to the general public.

In Australia, the following securities exchanges operate:

- Australian Securities Exchange (ASX), which provides listing and trading in securities and derivatives including shares, futures, options and warrants. It also provides clearing and settlement of trades through CHESS (I'll outline CHESS in chapter 5).
- National Stock Exchange (NSX), which specifically caters for the listing of small to medium enterprises. Not all brokers are licensed to trade on this exchange, so if you want to trade shares listed on the exchange you need to check.

- Cboe Australia (formerly Chi-X Australia) is a day-only trading exchange. This means orders can't be left overnight. Using Cboe may mean your orders are executed faster when compared to the ASX (as there can be less of a backlog of other orders to compete with). Cboe has exchange-traded funds (ETFs) and managed funds that aren't available on the ASX.

Notes:

- In some cases, a business may choose to list its shares on several exchanges. For example, some shares listed on the New Zealand exchange are also listed on the ASX. In this case you can trade shares in the business using the Australian exchange.
- The ASX is by far the largest and most widely used exchange in Australia, with over 90% of market share and more than 2000 listed entities, so it's the one I'll be concentrating on in this book.
- Nowadays, the ASX may shuffle share trades with one of the other exchanges in order to get a better deal, but this will make no difference to you as an investor.

Delisting and suspension

A listed company can be delisted; that is, it will no longer be listed with the securities exchange and the shares cannot be traded using its trading facility. A common cause of delisting is that a company restructures or is taken over and becomes a new entity. Other causes are bankruptcy, a major breach of legal requirements or exchange rules, or non-payment of fees. Delisting is usually permanent.

Voluntary suspension of share trading may also be imposed by the exchange at the request of the directors, usually because some major change is in the offing and the directors want to prevent speculative trading based on rumour rather than fact. This type of suspension is generally only temporary, usually for no more than a day or two. Such a suspension of share trading is known as a trading halt.

> **Tip**
>
> Voluntary suspension of share trading can be good or bad news for investors, depending on the nature of the change being considered by the directors. Enforced delisting is almost always bad news as any shares owned by investors become virtually worthless. Remember that the value of almost anything depends on what a buyer is willing to pay for it, so if it can't be sold it's essentially valueless.

Market cap

Market cap (market capitalisation) is a measure of the size of a company as reflected by the money invested in its shares. It's obtained by multiplying the number of shares on issue by the share price. When the share price changes, the market cap changes too. Large Australian companies have market caps of billions of dollars, whereas smaller ones may be only a hundred or so million dollars.

The value of a share

A company owns assets and has liabilities, and its assets should exceed its liabilities. This gives the intrinsic value of the company. If this value (assets – liabilities) is divided by the number of issued shares, the result is the intrinsic value of each share—which is known as the book value. This value changes only when the financial statistics are updated (usually twice a year).

> **Tip**
>
> There used to be a value similar to the book value called the 'par value' that was supposed to reflect the intrinsic value of a share, but this is now obsolete.

The true value of a security is what a willing buyer will pay a willing seller for it, which is known as the market value (or market price). This value changes continually with each transaction. For a profitable company, the market value of its shares is usually well above the book value—meaning the investors value their shares more highly than their intrinsic value. For example, at the time of writing, Commonwealth Bank shares were trading at about $160 but its book value was only about $45. This shows the huge premium shareholders are prepared to pay for these shares. On the other hand, a small struggling company had a book value of about 25 cents and the shares were trading at 23.3 cents. This shows that shareholders weren't very optimistic about the prospects for this company.

Tip

The market is focused forward into the future rather than backward into the past. Therefore, the market value of a share is strongly influenced by investors' perceptions of the future prospects of a business. Unfortunately, this is sometimes based on rumour or hype rather than fact.

Types of shares

There are many different types of shares, including the following:

- Ordinary shares (also known as fully paid ordinary shares or FPOs)—these are the most common shares owned and traded.
- Contributing shares (also known as partly paid shares)—these are usually issued so that part of the price is payable immediately and a balance is then due by an instalment, or instalments, payable in the future.
- Preference shares—these shares are given some preferential treatment over ordinary shares, such as first right to a dividend or company assets in the event of liquidation. They are similar to bonds in that they provide a regular income and usually have a fixed maturity date. Convertible preference shares can be converted to ordinary shares under defined conditions. They are also known as hybrids as they provide a fixed income as well as the prospect of capital gain income.

- Company-issued options—these give the holder the right (but not the obligation) to obtain shares in the company at some future point in time at a stated price.
- Rights—these are similar to company-issued options except the time period is usually much shorter and the rights are issued only to current shareholders.
- Bonus shares—these are additional shares issued free of charge to current shareholders. In the past, companies often issued these as an intended reward to shareholders, but bonus issues are now very rare, because in fact shareholders didn't benefit as the price fell proportionally after the issue.

Informal ways of looking at shares

As well as the officially recognised types of shares outline in the preceding section, investors and advisers often use an informal terminology to classify shares. There are some common terms you can expect to encounter:

- Blue chip—these are the shares of large, well-known and well-established companies that make a consistently good profit. They have a high market share, a relatively high market value (market price) and a high market cap. They usually pay a regular, worthwhile dividend that's franked (franking will be discussed later in this chapter). The shares are considered to be the safest, so they're also known as 'defensives' because they're less prone to large price falls. They're a favourite of 'mum and dad' investors; that is, average Australians with no special share investing or trading expertise who want a relatively safe haven for their savings.
- Green chip—these are shares in smaller businesses that have a relatively stable track record but are a little more risky than blue chips and less expensive. They include regional banks, medium-sized established retailers, industrials and others. Some pay a good dividend (which in some cases is fully franked) but others may not pay a dividend at all.

- Fallen angel—this is a blue- or green-chip share that has fallen on hard times, with a major reduction in profitability and consequently a big drop in the share price (and most likely a drop in its dividend).
- Growth—these are shares in a business considered to have excellent prospects for growth. They usually pay no dividend and re-invest profits back into the business to provide the funds needed for growth and expansion. If the anticipated growth does eventuate then the share price is likely to increase, so these companies present the possibility of good capital gains.
- Value—these are shares in a business that appear to be undervalued by investors; that is, they appear cheap relative to the earnings and can be trading at a price below their intrinsic value.
- Speculative—these are shares in smaller companies that don't have a proven track record of profitability. They usually don't pay a dividend and they're considered risky as they often trade on 'blue sky potential'; that is, possible future profitability (that may or may not actually eventuate). Companies in this category include pharmaceutical or health care companies whose fortunes depend on whether or not the drug or health technology they are developing proves to be successful.
- Penny dreadful—as the name suggests, these are shares that trade at a low price (sometimes only a few cents) and are risky investments. There is the possibility of large profits if there the company experiences a favourable turn in its fortunes but also the possibility of a total wipeout.

These informal share classes are not necessarily mutually exclusive. For example, a blue- or green-chip stock may appear undervalued, while a small mining company may be speculative and a penny dreadful at the same time.

Tip

If you're wanting to grow your wealth long term, I suggest you avoid speculative and penny dreadful shares. While they offer the prospect of large profits, you can also lose heaps in price downturns.

Volatility

Volatility is a measure of the extent and rapidity of percentage price fluctuations. For example, a $1 price change in a $10 share is a 10% change, and if this happened in one day it would indicate high volatility. However, a $1 price change in one day on a $50 share (a 2% change) indicates much lower volatility. Volatility can be applied to the market as a whole or to any sector of the market. It's usually high in times of uncertainty, when investors become jittery because the future direction of the market seems less predictable.

> **Tip**
>
> As I explain in later chapters, volatility and price risk are closely related, so the more volatile shares are also the more risky.

Trading and parcel

Trading is the act of buying or selling. When you trade shares, you buy or sell a 'parcel'; that is, a certain number of shares with a certain value. For example, you may place an order to buy (or sell) a parcel of 1000 shares that may be trading for $3.50 so have a parcel value of $3500.

> **Tip**
>
> It's important to remember that shares can't be bought without a seller (or sellers) or sold without a buyer (or buyers), and in all cases both buyers and sellers must agree on the price and quantity.

Trading hours

You can trade securities only at certain times:

- When your broker or broking site is open for business
- When the securities exchange listing the shares is open for business.

In Australia, ASX trading hours are 10 am to 4 pm on business days.

Tip

Sometimes your broker or exchange may accept an order outside of trading hours, which makes you first in the queue when the market opens. However, I never do this as I feel it is better to wait for a while after the market opens to obtain a feel for the direction of the market and the shares you're considering trading.

Board of directors

It's obviously impossible for shareholders in a public company to make consensus decisions on every important issue that arises, so these decisions are made by a group elected by the shareholders to make decisions on their behalf. This group is known as the board of directors (or board). They're often well-known Australians, such as retired politicians. The board periodically holds meetings (usually once a month) and considers matters of importance that have arisen and require the consideration of the board. The board also appoints the senior executives of the company who are responsible for the day-to-day operation of the business. The board is expected to act at all times in the best interests of shareholders without regard to their own personal interests.

Annual general meeting (AGM)

As well as monthly board meetings, the company is required to hold an annual general meeting (AGM) so they can elect board members, allow the shareholders to have their say and vote on important issues. The principle of one share one vote applies, so the major shareholders have the greatest influence. In practice, most shareholders don't attend AGMs so decisions tend to be made by a small number of large shareholders.

If you can't attend a meeting you can nominate a proxy to vote on your behalf. This could be a director of the company or, if you are a member of the Australian Shareholder Association (ASA), you can nominate the ASA to vote on your behalf. An increasing number of companies now provide shareholders with the option to attend AGMs online, so you can attend the meeting virtually. A recording of the AGM is often available, as well as personalised voting link(s) so you can vote electronically.

Tip

If you have time to attend an AGM in a location reasonably convenient to you, it's well worth doing so at least once. However, attending virtually is also a good option.

Annual report

Legally, companies are required to publish an annual report, which is a comprehensive report about the company's activities and financial performance. If you're a shareholder, you can elect to have a hard copy mailed to you or a digital copy emailed to you.

Tip

Annual reports can often run to about 100 pages, and you probably won't want to take the time and effort to wade through all the details and statistics. You're probably better off reviewing a summary report or reading the chairperson's briefing to shareholders.

Profiting from an investment

For most investments, profit is derived from capital gains; that is you sell at a higher price than you bought. More precisely, the net revenue from the sale is greater than the total cost of purchase. If you don't actually sell but your investment gains in value, the capital gain is a 'paper' profit (or unrealised gain), but if you sell the capital gain is considered to be taxable income (that is, a realised gain). This gain is the net revenue from the sale minus the total cost of purchase. Under current tax law, if you have held securities for more than one year, only half the gain is taxable income.

Tip

If you're thinking of selling securities you've held for nearly a year, it's worthwhile considering holding the security a little longer so you get the 50% tax concession on capital gains.

Note: At the time of writing, the government was considering changes to taxation on capital gains, in particular reducing the 50 per cent concession rate.

If you invest in shares, there's another source of profit—namely, dividends. Dividends are payments to the shareholders, usually from the after-tax profits of the company. Not all listed companies pay a dividend—smaller, more speculative ones in particular may not pay a dividend.

If there is a dividend it may be franked, unfranked or partly franked, depending on the amount of Australian tax paid by the company. From an investor's viewpoint, fully franked dividends are best because you obtain a full tax credit from the ATO for the profit tax paid by the company. Tax credits are known as imputation credits (or franking credits), and under current law you can receive them as a cash payment even if you don't pay income tax. However, this benefit has been under serious scrutiny as part of tax reform so this could change in the future. Your effective (after-tax) return from a fully franked dividend is higher than if the same dividend is unfranked or partly franked. In fact, under current company tax rates of 30% for large companies, a fully franked dividend gives you a return (after tax) that's effectively 42.9% higher than the unfranked dividend.

Dividends are usually paid every six months. Those paid in the first half of the company's financial year are known as interim dividends, and those paid in the second half of the year are known as final dividends. They may be equal, but the final dividend is often greater than the interim dividend. Some companies give shareholders the option of taking their dividends in shares rather than cash, sometimes at a discount price. This option, known as a dividend reinvestment plan (DRP), allows you to increase your shareholding over the longer term without injecting any more of your funds.

In theory, if a company doesn't pay a dividend, the capital gains achieved by shareholders should be higher than a company that pays one because no capital is being taken out of the business. In practice, this is not necessarily the case.

Tip

If you're investing for the long term, seek shares that have good fully franked dividends, as this is an indication that the business is a sound one and making good profits. If a DRP is available and you can manage without the cash payout, I suggest you join it, as it's a great way to build up your share wealth over the longer term.

Tip

Australian investors are accustomed to obtaining a worthwhile dividend from blue-chip shares, but this is not the case overseas. For example, in the USA many blue-chip companies pay no dividend or a smaller dividend than Australian blue chip would.

Return on capital

As an investor, you should always focus on return on capital rather than the dollar amount of profit. For example, a profit of $1 per share on a $10 share is a 10% return on capital (which is rather good), but if the share price is $50 the $1 profit per share reduces your return on capital to a paltry 2%.

Tip

Always focus on return on capital rather than the dollar value of capital gains or dividends.

Dividend yield

The dividend yield is the total dividend (interim + final) divided by the current share price and expressed as a percentage. It is effectively the return on capital invested from the dividend. Note that the dividend yield will change each time there is a change in share price even though the dividend may not have changed. If the price goes up the yield goes down, and vice versa.

Tip

When considering dividends, focus on the dividend yield. Bear in mind that a high dividend yield is not necessarily good if it's the result of a low or fallen share price rather than an increase in profitability.

Grossed-up yield

Because you get a taxation benefit from a dividend that's franked, the effective (after-tax) yield is higher for a franked share than for an unfranked share. This is known as the grossed-up yield (or GUY), and you can calculate it by multiplying the yield by a grossing-up factor. For fully franked shares, the grossing-up factor is 1.429 (at the present company tax rate of 30%).

Yields and grossing are discussed in greater detail in chapter 8, and there is a further comprehensive analysis in my book *Teach Yourself about Shares*.

Tip

Always take into account the benefit of franking when comparing dividend yields. For example, a 5% fully franked yield is better for you than a 7% unfranked yield.

Ex-dividend date

There's a cut-off date for the payment of the next dividend to shareholders, which is known as the ex-dividend date. If you hold (or buy) shares prior to this date you get the next dividend, but if you buy them after they have gone ex-dividend you miss out on the current dividend. Usually, on the ex-dividend date, the share price will fall by the value of the dividend, so if you buy on the ex-dividend date or later you'll buy at a better price but miss the current dividend.

If you sell shares after they go ex-dividend, you'll still get the current dividend. If you're in the DRP it's important to be aware of this implication, because sometime after you've sold your shares you'll be allocated the dividend in shares, and you'll be left holding a small parcel of shares that could be a nuisance because they may have only a small value.

Tip

Before you buy or sell shares, it's a good idea to check the ex-dividend date and be aware of its implications.

Obtaining or disposing of shares

The most common way to obtain or dispose of shares is by trading them; that is, by buying or selling them on the sharemarket. There are other ways your shareholding can change, such as:

- You can receive shares in lieu of a dividend payment (DRP).
- You can receive shares as a beneficiary of an estate.
- You can receive shares because of a demutualisation; that is, a change from a cooperative structure to a company structure.
- You can participate in an off-market transfer; that is, an ownership change that doesn't involve the market, such as from one family member to another.

Investor vs trader

While it seems obvious that a person who invests is an 'investor' and a person who trades is a 'trader', with shares there's a more subtle distinction. In most cases, before you become a share investor you need to trade because you can't invest in shares unless you own them, and you generally become a share owner by purchasing them. While an investor usually needs to trade, the frequency of the trades is the key factor in the distinction between an investor and a trader. Investors trade relatively infrequently and aim to hold their shares over the longer term, whereas traders trade frequently and aim to hold their shares for only a short time. As an extreme example, 'day traders' aim to hold their shares for no more than one day; that is, they buy and sell the shares on the same day.

Because a trader trades frequently there's little opportunity to profit from dividends, so a trader usually aims for capital gains profit only. For investors, dividends can be an important source of profit.

I've summarised the difference in table 1.1.

There's another important distinction between investors and traders. Investors contribute capital to a business enterprise; they are essentially part-owners of the business and therefore play an important role in the economy. Traders are essentially buyers who purchase with the aim of reselling at a profit and therefore do not make the same contribution to the economy.

Table 1.1: Investor and trader compared

	Trading frequency	Holding term	Source of profit
Investor	Infrequently	Long term	Dividends, imputation credits, capitals gains
Trader	Frequently	Short term	Primarily capital gains

Tip

If you're considering share trading on a daily basis as a means of deriving an ongoing income, I suggest you think again. Studies show that very few who attempt it are successful, and most end up with burnt fingers. It's almost impossible to guarantee a run of successful trades. The most dependable way of deriving a good income from shares is by longer-term share investing.

Brokers

You must be licensed to trade instruments listed with an exchange. If you don't hold this licence, you need to use a licensed agent to execute the trade on your behalf. Licensed share trading agents are known as stockbrokers, sharebrokers, or simply 'brokers'. Before a broker can execute trades on your behalf you need to enter into a contract with them in which you agree to the terms and conditions set out in their product disclosure statement (PDS). I'll explain how to do this in later chapters.

Brokerage

A broker who trades shares on your behalf charges a fee; this fee is known as brokerage. Brokerage is usually on a tiered basis according to the value of the trade, with a minimum fee for low-value trades. For high-value trades it may be based on a percentage of the trade value. In addition to brokerage, some brokers who provide a more comprehensive service to customers can charge a fixed fee that applies whether or not you trade. I'll discuss some of these fees and charges in later chapters.

Tip

In Australia, GST is almost always included in the brokerage fee so there's no additional cost.

Identification Codes

All tradeable securities are allocated an identification code. For ordinary shares, this code usually comprises three letters; for example, the code for Commonwealth Bank is CBA, for Woolworths it's WOW. For more sophisticated financial instruments, the code may be up to six characters long and include numbers as well as letters. If you're unsure of the code, you can easily obtain it online or from your trading website.

Tip

If you're a longer-term share investor, after a while you'll probably remember the codes of the securities you own. Nevertheless, it's a good idea to keep a list to hand, especially when contemplating a trade.

Indices

An index is a single statistic that amalgamates the price of a number of shares. Of itself, the index has no real meaning, but changes in the index provide an indication of the extent of market change.

There are two types of indices used with shares:

- A sector index applies to the type of business companies are chiefly involved in — for example, finance, materials or energy.
- A market index is a measure of the performance of the entire market. For example, an oft-quoted market index in Australia is the All Ordinaries index (code XAO), comprising the 500 largest companies (by market capitalisation) and so includes a wide variety of businesses.

Indices are explained in detail in chapter 10.

World markets

While Australia is isolated geographically our economy is not, and movement in world markets often impact the Australian market. In particular, our market often follows the lead of Wall Street as given by key US indices such as the Dow Jones and Nasdaq. Because China is a major trading partner, our market can be influenced by the Chinese economy and its market movements.

Tip

Whether or not our market follows the trend set by overseas markets depends on the mood of Australian investors, but very often US markets set the tone of our market (at least initially).

Share registries

A share register is a list of all shareholders in a company with all relevant details, such as their contact information, number of shares held, when the shares were obtained or disposed of, dividends and other payments received. Few listed companies maintain their own share register and most prefer to contract the work out to a specialist provider such as Computershare, MUFG (formerly Link Market Services) or InvestorServe (formerly BoardRoom). The important point is that if you have a query about your shareholding or dividend payments, you need to contact the share registry and not the company itself.

Shareholder information

When you become a shareholder, you can elect how you'll receive your shareholder information, such as dividend statements, annual reports, notice of meetings and reports to shareholders. You may choose to receive:

- all information by post
- all information online
- some information by post and some online.

Companies and share registries encourage online access to this information, as it considerably reduces the cost of mailouts and is more environmentally friendly.

Tip

In the future, shareholder information will likely be solely available online. It's a good idea to back up any files you save to your computer (or mobile device) so you can always retrieve your documents in the event of a device malfunction.

Why invest online?

The decision whether to trade and invest online really depends on how confident you feel and how much time you can devote to investing. If you don't feel very confident or you simply don't have the time, you may prefer to use the services of a financial adviser. A financial adviser can provide you with a full range of investment services, such as advising you of the securities to hold or trade, trading on your behalf, and keeping track of your portfolio and finances. On the other hand, you can decide to 'go it alone' online. Either way, the advantages and disadvantages of doing this are as follows.

The advantages are:

- You're in complete control and make all your own decisions.
- Online trading is much cheaper.
- The reduced cost makes small-parcel trading a feasible option and allows investors with small amounts of capital to set up a portfolio.
- A huge amount of relevant information is accessible online, very often for free. Trading data online is usually up to date and often available in real time. On the other hand, offline information will be up to date only 'at the time of writing'. You can often look at online data in chart or table form, which is much easier to analyse than text or information shared over the phone.
- You can access information and conduct your research 24/7—you're not restricted to office hours or the availability of another party.
- You can access trading data on the electronic device most convenient to you, such as a laptop, smartphone, tablet or even a smart watch.
- Online instructions and contracts lower the chance of verbal communication errors.
- You can easily experiment and test your systems at little or no cost.

The disadvantages are:

- You can't talk directly to a knowledgeable person. When you invest online, you're dealing with a dispassionate device that won't have a conversation with you. However, the huge growth in social networking sites and online forums makes online communication easy.
- There's a risk of hacking or a virus, so you need to be vigilant and have good virus protection software.
- You need a degree of tech literacy and financial competence in order to take full advantage of the information and facilities

available online. However, you don't need a great deal of knowledge to start with, and even if you're a rank beginner, after reading this book, you should be well on your way.

- You need to be careful to avoid errors that might otherwise be detected by an offline broker who's familiar with your situation.

Forecasts and tips

A large number of investing forecasts and tips can be found online. The data is usually accurate, especially if it comes from a verified source. But I suggest you regard forecasts and tips as having dubious value, even when they represent the consensus view of a number of 'experts'. Also, you need to be aware that the information or ideas expressed in online forums and on social media are personal opinions and inevitably contain a certain amount of bias.

Tip

Don't act on a forecast or tip without careful consideration and without first conducting your own research.

Information overload

There is a massive amount of online information that's constantly increasing and changing. There are about 2000 shares and other entities listed with the ASX, and you can access large amounts of data about each online. Whether you're a novice or an experienced investor, you can easily fall into the trap of 'paralysis by analysis', where you get confused and bogged down with too much information. On the other hand, you might decide to simplify your approach and concentrate on a selected number of statistics or indicators—and as a result omit consideration of some vital ones.

In other words, there's an optimum balance between insufficient information and information overload, as illustrated in figure 1.1 (overleaf).

The trick is to try to get yourself into the optimum zone where you have sufficient information to make good investment decisions but not so much that you get bogged down. In this book I'll try to guide you in this direction so you can focus on the essential information and avoid the peripheral distractions. This will get you started in the right direction, and as you become more experienced you can refine the information you access to best suit you.

Tip

Generally speaking, information simplification is better than overload. It's a mistake to believe that more is necessarily better. Some very successful systems have been developed that focus on only a handful of key statistics and indicators. I suggest you keep in mind the KISS principle: 'Keep it simple, stupid'.

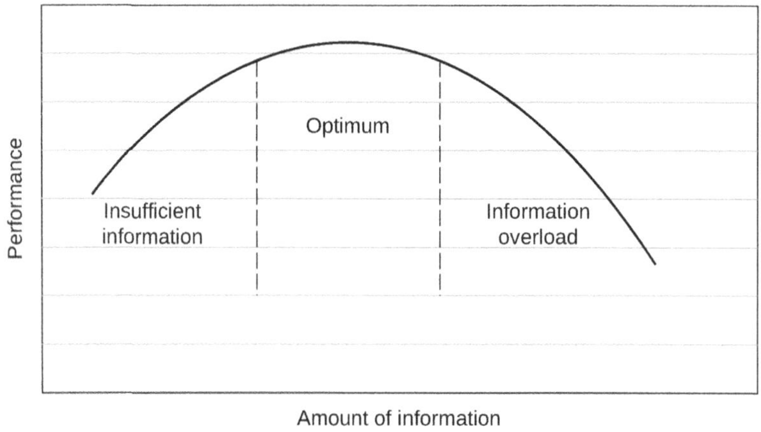

Figure 1.1: Optimum information

Key points

- It's easy and convenient to invest online, and there are many advantages to doing so.
- Increasing competition among online service providers is good news for online investors, who can expect continuing benefits from this rivalry.
- When you trade online, you're in full control, so you need to check carefully to ensure all details are correct before you place a trading order.
- There are many different types of shares, but if you're not an experienced investor it's generally best to stick to ordinary shares.
- Profit from an investment derives from an increase in value, and this is known as a capital gain.
- You can also profit from share investing via dividends. You obtain dividend income when shares you own pay you a dividend.
- Franking (or imputation) credits associated with a dividend boost its value to you considerably.
- You'll generally maximise your long-term returns from shares if you invest in shares that pay a good, franked dividend and at the same time provide worthwhile capital gains.
- Information obtained online is generally up to date and accurate. However, you shouldn't rely on any future predictions or tips, whether they are personal opinions presented in forums and on social media platforms or forecasts made by financial analysts.
- There's so much information and resources available online that you can easily get bogged down with information overload. Aim to strike an optimum balance, and remember that it's generally better to err on the side of simplicity rather than complexity. In other words, remember the KISS principle!
- There are a few pitfalls for the unwary online investor, but after reading through this book you should be well on your way to avoiding these and becoming a successful online investor.

Chapter 2
Using online resources

To get the most out of the available online facilities and resources for share investing, you need to know what they are. So, the first step to becoming a successful online investor is to understand the online resources available to you so you can tap into and use the ones you feel are most appropriate for you.

In this chapter I outline some of the most valuable resources you should be able to access online. The discussion here is only brief because I elaborate on these in greater detail in later chapters.

Resources available online

The online resources available to share investors are summarised in table 2.1 (overleaf). The list is not exhaustive, but it includes the most important resources and facilities you may find useful. In chapter 3, I talk more about specific websites that may help you grow your investing knowledge.

General information

Many websites provide general information about shares or other investment instruments. International sites often contain useful information and facilities, but it's generally best to access Australian sites as these focus more on our market and the facilities available to Australian investors.

Table 2.1: Main resources and facilities available online for share investors

General information	Research tools
Listed companies and their codes	Watchlist
Delisted entities	Portfolio
Upcoming floats (IPOs) and listings	Alerts
Sectors and indices	Online forums and social media
Market news	Recommendations
Company announcements	Online brokers
Director trades	Managed funds
Shareholder briefings (presentations)	Exchange-traded funds (ETFs)
Company profiles	Self managed superannuation funds (SMSFs)
Financial information	Margin loans
Forecasts	Contracts for difference (CFDs)
Online trading facility	Paper trading
Charting	Trading games

Listed companies and their codes

As described in chapter 1, when a tradeable instrument is listed with a securities exchange it's assigned a unique code, which for ordinary shares usually comprises three letters. You need to use the codes when you trade or look up information about shares or other investment instruments. I suggest you keep a master list of the ones you own (or are interested in) for easy reference.

You can obtain a master list of all companies listed with a securities exchange with the relevant code from the exchange's website (refer to chapter 1 for more on identification codes). Many other sites (including online trading sites) enable you to obtain the code if you enter the name of the company or investment instrument you're interested in.

Delisted entities

As noted in chapter 1, a listed entity can be delisted by an exchange for a number of reasons. If you try to trade an entity or access information about it and find you can't do so, delisting is the most likely reason.

You can obtain a list of delisted entities on the exchange's site with an explanation for the delisting.

Upcoming floats (IPOs) and listings

If you're interested in investing in an upcoming float (also known as an IPO, or initial public offering), you can find out about it and the key dates online. You may also be able to download the relevant prospectus. If you wish to subscribe, you'll need to complete the application form in the prospectus and arrange payment.

Sectors and indices

You can find out the sector group in which a company is included, as well as which shares are included in each of the market and sector indices. You're also able to track trends in sectors or market indices, for both Australian and overseas markets.

Market news

This facility enables you to obtain the latest market news for both Australian and overseas markets. Generally, you're given a broad overview of markets, including general market trends, as well as trends in the major indices and commodities and any significant changes in investor sentiment. Some websites also give brief details of companies in the news because of some recent major or pending change.

Company announcements

One of the securities exchange listing rules is that listed entities cannot release details of any major changes in the offing without first releasing the information to the exchange. The information is submitted to the exchange in the form of an announcement published on its website, so is available to anyone with access to the site. In Australia the ASX site is the major exchange, so it's the logical place to search for announcements. However, many other sites (including online trading sites) tap into the ASX site and list recent announcements. They may also provide links so you can access the announcement if you wish.

Announcements are made every day, and if you try to read them all you'll be overwhelmed. It's important to restrict your search to shares in which you have an interest and to specific timeframes. Many websites allow you to search today's announcements, or announcements for specific shares over the past week, month, six months or year. Some websites will email you headline announcements if you register and request this service. This facility allows you to quickly scan a list to see if there are any that interest you.

On the ASX site, announcements made by a particular company can be found in the company information section. There is also a list of all announcements as a sub-heading under the 'Markets' tab. In this list, announcements considered to be price sensitive are differentiated from those that aren't by marking the price-sensitive ones with a dollar symbol.

The various types of company announcements include:

- lodging of financial reports (such as interim or final reports)
- shareholder presentations
- dividend announcements and DRP price allocations
- substantial changes in share ownership (including directors' interests)
- restructuring plans (such as acquisitions or the sale of divisions or subsidiaries)
- substantial changes in business activities
- substantial sales or acquisition of assets or devaluation of assets
- significant litigation cases that have commenced or concluded
- a significant find by a resource company or a decision to abandon a well or mine

- changes in company governance
- changes in share ownership of directors
- issue of new shares (such as a rights issue)
- earnings estimates or preliminary financial results
- responses to inquiries made by the exchange (for example, regarding sudden unexplained rises or falls in the share price)
- trading halts (suspension of share trading)
- appointment of receivers (for businesses declared bankrupt).

Tip

If you notice a sudden dramatic share price movement, it is a good idea to check to see whether the company has released an announcement that could explain it.

Director trades

In Australia, directors of listed companies can legally trade shares in their own companies. Knowledge of director trades can provide a useful insight because a director of a company should be well aware of the current financial situation and likely future performance of the business.

Tip

Director trades aren't necessarily significant because, like anyone else, a director may have their own reasons for buying shares for investment purposes or selling them to access cash.

Shareholder briefings (presentations)

At the AGM, the chairperson of the board and the CEO usually make a presentation to shareholders (often presented in slide form for visual impact). This presentation summarises the activities and performance of the company over the past financial year. It usually incorporates sales and profits trends, as well as providing some indication of the likely outlook for the business. Most shareholders don't attend AGMs or wade through a detailed annual report, so these presentations can give shareholders a useful and accessible overview.

Company profiles

A company profile provides information about the principal activities of a listed company. The profile contains basic details such as the location of the head office, the business's main products and where they are sold, how long the business has been in operation, who the directors are, and what acquisitions or mergers the company has been involved in.

Tip

A company profile provides a convenient 'snapshot' of the business.

Financial information

This facility enables you to access current and past financial data, such as profit and earnings per share, dividend per share, assets, liabilities, loan capital, equity capital and gearing. This type of information is also known as fundamental statistics.

Tip

In chapter 8, I provide more details about company profiles and important financial statistics.

Forecasts

Data in financial records is historical. The sharemarket, however, is forward looking, and investors are more focused on future prospects than past results. Many websites publish forecast earnings and growth figures compiled by financial analysts based on available information and trends.

Online trading facility

This facility allows you to trade online using a computer or mobile device. There are many sites you can access in Australia, from the large and dominant ones affiliated with the major banks to the smaller ones that have a low market share. Many of the trading sites have a facility enabling you to trade other instruments, commodities and currencies (forex), as well as Australian shares. Some also provide CFD trading (contracts for difference). Many sites provide lots of other information and facilities, but in order to access these or use the site you will need to register.

I discuss online trading in detail in later chapters, so I won't elaborate further here.

Charting

Information such as share price movements and volume of trades is easiest to interpret when presented in chart form. Most online trading sites have a charting facility and there are also dedicated charting sites you can access.

Tip

The analysis of charts is known as 'technical analysis', which I discuss in chapter 9.

Research tools

Because of the large number of listed shares, it's obviously very time-consuming to trawl through them all when you're searching for those you're interested in. Many sites have a research tools facility that allows you to obtain a list of shares that satisfy your stipulated requirements.

For example, you can obtain a list of shares whose price relative to earnings (P/E) or dividend yield is within a certain range stipulated by you.

Tip

A research tools facility can save you a lot of time.

Watchlist

As the name suggests, a watchlist is a list of shares or other instruments you want to keep tabs on. When you access your list, you can quickly see how the shares or instruments have been performing. Most online trading sites have this facility, and there are also other sites (as mentioned in chapter 3) that have this facility.

Tip

A watchlist is a great time-saver as it allows you to keep tabs on a number of shares or other instruments without having to look up each one individually.

Portfolio

Your portfolio lists all the shares you own. Online trading sites usually set up a portfolio automatically for you when you buy shares through the site or have shares allocated to you in lieu of dividends (a DRP). When you purchase shares these are added to your portfolio, and if they are shares in the same stock they will be added to your holding. When you sell shares through the site, these are deleted from your portfolio.

Your online portfolio is usually updated in real time, so it shows the last sale price of each of your shares, the value of each parcel and the total value of your portfolio. It often shows the profit or loss on each parcel and the total profit and loss of your portfolio. This is trickier if you've bought shares in the same stock at different times and at different costs, or if you've had shares allocated to you in lieu of dividends. In these cases, the portfolio profit or loss as shown on your online trading website may not be completely accurate.

As well as your online trading site, there are other public-access sites that allow you to set up the portfolio of shares you own or a hypothetical portfolio, in which case the portfolio you set up will be much the same as a watchlist.

Tip

As well as my online portfolio, I keep my own portfolio spreadsheet and I check to ensure that they both agree on the number of shares I own in each stock and their value; if not, I investigate any differences immediately. I find it's often convenient to check my portfolio at times when the exchange is closed and this has the added bonus that prices don't change while you're looking at it. I make a point of checking my portfolio at least once a week and more often if any major change has occurred or is in the offing.

Alerts

It's possible to arrange email or mobile phone alerts for shares or other instruments you nominate. You may have to pay for this service, but some sites provide it free of charge. You can be alerted for different criteria, such as:

- *Price alert*—when the share price reaches a threshold value set by you.
- *Announcement alert*—when the company makes a new announcement.
- *Volume alert*—when the number of securities traded reaches a threshold value set by you.

Tip

Before you arrange for any alerts, it's worth checking if there's a fee involved.

Online forums and social media

Many websites provide online investing forums that allow you to communicate with others who are also interested in online investing. You can also find like-minded investors on social media, but the advantage of using an investing website is that the messages (and audience) are specifically focused on shares and investing.

Messages are usually filtered to block inappropriate language and ensure authenticity. Sometimes messages are posted or responded to by company executives, but this is unusual.

Tip

The accuracy of any information on online forums and social media should not be taken for granted, as cases of deception have occurred in the past.

Recommendations

Some websites provide buy, hold or sell recommendations for shares. Sometimes the recommendations are broken down further into categories such as 'strong buy', 'moderate buy', 'buy', 'hold', 'sell', 'strong sell', 'add' or 'reduce'.

The 'hold' recommendation is usually interpreted to mean there are no clear reasons to trade the shares, so you should adopt a 'wait and see' stance.

Tip

Don't adopt any recommendation without your own careful consideration. It's not uncommon to receive a 'buy' recommendation from one source and at the same time a 'sell' or 'hold' recommendation from another.

Online brokers

There are many online brokers to choose from. While they all provide similar trading services, costs can differ considerably. There can also be differences in the facilities and information provided.

Tip

I discuss online brokers in greater detail in chapter 4.

Managed funds

Managed funds allow you to invest in a variety of entities by buying into the fund. The types of funds available vary greatly. Examples of managed share funds are:

- Australian funds that invest in a variety of Australian shares
- index funds that are designed to track an index
- sector funds that invest in a specific sector (such as the financial sector)
- special funds that invest only in businesses that conform to specific criteria, such as environmental friendliness
- international funds that invest in particular countries (such as the USA, China or India).

In addition to shares, many funds diversify their capital by investing in other instruments such as bonds, property, fixed-interest securities, forex and even cryptocurrencies. The advantages of investing in a fund are that you can diversify through a single investment and that your investment is managed for you by one or more financial analysts who should be experts in their field. The main disadvantage is that the fund charges a fee for providing this service. This fee is known as the MER (management expense ratio) and for smaller, unlisted funds it can be significant.

Rather than issuing shares, funds issue units that you purchase in order to invest in the fund and that you need to cash in if you decide to exit the investment. Many funds are unlisted; that is, they're not listed with a securities exchange. If the fund is unlisted, you need to apply to the fund in order to purchase units or cash them in. To buy into the fund, you'll need to complete the application form in the prospectus (which is usually available online).

Tip

Managed funds are an easy way to invest in shares without needing to do anything else except purchase units. Also, you don't need to have any particular expertise in share investing. However, before you invest in a managed fund it is advisable to check the MER to ensure that it will not erode your profitability significantly.

Exchange-traded funds (ETFs)

Many of the larger funds are listed, in which case you can trade fund units in exactly the same way that you'd trade shares. These funds are known as exchange-traded funds (ETFs). Many of the larger ETFs have been around for many years and have a proven track record of profitability. A great advantage of investing in a large ETF is that the MER is usually only a small proportion of the value of the assets held in the fund and so it doesn't detract significantly from the ETF's profitability. For example, ARGO, a large Australian fund, has an MER of only 0.14%.

Tip

It's easier, faster and more convenient to invest in a listed fund rather than an unlisted one. I recommend you hold at least one or two ETFs in your portfolio.

Self managed superannuation funds (SMSF)

Many investors with substantial capital to invest set up their own superannuation fund. There are many advantages to doing so and also some disadvantages. You need to look at all aspects and weigh up the pros and cons to decide whether it's a worthwhile proposition for you. One limitation is the amount of investment capital you have, because it's generally not worth setting up an SMSF unless you have substantial investment capital. The most cost-effective way of setting up and managing an SMSF is by using an online facility.

Tip

If you're thinking about setting up an SMSF, I suggest you consult with a specialist in this field. To give you a headstart, I discuss the advantages and limitations of a self managed superannuation fund and how you can set one up online in greater detail in chapter 5.

Margin loans

Many online brokers, especially those affiliated with banks and major financial institutions, provide a margin loan facility. A margin loan is a way of increasing your investing capital without using your own money because it allows you to use your share portfolio as collateral. The catch is that the interest rate for a margin loan is considerably higher than that interest rates that apply to other loans such as home loans. Also, in the event of a market fall you can get caught out with a margin call if you're highly geared. This means some of your shares will be sold in order to boost your cash balance, and this can be unprofitable if the value of your portfolio has taken a downturn.

Tip

If you're considering a margin loan, I suggest you don't gear too highly—that is, borrow right up to the available limit—because by doing so you're risking a margin call should there be a market downturn. A margin loan can boost your profits in a rising market but will generally be counterproductive in a falling one.

Contracts for difference (CFDs)

A contract for difference (CFD) is similar to a margin loan in that it enables you to increase the amount of capital you have available for investment. With a CFD, you don't actually trade shares or other investment instruments; instead, you enter into a contract with a CFD provider for the value of the trade. CFDs have been a growth area of investment and many providers now offer trading in CFDs online.

Tip

CFD trading, discussed in greater detail in chapter 5, is a way of leveraging your share investing/trading profits. It will boost your profit considerably if you get it right, but if you get it wrong CFD trading can magnify your losses.

Paper trading

Paper trading is where you set up a hypothetical portfolio and buy or sell shares hypothetically without using any real cash. A few websites provide this facility, which allows you to test your system and see whether or not it is a profitable one.

Tip

Paper trading is a good way to test your trading/investment system, but a word of caution is appropriate. Paper trading can't simulate your responses under stress, so it doesn't necessarily provide an accurate guide to the decisions you'll make when your real hard-earned money is at stake. Research shows that decisions made under stress are often very different from those made in a stress-free environment.

Trading games

Some websites (such as the ASX site) periodically run a trading game that you can play to match your skills against those of other investors. You might find this to be an enjoyable way of testing your trading skill compared to others.

Key points

- There's a great deal of investing information and facilities available online. Many of these will be discussed further in later chapters.
- If you're starting out as an investor, I suggest you don't try to access all the information and resources available straight away. Instead, start out small and simple, and then expand your horizons as your experience and knowledge grows.
- Consider using the information in this chapter in conjunction with the list of websites presented in the next chapter to carry out your own research.

Chapter 3
Profiting from useful websites

In this chapter I outline some websites you may find useful. I haven't included sites that are discussed in greater detail in later chapters; for example, online broking sites and charting sites.

Types of investing websites

Broadly speaking, websites can be classified into three main groups:

- user-pays sites
- free sites
- hybrid sites.

User-pays sites

User-pays sites provide information or facilities accessible to paying subscribers only. This may be a program or trading system that's claimed to be superior in some way, periodic newsletters or trading advice (tips). The fee may be a once-only charge—for example, to undertake a training program—or an ongoing charge in the form of a monthly, six-monthly or annual fee, if you want to maintain your subscription.

If specialist or unique share investing information or resources are available on a website, you can expect to pay a fee to access it. After all, an inventor or creator who puts time, effort and expense into creating an original product or resource that offers significant benefits is entitled to compensation from those who use it to their advantage. Accessing the resource online doesn't change this; it just makes the product or service easier to access.

Once you pay and become a subscriber (or customer), you'll most likely need a log-in code and password. Fees vary widely, from a few hundred dollars to several thousand.

Tip

Sites offering trading systems or software packages often make grandiose claims and present glowing testimonials but usually provide very little (if any) independent or authoritative verification of these claims. So, I suggest you exercise caution before you pay to use any website or purchase any online system or resource.

It's easy to prove any system or method produces superior results by going back in time (the wisdom of hindsight). For example, past results can be biased towards higher returns simply by selecting the most favourable time periods or investments that were superior and omitting the others. Even if past performance has been consistently better than market, bear in mind this important share investing principle: *past results don't guarantee future performance.*

Free sites

Free websites are accessible to anyone at no cost. Some sites will require you to register and provide some personal details and perhaps to use a log-in code and password; others don't even require this. Some free sites will send you emails each day, week or month, providing share investing information or trading tips or links to information or resources you can access.

Setting up and maintaining a website involves cost, so the question arises: why would anyone go to the trouble and expense of setting up a website that can be accessed by anyone free of charge? There are several reasons:

- A website can be set up as a vehicle for advertising a business or product or for customer liaison. Most listed companies and securities exchanges maintain a website for these reasons. Websites often provide a 'Contact us' tab where customers or potential customers can provide feedback or information that may be useful for marketing purposes.

- When you register on a website, you're sharing personal details that can provide valuable marketing information. Even if you can access the site without registering, the number of hits on the site and the trend of those hits in themselves offer useful marketing information that may have a saleable value.
- Many free websites carry advertisements that may tempt you to respond or purchase, but even if you ignore them they can have a subliminal impact you might not be aware of. It's rather like a roadside billboard: you're not consciously aware of it while driving by, yet it can have a subliminal impact on your product awareness. Sometimes inadvertently passing your cursor over an advertisement or your finger over a smartphone or tablet screen will link you to a website you didn't intend to look at.
- Free information or resources are offered in order to 'lure you into the shop' both to sample the freebies and, it is hoped, pay for the user-pays services they provide at a later stage. It's the principle used by stores that advertise a few specials to get you through the door, knowing that once you're there you'll most likely make additional purchases.

Tip

If you're not sure whether to register with a site and receive free resources, such as newsletters, I suggest you do so. You can always opt out at a later stage if you get bogged down with too many emails or text messages.

Hybrid sites

The distinction between user-pays and free sites isn't as clear cut as it might appear, because many user-pays sites contain a certain amount of information and facilities accessible to non-subscribers. This free information is often provided to 'get you hooked', while additional, more comprehensive information and resources are available to paying subscribers only—which is why these websites can be more accurately considered hybrid sites.

Tip

Hybrid sites can contain a large amount of useful information and great resources free of charge, making them worth a visit even if you don't subscribe to the fee-paying facilities on offer.

Your choice

It's entirely your choice whether you pay for online information or resources. The creator of a unique facility or resource that offers significant benefits is entitled to compensation from those who reap the benefits. However, it's often the case that what appears to be a unique facility or resource on one site is actually freely available on another, where it has been slightly changed and/or rebadged. I just can't see the sense in paying for something that's available for free elsewhere. I call this the 'Kinsky Principle', which in essence is this: *Don't pay for something you can get for free.*

A corollary of this principle is:

Don't pay for information or the use of an online facility or resource unless you're satisfied that the following two conditions are met:

- *You really need the information, resource or facility.*
- *There's some benefit from the information, resource or facility you're paying for that can't be obtained elsewhere for free.*

Tip

A good approach is to learn as much as you can about share trading and investing, then formulate your own system or method that you really understand and know how to use. It's also a good idea to be flexible and to refine and improve your system as you use it or test it.

Company websites

Many companies maintain a website containing information that can be useful to an investor (or potential investor), including the history of the company, its location, size, products and services, directors and executive officers, financial details and share registry. Typically there'll be a 'Contact us' tab designed with potential customers in mind, which you can use to obtain share investing information. For example, I've often sent emails to company executives with share investing queries, and I usually receive a reply. Needless to say, in larger organisations you're unlikely to get a response from the chief executive officer, but you may if the organisation is a smaller one. In any case, it's worth the attempt.

You can obtain the web addresses for listed companies in several ways:

- Have a stab. It is a fair bet that www.'companyname'.com.au will produce a result.
- Check the Australian Securities Exchange (ASX) site where the details of all ASX-listed companies—including web addresses—are given.
- Enter the company name in a search engine.

Tip

If you're considering investing in a company, it's worth checking out its website to get a general feel for the company and its products. You may be able to contact them directly if you have any questions.

Securities exchange sites

Securities exchanges both in Australia and overseas maintain websites containing useful share investing information particularly relevant to companies listed with the exchange, and these sites are well worth visiting. In Australia most shares are listed with the ASX, which makes it the premier site for information relevant to Australian share investors.

Online trading sites

The main purpose of a trading site is to provide an online trading facility. Most trading sites provide heaps of additional facilities and information. This provides a 'one-stop shop' so customers have all the information they require to make trading and investment decisions without needing to search elsewhere. In some cases, even if you're not a subscriber, you can access the site and obtain useful information. You may also be able to 'take a tour' of the site, which can be a valuable exercise regardless of whether you go on to use the website to invest in shares.

Share registry sites

Share registries maintain websites that contain relevant shareholder information about companies that use the services of the registry. To access your information, you'll need to register and log in with your registration code and password. The site will show your portfolio and dividend information. The site may also show the price of each share in your portfolio and your total portfolio value.

Tip

A share registry site will contain information about the companies that use the share registry only, so it's a good idea to note which registry applies to each of the different shares in your portfolio. Then, if you have a query, you're able to log in to the appropriate one.

Forums and social media

The popularity of social media over the past few years is reflected in the world of online share investing. There are many online forums and social media platforms that allow you to share ideas and information with other investors. Some online trading sites also provide a space to exchange ideas with other subscribers.

Charting sites

Most online trading sites have a charting facility; there are also several dedicated charting sites. Almost all sites that provide charting allow users to customise their charts, such as by changing the format of the chart or the time period over which the chart is drawn. You can often save your preferences, so the next time you visit the site the chart will conform to your specifications.

> **Tip**
>
> Charting is discussed in detail in chapter 9.

Recommendation sites

Also known as tipster sites, these sites provide trading tips and advice about shares or sectors to invest in. They are most suitable for investors who feel they don't have the expertise or time they need to make profitable trading and investment decisions, so they turn to others who they believe do have this knowledge and expertise. I once fell into this trap and subscribed to an expensive tipster service that had a long history and a good reputation. Most recommendations turned out to be less than spectacular, and one in particular was disastrous. Needless to say, I didn't renew my subscription!

Many subscription sites provide free access to past publications or recommendations to give you an idea of the type of service they provide. As I have pointed out, you need to be wary of these examples of past performance, as it's very easy to trade shares profitably with the wisdom of hindsight. Some sites offer a free, no-obligation trial. If this option isn't available, you may be able to evaluate the service by seeking the opinions of subscribers—but be wary of glowing testimonials on the site itself, as they may have been curated to reflect the site in the best possible light (adverse comments are unlikely to appear). You may find it helpful to search forums or social media for more independent information about the sites you're interested in, as well as post your own questions to gather specific insights.

If all else fails and you're still keen, you could test the service by subscribing for the minimum period and cost. When renewal time comes around, you can do your sums and decide whether subscribing to the service was a profitable exercise.

> **Tip**
>
> The bottom line is that no matter what advice you get from anyone, ultimately you are responsible for your investing decisions. I suggest you try to adopt this mindset rather than believing that others can (or should) make decisions for you that will be consistently better than the ones you could make for yourself.

Useful websites

Following is a list (in alphabetical order) of some useful websites. It is by no means an exhaustive list, as there are many thousands of websites that contain share investing information, and if I tried to provide a synopsis of them all there'd be no room in this book for anything else. So, I've included only the sites I think you may find most useful as an Australian investor. I've provided a brief synopsis only, so for more detailed information you'll really need to browse any sites of interest for yourself.

Bear in mind that websites will change over time, so while the information I provide here is accurate at the time of writing, it may have changed by the time you check it out.

> **Tip**
>
> You may feel overwhelmed by the sheer number of sites and the amount of information available, so I suggest you browse through and bookmark those of the most interest to you and later, when you have time, explore them at your leisure.

AMP

AMP (amp.com.au) is a well-known company that provides information about investing, financial planning and superannuation, as well as access to lots of managed funds. Of course, it's tailored to AMP products, but it may be worth exploring when you're in the planning stage.

Australian Financial Review (AFR)

This is the website of the publication *The Australian Financial Review* (afr.com). You can read a short synopsis of articles for free, but you can't really get much information unless you subscribe and pay the subscription fee.

Australian Securities and Investments Commission (ASIC)

ASIC (asic.gov.au) is charged with enforcing and regulating company and financial services laws. The site is more useful for companies than for individual investors.

Australian Securities Exchange (ASX)

The ASX (asx.com.au) controls the activities of listed companies and has its own set of listing rules companies must conform with in order to be listed or maintain their listing. If you go into the 'Investors' section of the site you can obtain a lot of free information about getting started with share investing and trading shares. You will also see a useful subsection called 'Find a broker or adviser', and you can also participate in the sharemarket investing game the ASX runs periodically.

Incidentally, the ASX is a public company and you can trade its shares in exactly the same way as any other listed company.

Australian Shareholders' Association (ASA)

The Australian Shareholders' Association (australianshareholders.com.au) is a not-for-profit organisation that keeps tabs on listed companies and ensures that shareholders' rights are protected in areas such as corporate governance, transparency and accountability, executive remuneration, risk management and dividends.

You can become a paying member or subscribe for free and receive a weekly newsletter that provides up-to-date information for shareholders. If you become a member, you can appoint the association as your proxy to vote on your behalf at the AGMs of all the listed companies in your portfolio. If you have a query or complaint about a company, you can contact the association and ask it to investigate.

Australian Stock Report

This website (australianstockreport.com.au) contains a number of useful articles about sharemarkets and shares. If you register you gain free access to the latest traders' report, which gives a snapshot of market action and a market commentary. The website provides a number of free webinars, as well as an online tool called 'HALO' that is marketed as giving consistently good buy and sell trading signals. You need to purchase HALO, though you can try before you buy.

Australian Taxation Office (ATO)

Many taxation laws and regulations have a significant impact on net share investing income and profit, and on estate planning. Tax laws and government policy related to tax and budgets change frequently, so if you are to make informed decisions you really need to keep updated. You can obtain lots of information about tax matters from other websites, but the most authoritative source is the ATO itself (ato.gov.au). On this site you can view legislation and changes to legislation, and search for any tax topics of interest.

Tip

The real profit you make from shares is your after-tax profit, so you need to be aware of, and keep up to date with, the tax implications of your share trading/investing and estate planning strategies.

ChatGPT

Unless you have been offline for a few years, you probably know that ChatGPT (chatgpt.com) is a free online chatbot (also available as an app) that uses AI (artificial intelligence) to do almost anything. It can save you time, as you can get it to search for the investing info you require. For example, I asked ChatGPT to find me some Australian shares that paid a good dividend, and it quickly responded with three blue-chip income generators and five less mainstream ones. Furthermore, it provided some important considerations regarding yield.

AI is now being widely used for many reasons, including for researching shares, so ChatGPT is well worth checking out. There are also several other chatbots that are available to you and that you may be familiar with.

Tip

While using AI may save you a lot of time, the results generated may not be 100% reliable or accurate, so you should always check the facts independently and verify them for yourself before taking action.

Clime

Clime (clime.com.au) is an independent Australian fund manager that has a number of managed investments funds with different profiles. The website contains some useful investing information.

deListed Australia

This site (delisted.com.au) is helpful when a share is no longer listed with the exchange where it was originally listed. Information about delisted companies is often difficult to obtain, because the ASX ceases to provide it once an entity is removed from its listings. The deListed site includes an alphabetical list of delisted entities; alternatively, you can search by entering the code or name. There's also some useful general information, so this site is worth a visit. If you are unfortunate enough to hold any permanently delisted stocks or funds then you have an additional problem, because you're not able to declare losses to offset capital gains in your tax return until the receivers and administrators have made official declarations, and this is often a lengthy process. This site enables you to sell such shares (at a low nominal price) so you can claim the capital loss. However, you will have to pay a fee to use this service, and the cost of doing so could well exceed the tax benefit you might subsequently derive.

Educated Investor Bookshop

This is an online bookshop catering especially to traders and investors (educatedinvestor.com.au). It has a huge range of titles that you can purchase online.

Esuperfund

This site (esuperfund.com.au) allows you to set up a Self Managed Super Fund (SMSF). Before you do so, you can download factsheets from the site that provide information about SMSFs and the service Esuperfund provides.

> **Tip**
>
> You can obtain more info on SMSFs in chapter 5; however, before you set up an SMSF, I strongly advise you to consult a financial adviser and make sure that an SMSF is appropriate for you.

Fat Prophets

Fat Prophets (fatprophets.com.au) is a tipster service that provides share trading advice. The site contains some free information, but primarily it promotes the use of its service. Subscribers receive daily and weekly emails and alerts. If you register you can also receive some free reports.

FIIG

Diversification of your investments is a recognised strategy to spread the risk so that you're 'not putting all your eggs in one basket'. Investing some of your capital in bonds is one way you can spread the risk. If you're interested in investing in bonds, FIIG (fiig.com.au) is a great site to visit as it contains lots of information on this type of investing. Unlike shares, bonds provide a fixed rate of return that does not depend on the share price, so bonds are regarded as a safer investment than shares.

> **Tip**
>
> Diversification as an investing strategy is discussed in more detail in chapter 11.

Finder

This site (finder.com.au) contains information about internet share trading and a comparison of the many share trading platforms available, providing insights and a discussion about the different sites you can choose from.

> **Tip**
>
> The various share investing platforms available for online investing are discussed in detail in chapter 4.

FNArena

This site (fnarena.com) contains a fair bit of free information and is worth a visit. However, most of the information is available only to paying subscribers.

Fool (Motley Fool)

This site (fool.com) is primarily a subscription site, although some free information is available. It provides many specialist subscription services at different costs.

Guppy Traders

This is the site of Daryl Guppy, a well-known Australian share investor and author (guppytraders.com). He conducts share investing seminars and online workshops that you can subscribe to. He has also developed several proprietary technical indicators, such as the Guppy Multiple Moving Average. If you subscribe, you can obtain a regular newsletter from him.

HotCopper

This site (hotcopper.com.au) is a popular forum for Australian share traders, with many posts each day. To place or reply to a post you need to join, but you can register without charge. You can search for notices posted about any shares you're interested in over a timeframe you can specify.

This site is well worth visiting if you want to seek the opinions of others or when you want some ideas about shares that could be candidates for a speculative trade. There is also quite a lot of general information about shares.

InfoChoice

This site (infochoice.com.au) is primarily a financial comparison site that allows you to obtain guidance on some financial issues such as the best personal or home loans, the best bank account or term deposit interest rates, and even car, home and life insurance. Although this site isn't devoted to share investing, it contains plenty of financial information as well as financial calculators so is well worth a visit.

Intelligent Investor

This site (intelligentinvestor.com.au) is a well-established subscription advisory service that offers advice about Australian share investing. You can subscribe to the service to obtain buy, hold or sell recommendations. You can also sign up for free to obtain regular emails.

InvestoGain

This is a free site (investogain.com.au) with heaps of information about Australian and New Zealand shares and managed funds. You can browse listed Australian companies and managed funds or search for companies or funds by name. There's information about superannuation, floats and a listing of the latest director's share purchases and sales. You can join if you wish, but much of the information is freely accessible.

InvestSMART

This site (investsmart.com.au) is essentially an Australian portfolio management site, and if you subscribe you can access the company's expertise to set up a portfolio of Australian and global shares, ETFs, bonds and property, and manage it for you. The site caters for individuals, joint accounts, family trusts and SMSFs. Naturally, there is a fee if you decide you want them to act on your behalf.

Tip

The basic goal of this book is to provide you with the information that will enable you to make your own investment decisions using the resources available online. Therefore, I don't encourage you to pay for a service that manages your finances for you until you have read right through this book and decided that is the way you want to go.

JustData

On this site (justdata.com.au), you can purchase software for trading, charting and technical analysis.

Lincoln Indicators

This is the website of Tim Lincoln (lincolnindicators.com.au), who provides an advisory service for shares based primarily on a software program called Stock Doctor, but you need to subscribe in order to access and use the facilities available. You have a choice of several managed funds. This is a service for investors who prefer to have their portfolio managed professionally.

Market Index

This is a very useful site (marketindex.com.au) that has lots of information about the Australian market and its performance. You can also find information about individual shares and their performance, as well as a complete listing of all the market and sector indices used in Australia and their performance. Various investor plans are also available (one is free, but fees apply to the more comprehensive plans). This site is well worth browsing and perhaps using on a regular basis as you learn more about share investing.

MarketWatch

This is a US site (marketwatch.com) and therefore primarily contains information about US shares and global markets. However, our market is strongly influenced by the US market so this site is worth a visit, particularly when topical issues in the USA are having a flow-on effect to us.

Moneysmart

This is an Australian government site (moneysmart.gov.au) that provides totally unbiased information for investors on a variety of topics, including money management, debt reduction, borrowing, superannuation (including self managed), retirement, investment and scams. There are many tools and resources that you can use to help you save money and invest wisely, including a budget planner, a compound interest calculator and mortgage switching tools. The site also provides an overview of banking and credit scams and how to best avoid being scammed.

Morningstar

This site (morningstar.com) has some free information but, in order to access most of the facilities available, you need to subscribe. There is information about our market but also USA, European and Asian markets.

Next Investors

This site (nextinvestors.com) provides free information on small cap stocks. You can receive free daily newsletters if you subscribe.

Reach Markets

This is an Australian investing organisation (reachmarkets.com.au). It is primarily a subscription site, but you can also receive a free weekly newsletter.

Roger Kinsky Shares

This is my website (rogerkinskyshares.com.au), which provides information on and links to buy my share investing books. I also post articles on general share investing on the 'Sharing Shares' that I add to periodically.

Scamwatch

This is an Australian government site (scamwatch.gov.au) that has heaps of information about scamming, including how to recognise a scam and how to avoid being scammed. It's a very useful website for everyone who invests online.

ShareCafe

This site (sharecafe.com.au) has lots of share investing and trading information about market action and specific shares and sections of the market. You can register for free and receive a weekly newsletter.

Small Caps

As the name suggests, this website (smallcaps.com.au) is great for investors primarily wanting information on smaller cap and speculative shares. It contains a number of articles of general topical interest as well as more specific articles on various types of shares and upcoming floats (IPOs). You can subscribe for free and receive regular emails.

S&P Global

Standard & Poor's (S&P) is a US compiler of financial credit ratings and market indices for stock markets and investments throughout the world (spglobal.com). It's used by the ASX for compiling Australian market and sector indices (which is why these indices are prefaced by S&P). This website is a useful reference for information about credit ratings and indices.

Stockhead

This is a free site (stockhead.com.au) that will send you three emails on each day of trading: one prior to market open, one at midday and one at market close. This site is primarily devoted to small cap, speculative shares but also provides some interesting general financial information from time to time. Every weekend, Stockhead shares trading tips from several advisers with buy, sell and hold recommendations.

Stockspot

This website (stockspot.com.au) has informative articles about shares and share investing. If you register you will receive regular emails and gain access to all the articles on the site. Stockspot also manages several funds with different levels of risk in which you can invest if you feel so inclined.

The Bull

This website (thebull.com.au) contains lots of free information about shares and other trading instruments and is well worth a visit. You can subscribe for free to receive a weekly newsletter and access to a number of articles that might interest you. There is a weekly article entitled '18 share tips' written by a number of financial experts that provides buy and sell suggestions you may wish to consider. The Bull also offers a subscription service you need to pay for called 'Bull Premium' that claims to offer additional benefits.

TradersCircle

This site (traderscircle.com.au) primarily provides financial training courses that you can subscribe to if you feel you would like to receive specialist training to deepen your understanding.

Vanguard Australia

This site (vanguard.com.au) allows you to open an account and invest in a variety of managed funds and ETFs as part of your portfolio of Australian shares. As I have already noted, I don't recommend you pay for an investment service until you have decided it's the best option for you.

VectorVest

This is an online share investing advisory service (vectorvest.com.au). You need to subscribe, but it provides a one-month free trial to enable you to decide if you want to become a subscriber.

Wiley

This is the website of Wiley Australia (www.wiley.com), which publishes a large range of trading, personal investment and finance books for the Australian market (including this book). The catalogue includes many relevant titles on share investing, charting and stock analysis. Titles can be purchased online.

Yahoo Finance

This is a US site (finance.yahoo.com) that contains free articles and information relevant to Australian investors. It has information about Australian and international markets as well as commodities, indices and cryptocurrencies. You can also set up a watchlist and portfolio.

Key points

- In this chapter I've outlined some of the sites that I consider of interest and value for online share investors. It is by no means a comprehensive list, and there are many other sites of interest and value that I have not included (purely for practical reasons).
- I have provided a brief outline of the sites. You need to browse for yourself to get a better idea if the site is of value to you. I suggest you do so in stages so you don't get overwhelmed.
- Sites come and go and are constantly changing, so when you access a site some details may differ from those I've described.
- In many cases you need to register to access the site, but as registration is often free this isn't a great disadvantage. Of course, you can cancel your registration at any time.
- Some sites provide emails, newsletters and alerts at no cost, and these are usually worth receiving.
- Many sites require you to pay a fee for the facilities and information provided. Sometimes this is only a small amount, but in other cases it can be big dollars. Remember the 'Kinsky Principle' and don't part with your hard-earned money unless you're sure that the benefit outweighs the cost and that you can't obtain the information for free or at a lower cost elsewhere.
- Some sites allow you to set up watchlists and portfolios, which allows you to monitor the performance of your portfolio and to 'keep an eye' on shares you're interested in. Your online broker will probably offer this facility, but there are many public-access sites that also offer it for free.
- You can get opinions from other traders and investors through a forum or on social media, but remember that the advice or information you receive isn't necessarily reliable and may be based on personal opinion.
- I suggest caution regarding testimonials or claims about past performance, as there's usually no independent, unbiased audit available. Also remember that it's easy to get great results with the wisdom of hindsight.

- I suggest you access some of the free information available but also adopt the mindset that, rather than relying on others, you'll develop your own strategies as your knowledge and expertise increase. Presumably that's why you're reading this book—so please read on.
- As well as the advice in this book, you will find many strategies and suggestions for improving your share investing profitability in my book *Teach Yourself about Shares*. Both books aim to provide a firm foundation for profitable share investing.

Chapter 4
Online brokers and facilities

In this chapter I discuss the various brokers operating in Australia and the various facilities available when you sign up with them. This should help you choose the broker and trading platform to best suit your research and trading needs.

If you're already trading online, you can use this chapter to widen your horizons and perhaps register with another broker that offers additional benefits. Usually there's no cost involved in becoming a customer with an online broker; if this is the case for the brokers you are interested in, you may decide that you'd like to try more than one broker in order to make a real-life comparison. Later on, you could then focus on the one you prefer. However, if you do this and you buy a security using one broker you must also sell the same security using the same broker.

Tip

You might like to explore more than one broking site, as most provide some free information that makes them worth visiting even if you don't use them for trading.

The cost factor

Brokers usually have a brokerage fee structure (including GST) with a minimum charge in the form of a flat fee for smaller parcel values until you reach a threshold, after which the brokerage is proportional to the parcel value. Sometimes there's a tiered threshold parcel value—for example, one fee for parcels up to $1000, another fee for parcels up to $10 000, another for parcels up to $25 000, and a percentage fee for parcel values above $25 000.

When choosing a broker, the first thought in most people's minds is: how can I get what I want at the lowest possible cost? For the process of share trading, this question becomes: how can I trade shares and pay the lowest possible brokerage? While I endorse this general principle, as it's really an extension of the 'Kinsky Principle' (as outlined in chapter 3), with share investing you need to consider other factors as well as brokerage fees. So, it's not just a matter of finding the lowest brokerage fee.

To put it in perspective, suppose you want to buy a used motor vehicle and are looking at one with an asking price of $10 000. Would you enter into negotiations with the seller to reduce the price by $10? I think you'd agree that a saving of $10 on an outlay of $10 000 isn't really worth thinking about, as it represents only 0.1% of the price. It's the same with online share trading, because the difference in brokerage between the various major online brokers is only about $10 for share trades that are $10 000 in value. The 0.1% difference is trivial when you consider that many share trades are made with the aim of a capital gain of 10% or so, and share investors can obtain ongoing grossed-up dividend yields of around 7% per year with many shares.

The economics is rather different if you're trading a $500 parcel of shares; in this case, a $10 saving is 2% and is more significant. The economics is also different if you're a frequent trader averaging, say, five trades a day, because a $10 saving per trade would be a daily saving of $50 and could be a lot more significant.

To summarise, the importance of the brokerage cost depends on two factors:

- Frequency of trading—how often will you trade? The more often you trade, the more significant the brokerage charge.

- Parcel value—what's your average parcel value? Remember, the smaller the parcel value, the more significant the brokerage is in proportion to the value of the trade.

Tip

Some online brokers charge a monthly fee (as well as proportional brokerage) in order for you to maintain customer status and use their site, so it's a good idea to check this before signing up. You don't want to pay account-keeping fees unless you're a very active trader, in which case the fee could be offset by a reduced brokerage cost.

Your broker wish list

Before you go shopping, it's generally best to have an idea of what you're looking for; that is, a list of items or specifications for them you've thought about in advance. The situation is no different when you're shopping for an online broker: to get what you want, it makes sense to think first about your requirements. Then you can search more purposefully for a broker who could best fulfil these requirements.

Certain essential features are provided by all online brokers, and it's easy to take these for granted—but this is what you are paying for. These features include:

- *Trading facility*—the ability to make trades online using the broker's trading platform.
- *Trading information*—the provision of all the information you need to make trading decisions, such as a trading depth list showing the buy/sell orders at market with prices and volumes (quantities), completed trades with prices and volumes, and last sale price.
- *Order status*—the ability to check the progress of your open orders (orders in market that haven't been transacted) as well as your orders that have transacted.
- *Trading history*—the trades you've made with that broker.

- *Account balance*—the available funds in your trading account. Remember that cash transfers occur two business days after the day of the trade transaction.
- *Portfolio*—the list of shares you own that you purchased with the broker along with price, quantity and value. Sometimes your portfolio may also show the profit or loss on each parcel.
- *Market news*—an indication of market action.

One-stop shop?

When you go shopping, it's convenient to be able to get all you want in one location as it saves a lot of time and effort (not to mention the cost of transport). With online share trading, the same idea applies: it saves time and effort to get all the resources you need for share trading from one site. However, when you're online you can access a number of websites simultaneously and toggle from one to another in no time (or easily move from one app to another on your mobile device). When you're online, the range of facilities provided by your broker isn't such an important consideration because you can use your broking site for trading while using other websites or apps for research.

For example, the charting facilities available on an online trading site aren't an important consideration for many traders because they use a dedicated site for charting. Before trading, they access the charting site and toggle between the charting site and their trading site as they contemplate each trade. However, some dedicated charting sites charge a fee, so you may like to explore the charting options available on your online trading site first before you sign up and pay for a dedicated charting site. I discuss using charting further in chapter 9.

Features to consider

To help you set up your wish list of broker requirements, I've made a list of features to consider that can vary between different online brokers:

- tradeable securities
- types of orders
- securities exchanges

- brokerage and fees
- fundamental analysis data
- charting and technical analysis data
- research tools
- market data
- alerts
- announcements
- watchlist
- recommendations and forecasts
- margin loans
- mobile device apps
- taxation summary
- customer service.

Tradeable securities

You need to consider the range of securities you plan to invest in. All online brokers offer trading in ASX-listed shares and company options (renounceable issues). As a general rule, most online brokers also provide trading of ASX-listed warrants and managed funds.

Fewer online brokers provide trading in international shares or derivatives such as exchange-traded options (ETOs), futures, contracts for difference (CFDs) or currencies—also known as foreign exchange rates (forex) and cryptocurrencies. If you want to trade these instruments, you need to ensure your online broker provides the facility to enable you to do so.

Tip

If you're not an experienced investor, the range of tradeable securities available on your trading site won't be important because you'll most likely want to trade ASX-listed shares only.

Types of orders

All online brokers cater for the two most common types of orders: limit and market orders. In the past, few brokers would accept conditional (deferred execution) orders, such as stop-loss orders, but an increasing number are now doing so. If you want to include these types of orders (or other more complex deferred execution-type orders) as part of your trading strategy, you need to ensure your online broker provides this facility.

Tip

The different types of orders you can place (including conditional orders) are discussed in detail in chapter 7.

Securities exchanges

In Australia (at the time of writing) there are four securities exchanges in operation:

- ASX (Australian Securities Exchange)
- Cboe Australia (formerly Chi-X Australia)
- NSX (National Stock Exchange of Australia)
- Sydney Stock Exchange (SSX).

Of these, by far the most trades take place on the ASX.

Tip

The ASX uses a smart order router that can automatically switch trades between the various exchanges to get you the best deal, but if you want to ensure you trade using a securities exchange other than the ASX, you need to find brokers that are licensed to use the exchange.

Brokerage and fees

There are differences in brokerage and fee structures between online brokers. The brokerage cost for a trade may or may not be an important consideration for you; as I've already mentioned, its importance depends on parcel size and trading frequency (how often you will trade).

A complication when comparing trading costs is that some brokers offer discounts for frequent trading. There can also be charges you may not be aware of until you trade; for example, there may be additional costs for trading using a margin loan account. Different types of trades may have different brokerage and fee structures too—for example, an additional fee may apply for conditional order trading.

Tip

As you can see, there are a number of different factors to consider when estimating your trading costs, and an exact apples-to-apples comparison is not easy to make. However, you can come up with a reasonable estimate if you know the types of orders you intend to make, what instruments you intend to trade and how often you plan to trade. (I discuss planning in detail in chapter 6.)

Fundamental analysis data

Fundamental analysis data is basic information about the business as well as its financial performance. Most company websites, as well as online brokers, provide this type of data, but there can be considerable differences in the amount of data and how it's presented.

Tip

Using fundamental analysis for investment decisions is discussed in detail in chapter 8.

Charting and technical analysis data

Most online brokers provide a charting facility but, as with fundamental analysis data, there can be considerable differences in the types of charts and technical analysis tools available, and the extent to which you can customise a chart.

Tip

Using charting for investment decisions is discussed in detail in chapter 9.

Research tools

This facility allows you to search the website database and obtain a shortlist of shares that satisfy criteria you set. This can be based on fundamental data such as dividend yield or technical analysis data such as moving average crossover points. Research tools are provided on many (but not all) online broking sites. There are also other websites (as well as AI chatbots, such as ChatGPT) that enable you to research shares to satisfy your criteria.

Tip

Using research tools can save you a great deal of time and effort when you're looking for shares that satisfy fundamental or charting criteria you specify, so it's a facility worth including in your requirements list.

Market data

When you trade online you can rest assured that all licensed brokers are treated equally and can access the latest market data at the same time. That is, regardless of whether your broker is a small operator or a very large business, you will access the same orders at market as anyone else with prices and parcel volumes for each purchase or sale. This data is current and valid at the moment you access it, with no time delay. However, it can change constantly, and you may need to refresh your screen to keep up with the changes.

With data other than trading data (including charts and financial statistics), there can be variations in the currency of the timeline and how frequently it is updated.

Data can be:

- *Dynamic*—the data is completely up to date at all times.
- *Real time (live)*—the data is up to date when you first access the site; however, if the data changes while you're on the site, you won't see the most recent data unless you refresh your screen.

- *Delayed*—the data is delayed, most often by 20 minutes, so the data you see when you access the site is delayed by this amount of time.
- *Previous day*—the data is updated daily so it's current at the close of trading the previous business day.
- *Full-day delay*—the data is delayed by a full business day. For example, you won't receive the data applying to close of trading on Friday until Tuesday morning.

Many free websites provide delayed, previous-day or full-day delay data only. Some brokers offer different trading platforms at different costs depending on the data timeline you specify. Trading data is usually real time, and for other data the delayed-data option is usually the default one. If you require dynamic data you may have to pay a fee, so you need to check this out.

Financial data (as opposed to market data) is usually updated twice a year, when the company releases its interim and final reports. Therefore, the financial data shown online could be more than six months old when you access it, whether through your broker or another site.

Tip

It's a good idea to check the timeline of any data you access online and be aware of the implications. Generally speaking, data delays of a day or more aren't critical for fundamental data that's not price-based, because the vital statistics released about a company's operations change infrequently.

Alerts

This facility provides for SMS or email alerts to be sent to your mobile device or computer for shares you nominate and for events you nominate—for example, when a share price rises or falls to a certain level or when a company makes an announcement. This facility may not be included for free in a basic trading package but may be available if you're prepared to pay, either as a fee per alert or as a monthly charge. The facility may also be included in a higher-cost trading platform.

The importance of this facility depends on how active you are as a trader and how closely you are following the market, so you should decide if you really need this facility and are prepared to pay for it.

Tip

Some sites provide an alert facility free of charge, so you need to check this out before you pay to receive alerts.

Announcements

This facility provides a list of the announcements made by the company over the past few months (or another period you specify). The announcement usually has a marker that tells you whether the announcement is considered to be market-sensitive or not; that is whether the announcement is likely to affect the price.

Tip

When a share price changes dramatically, it's a good idea to check if there have been any announcements that might explain the change. Frustratingly, even though you can tell something is going on, it may be difficult (or impossible) to pin down exactly what it is.

Watchlist

Many online brokers allow you to set up a watchlist of shares you're interested in so you can easily keep track of price movements or other changes. In some cases, you can also have an email or text message sent to you when one of the companies on your list makes an announcement.

Tip

You could set up a watchlist of your own by keeping a list and checking prices periodically, but a watchlist set up online (especially with your broking website) is quicker and easier to check.

Recommendations and forecasts

Some online brokers provide financial analysts' recommendations and forecasts for selected shares. Whether or not you value this facility depends on the extent to which you follow recommendations or rely on forecasts. It isn't very important for me because I prefer to do my own research using a variety of sources for my information. Also, I've found from bitter experience that the recommendations of financial analysts can't be relied on, so it can be counterproductive if you act on them without conducting thorough research of your own. Sometimes, when you receive recommendations from a number of analysts at the same time, you may find that one analyst recommends a buy whereas another recommends a sell. Or you may find you get a buy recommendation but a short time later this is changed to a sell recommendation.

Tip

As I've said before, recommendations and forecasts can't usually be relied on, even though there may be a consensus opinion among a number of informed financial analysts. However, they may provide a useful guide.

Margin loans

Many online brokers have a margin loan facility; if not their own, they may provide it via some other financial service with which they are affiliated. A margin loan allows you to increase your trading capital by using your existing share portfolio as collateral. This can be a good idea in times of bull markets, but it is fraught with danger in bear markets or when the market is very volatile.

Tip

I suggest you avoid using a margin loan unless you're an experienced trader.

Mobile device apps

Most online brokers have free apps for several types of smartphones and tablets that allow direct and convenient access to the site. Some of these apps also provide for trading in more sophisticated instruments such as CFDs.

> **Tip**
>
> It's well worth checking the apps that are available with your online broker for your preferred device.

Taxation summary

Many brokers (both online and offline) provide a free taxation summary. This can be very useful at the end of the financial year, as it provides all the data you need relevant to your share investing and trading in order to be able to complete your tax return. This includes all dividends (franked and unfranked) with appropriate franking credits. The taxation summary you obtain from your broker may also provide a list of shares sold during the year, with purchase costs and selling revenues, and so provide the capital gains tax information you need.

The dividend summary provided by your broker will usually be accurate, but capital gains tax information is more difficult to obtain accurately from your broker, particularly if you were allocated shares through a DRP (dividend reinvestment plan). Another problem is that the length of time you hold the shares affects the taxable capital gain. Remember that when you receive shares through a DRP, the cost of those shares needs to be included in the cost price of the shares you own—even though you didn't actually purchase them.

> **Tip**
>
> If you use the ATO's online tax facility to complete your tax return, the dividend data should already be held by them and you can opt to have this data prefilled, which can be a great time saver for you at tax time. The ATO has this data because you are required to submit your TFN (tax file number) when you set up your trading account.

Customer service

A very important consideration is the extent of the customer-friendly service provided by your online broker. The chances are that sooner or later you'll want to question some detail of an order or your share account. Your online broker should provide telephone contact details and an email address so that it can answer your queries in a prompt and efficient manner. There may also be a chat support on the website so you can obtain prompt answers to any queries you might have.

> **Tip**
>
> The customer service provided by an online broker is an important consideration but is difficult to evaluate beforehand; you won't really know how good or bad it is until you actually need to use it. You can try social networking to tap into others' experiences with the broker. Bear in mind that any queries about your shareholding or dividends are a matter for the relevant share registry and not your broker.

Online brokers affiliated with banks

When you have decided what features you would like to include in your wish list for an online broker, you can look for a broker who satisfies those requirements. I suspect that in many cases the decision will be an easy one, as the vast majority of investors tend to give first preference to the broker associated with their bank. This makes personal identification and cash transfers for trades easier, quicker and hassle-free, so it's a good option for most investors. Over recent years there has been a convergence between the various online broking sites affiliated with the major banks, and there's seldom much difference in the fees charged and the features provided.

> **Tip**
>
> In the past, most regional banks had an online share trading facility, but nowadays they outsource this facility.

Unless you're an advanced trader with special requirements or you're obtaining finance from some source other than your bank, there's no compelling reason to choose an online broker other than the one affiliated with your bank. Australian banks affiliated with online brokers are listed (in alphabetical order) in table 4.1.

Table 4.1: Online brokers affiliated with major banks

Bank	Online broker
ANZ	CMC Markets
Commonwealth Bank	CommSec
Macquarie Group	Bell Direct
National Australia Bank	nabtrade
Westpac	Westpac Share Trading

CMC Markets

In 2021, ANZ Share Investing was sold to CMC Markets, which now operates the trading platform on behalf of ANZ. The site is a comprehensive one and offers trading in a wide suite of securities, including Australian and international shares, ETFs (exchange-traded funds) and options.

CommSec

For many years CommSec has been the most popular Australian online share trading and investing site, catering for the needs of the majority of Australians. The site has many useful features and is constantly being updated and improved. CommSec offers trading in a wide suite of tradeable securities both here and overseas. A margin loan facility is also available for approved customers.

Bell Direct

Formerly Macquarie Online Trading, the Macquarie Group's broking platform is now operated by Bell Direct. This platform offers trading in all the instruments you would usually expect, such as Australian shares, ETFs, ETOs, warrants and managed funds at the same cost as most other sites. However, money transfers are still made using a Macquarie cash management account.

Nabtrade

Nabtrade provides online trading for National Australia Bank customers in shares, ETOs, ETFs and warrants on the ASX, as well as international trading.

Westpac Share Trading

This site offers online trading in Australian shares, international shares, options, warrants and ETFs.

Tip

If your online broker has several different trading platforms available, I suggest when starting out you choose the simplest (and cheapest) one. Later on, as you gain experience, you may want to step up. All brokers have mobile apps available as well as the standard online platform.

Other online brokers

Apart from the brokers associated with the banks outlined in table 4.1, there are many other online brokers accessible to Australian traders and investors. It is a very competitive area of share trading and investing, and one that is constantly changing as new brokers enter the field and established ones leave or amalgamate with other brokers. At the time of writing, there are approximately 30 online brokers operating in Australia offering about 40 different trading platforms between them.

Comprehensive comparison sites you can use to compare different brokers include Canstar and Finder. These sites are well worth visiting if you are looking for a broker.

You can also use the ASX site to find a broker. Click the 'Find a broker or adviser' link in the Investors section to find a list of online and full service brokers, plus a list of futures brokers. You can click on any broker you're interested in to obtain further information.

The information obtained from comparison websites and the ASX is in summary form and just tells you whether or not a facility is available.

The problem with this is that the summary might show that the online broker provides a certain facility, but you won't know the extent of it. For example, the summary may show that a broker provides a charting facility, but you won't be able to determine the types of charts provided or the extent to which the charts can be customised. Similarly, the summary may show that financial and statistical information is available, but you won't know exactly what data is included and how it's presented. Another problem with these summaries is that they don't necessarily apply exclusively to online services. For example, the summary may show that an online broker provides the facility for trading derivatives, but in fact this facility may be a telephone service only.

Tip

Comparison sites provide a general overview, but they may not provide the detailed information you need to make a truly informed choice.

Market share

Online brokers are an example of Pareto's Principle (also known as 'the 80–20 rule'), because a relatively small number of large brokers dominate the market and have the largest market share, whereas a large number of small brokers have a smaller market share. Brokers affiliated with the banks have the major market share and, of these, CommSec has for many years held the dominant market position. Some of the lesser-known brokers have a small client base and usually occupy a niche in the market for traders and investors with particular needs.

Online share trading accounts

Many online brokers offer financial incentives to encourage you to set up a dedicated trading account with them or with a bank or financial institution of their choice. In most cases, you can utilise an existing account for your online trading by giving the broker authority to access the account for trading deposits or withdrawals, but you may not get the lowest trading cost if you don't have a dedicated trading account.

When you buy shares (or other investment instruments) online, you need to have sufficient funds available in an account the broker can access online on settlement date. The funds need to be sufficient to cover the total purchase cost (including brokerage). When you sell, the broker needs access to an online account into which the net funds can be deposited.

Tip

When you get started with online trading, it may be more convenient for you to use an online broker affiliated with a bank or financial institution that already has your custom. As you gain experience, you can explore other options.

Brokerage

You can trade Australian shares online for as little as around $5 a parcel with a number of brokers. Broking is very competitive, so there is continual pressure on brokers to keep their rates low.

Tip

As I've previously pointed out, many factors other than broking cost are important when using an online share broker.

Making your choice

It's difficult to make a precise evaluation of an online broking site unless you become a customer. Many online brokers have a 'take a tour' or similar feature on their website, and this can be a good way of obtaining some idea of the cost structure and facilities offered, but you still won't get a precise idea of the user-friendliness of the site. If no registration charge or ongoing monthly charge is involved, a good way to finetune your choice is to register with one or more online brokers. This allows you to access their sites as a bona fide customer and get a better idea of the resources available and how data is organised and presented.

Tip

It's possible to use a low-cost online broker for trading while using other websites for research and information. This strategy allows you to trade at a low cost and still obtain all the info you need.

Key points

- With so many online brokers and trading platforms available in Australia, investors have a great deal of choice.
- There are many similarities between online brokers, but there can also be appreciable differences in cost structure, securities traded, types of orders accepted, fundamental research tools and technical analysis indicators, as well as differences in the availability of apps for mobile devices.
- If you want to make an informed choice, it's a good idea to prepare a 'wish list' of features you'd like your online broker to provide. I've outlined the ones you may want to consider.
- Unless you're a frequent trader (particularly in small parcel values), brokerage cost difference may not be a significant factor and other considerations may be more important.
- Several websites have online broker comparison summaries with links to each site. Comparison websites are a good way of getting a general impression, but they won't provide you with the full picture and may not be completely up to date.
- To finalise your choice of online broker (or multiple brokers) you really have to 'suck it and see'. Most often you can become a customer without incurring any costs. This will give you full access to the site and you won't even need to trade.
- You may be able to use an existing bank account for your trading by giving the online broker authority to access the account for trading deposits or withdrawals. Many brokers offer incentives to encourage you to set up a dedicated share trading account, and it is often in your best interests to do so.
- Some online brokers charge a monthly fee that's payable even if you don't trade and can be waived or reduced if you trade frequently. Unless you're a frequent and experienced trader, I suggest you avoid sites or platforms that charge monthly fees (at least initially).
- It's possible to use more than one broker, which is not a problem provided you buy and sell the same shares with the same broker.
- While a 'one-stop shop' is the most convenient option, when trading online you can have several sites or apps open and toggle between them while you're contemplating your next trade.

Chapter 5
Becoming an online investor

Once you've chosen an online broker, you need to set yourself up with the broker so you can trade and invest online. In this chapter, I discuss in further detail how you can get set up ready to start trading. I also outline the various ways you can trade online, including margin loans, CFDs (contracts for difference) and SMSFs (self managed superannuation funds), as well as also some of the securities you can trade online, including listed managed investments.

Signing up with an online broker

When you apply to be a client with an online broker, you'll need to complete an application form in which you divulge relevant personal details. You may be asked to nominate a password that allows you to access your customer account, but you may initially have a password allocated to you that you can change later if you wish.

If you have an existing account with a bank or financial institution affiliated with the broker, the whole process is easier as your personal ID will already have been verified. If not, you can still verify your ID using e-verification if you have an Australian passport and tax file number (TFN).

Later in this chapter, I walk you through the sign-up process with CommSec, a popular online broker.

CHESS

If you want to invest in shares, your online broker will ask if you want to be sponsored into the Clearing House Electronic Subregister System (CHESS). In this system you're sponsored into CHESS by a broker, so it is also known as dealer (or broker) sponsorship. You'll be allocated a Holder Identification Number (HIN). This number is the same for all shares or other securities you trade with this broker. You'll be issued a CHESS holding statement for each of the equities you own, and it's automatically updated when your holding changes for any reason, such as additional purchases, sales or issues of shares (such as those received through a DRP—a dividend reinvestment plan). While there'll be some time delay before the new CHESS statement is issued, this doesn't affect your ability to trade because you don't need the statement to trade.

Tip

Some time ago, the ASX spent a heap of time and money trying to supersede CHESS with a new system that would provide instant transfers (no time delay), but eventually the idea was scrapped. However, changes to CHESS could be on the horizon in the coming years.

Issuer sponsorship

Before CHESS, shareholders were issuer-sponsored. When you bought shares, you received a statement from the share registry with a Shareholder Reference Number (SRN). This number was the same for all your shares in this particular stock; for shares in any other stock, you were allocated a different SRN. This system still operates today. If you register with a broker and don't apply for CHESS sponsorship, you'll automatically be issuer-sponsored.

Some Australian shareholders still hold issuer-sponsored shares—usually for one of the following reasons:

- The shares were purchased prior to the introduction of CHESS.

- The shares were acquired because of demutualisation; that is, when a member-owned organisation, such as a building society, converted to a company owned by shareholders.
- Longstanding shares were acquired as a beneficiary from a deceased estate.

> **Tip**
>
> If you're not sure whether shares you hold are issuer-sponsored or broker-sponsored, check the holding statement to see whether your identification number is given as an SRN or HIN.

Advantages of CHESS

CHESS has two main advantages:

- Once you've been allocated your HIN, you can place both buy and sell orders almost instantaneously for the same shares (provided you use the same broker for both transactions). In other words, you can buy shares and, as soon as the order transacts, you can place a sell order for the same shares. This is particularly useful if you're a very active trader or prices are volatile and you want to cash in profits or reduce losses quickly. If you're not CHESS-sponsored, you can't sell any shares you buy until the SRN is allocated to you, and that can take several weeks.
- You have only one number to keep track of for all your share transactions using your online broker, and you don't even need to quote this number when you buy or sell. With issuer-sponsored shares, you need to keep track of (and quote) your SRN for each parcel of shares you sell, because it's a different number for each stock you hold. Note, however, that if you use more than one online broker, you will have a different HIN for each broker.

Transferring from issuer sponsorship to broker sponsorship

If you hold shares you bought or acquired prior to joining CHESS, you can easily transfer them into CHESS. To do this typically involves contacting your broker and filling out a transfer form. Of course, you'll need to provide the broker with your current SRN. It may take a few days, but it doesn't cost you anything. It's not considered an ownership transfer and there are no capital gains tax implications unless you're transferring shares registered in one name to a different name. If you've acquired shares from a deceased estate, capital gains tax liability doesn't occur at the time of transfer but only as and when you decide to sell any of the shares.

Tip

It doesn't cost anything to join CHESS. It is one of those rare things in life that has multiple advantages and no disadvantages. There's no reason not to be in CHESS—unless, for some devious reason, you're trying to make your share transactions more difficult to trace.

Holding statement

When you buy shares, you'll be issued with a holding statement sometime later. If you've joined CHESS, you'll receive a CHESS statement; otherwise, you'll be issued with a holding statement from the share registry. Normally these are paper documents that will be mailed to you free of charge, but you may be able to obtain them online.

When your shareholding changes because you buy or sell shares or receive additional shares in lieu of dividends, you'll receive a new holding statement.

Tip

When you receive a holding statement, always check your own records to ensure there's complete agreement between them, and investigate any discrepancy immediately. If you detect a discrepancy, you'll need to lodge a query with the share registry (not with your broker or the ASX).

Using more than one broker

As I suggested in chapter 4, you may wish to open an account with more than one online broker so you can thoroughly compare the facilities and services offered by different brokers. If you use more than one broker with CHESS, you'll have more than one HIN. This is no problem provided you buy and sell shares in the same stock with the same broker. This is easy to keep track of because the name of the sponsoring broker appears on the CHESS statement for each stock you own. For example, if you buy shares in Stock XYZ using Broker A, you can't then sell those shares using Broker B. To do so you need to first transfer the shares by filling out a broker-to-broker transfer form. If you're holding shares you purchased using an offline broker but want to sell them online (because it's cheaper to do so), you need to transfer them to your online broker before you can arrange the sell order.

If in time you decide to deal with only one online broker, you can transfer shares bought using other brokers by filling out a broker-to-broker transfer form obtainable from the broker you're transferring to. If you're transferring all your shares and you're in CHESS with both brokers, you won't even need to state the name or code of each stock and the numbers of shares in each—you simply indicate that you wish to transfer your entire shareholding. The system can do this automatically and you'll receive new CHESS statements for all shares transferred (at no cost to you). There are no capital gains tax implications from such a transfer.

Tip

If you're currently trading offline, you may wish to continue your relationship with your offline broker while establishing an online broking account, so you can get into online trading yourself and test the water before deciding whether or not this is the way you wish to go.

Your trading account

A trading account is a cash account (just like a bank account) where the cash for your share purchases is withdrawn from and the cash from a sale is deposited. Many online brokers provide financial incentives to encourage you to open a trading account with them or with a financial institution they nominate. To open the account, you may be required to provide a minimum deposit. In the past this may have been several thousand dollars, but nowadays some brokers allow you to open the account with a token minimum deposit.

If you don't open a trading account with the broker, you'll need to authorise cash transfers; that's to say, you need to allow the broker to access the necessary funds so you can pay for the shares you buy and also provide the broker with an account into which cash can be deposited for the shares you sell. This involves quoting a BSB number, account number, branch location and so on.

Completing your application

Once your application to become a client with the broker has been processed, you'll be allocated a customer account number and an HIN (assuming you've opted for broker sponsorship). You'll need a password in order to access your customer account. If you want to place an order, some brokers also require a trading password before they'll process your order, which provides an added level of security. If you're opening a trading account, you'll also be given a BSB and account number. This trading account number will generally not be the same as your customer account number, but the password may be the same if you so choose. You should also be given your broker's phone contact and email details in case you have any questions about your account or experience any difficulties.

Once your application has been processed, you're ready to start online trading. At least this is true in theory, but in practice you may encounter difficulties that take a phone call or email to sort out.

> **Tip**
>
> If you're new to online trading, I suggest you resist the temptation to trade immediately, and do so only after you've read through this book in its entirety. It may prove to be a profitable delay!

Keeping track of your numbers

You need to keep track of quite a few numbers when you invest online, including:

- your customer account number
- a password to access your customer account
- a trading password (if required)

- your CHESS HIN
- your trading account number(s).

Customer account number

This is the number you use to log into your customer account with the broker.

Password

This is the personal password you need to log into your customer account.

Trading password

This is an additional password some online brokers require you to quote when you're placing a trade order with them.

CHESS HIN

This is the number allocated to you when you join CHESS.

Trading account number(s)

These are the numbers that apply to your trading account (where the actual cash transfers occur) and include both your BSB and account number.

If you're going to use more than one broker, you'll have a set of these numbers for each one, so you'll have a lot of numbers to keep track of. Therefore, you need a convenient and secure way of accessing these numbers when you need them.

> **Tip**
>
> I suggest you keep a paper or external electronic copy of the relevant numbers and information you need so you won't lose them in the event of a device malfunction. Your next of kin should also be able to access this information if necessary. As you age, this becomes a more important consideration.

Cash transfers

Some brokers require adequate funds in your nominated account before they'll accept purchase orders, while others may provide temporary credit.

In any event, you need to ensure that adequate funds are in your account to cover the total net cost of purchases at the time of settlement (when the funds transfer to complete a share trade).

The transfer of funds for a share trade occurs two business days after each transaction (T + 2 settlement). It's not hourly based but simply daily based. For example, it makes no difference whether you buy shares at 10 am or 3.30 pm on a Thursday, it's regarded as a Thursday trade and you need to have the funds available in your account on Sunday night as the cash transfer will occur the following Monday to settle the trade.

Tip

For many years the 'settlement period' was three business days, but in 2016 it was shortened to two business days. It's certainly possible that at some time in the future, instant settlement will become a reality.

If you buy and sell shares on the same day, you need the funds in place on settlement day to cover any outstanding net amount only. For example, if you buy shares to the value of $10 000 and sell shares to the value of $8000 on the same day, and the brokerage on each transaction is $20, you need $2040 available in your account two business days later (on day T + 2). However, if the buy transaction took place, say, on a Monday and the sell transaction the next day, on the Tuesday, you need $10 020 in your account on Tuesday night to cover the debit occurring on Wednesday. Then, on Thursday, your account would be credited with $7980.

Tip

Make sure adequate funds are in your account at the time you place any purchase orders, especially if you're a new customer. If this involves transferring funds from one financial institution to another, a time delay may be a factor. I usually play it safe and transfer funds for a buy order into my broking account before I place the order.

Minimum parcel value

Most brokers have a minimum parcel value for orders to buy or sell a security, especially sell orders. Your order can be declined if you own shares that fall in value to the extent that their value is lower than the minimum parcel value. If this happens, you'll need to contact your broker to sort things out. Another option is to buy some more of these shares to add to your shareholding, which can then be amalgamated with the shares you already hold. You can then sell the whole lot because the parcel value is now above the minimum parcel value.

Securities you can trade online

In today's globalised world there's a wide range of securities you may be able to trade online with your broker. I use the word 'may' because not all brokers trade all securities, so (as mentioned in the previous chapter) if you want to trade any securities other than listed Australian ones, you need to ensure your broker provides the facility to trade them.

Securities can be classified broadly into two types: listed and unlisted. A listed security is one that's listed on an Australian exchange. In this case, prices will be quoted on the exchange in Australian dollars and trading takes place using the trading facility provided by the exchange. If your broker is licensed to operate with the exchange, trading should be relatively straightforward and will be arranged by your broker according to your requirements. If the security is unlisted, it means it's not listed on an exchange and trading of the security becomes a matter for you (or your broker) to arrange personally.

Tip

If a security is listed, trading is much easier than if it is unlisted, so I suggest you stick to listed securities unless you have special reasons to invest in unlisted ones.

The securities that may be available for you to invest in are:

- Australian shares
- international shares
- initial public offerings (IPOs)

- listed managed investments:
  - listed investment companies (LICs)
  - listed managed funds
  - listed investment trusts (LITs)
  - exchange-traded funds (ETFs)
- company-issued options
- exchange-traded options (ETOs)
- warrants
- futures
- contracts for difference (CFDs)
- forex (currencies)
- cryptocurrencies.

The advantages and disadvantages of investing in these various securities and the ways you can do so can be quite complex. In this book I concentrate on Australian shares, as to fully explain the complications involved with some of these securities is well beyond the scope of this book. However, in the following sections I briefly outline the other tradeable securities as well to give you an idea of what can be involved, so you can delve further if you're interested.

Tip

The bottom line for you as an investor is that it doesn't really matter what type of security you invest in. There are really only two issues you need to focus on:

- *The riskiness of the investment.* It should match your risk profile—that is, the amount of risk you're prepared to accept. I talk more about risk profiles in chapter 11.
- *The return on investment after tax.* Obviously, you would like the return on your investment to be as high as possible (provided the risk level is acceptable to you).

Australian shares

In addition to property, Australian shares are the primary investment vehicle for Australian investors. There are around 2000 listed Australian shares in a wide range of different sectors, so you have lots of choice. All online brokers have the facility for trading them, and trading is straightforward. The main thing to watch is that you have the funds available if you want to buy. When you sell, the funds will automatically be credited to your nominated account, with no further action needed from you.

International shares

In the past the Australian sharemarket has performed well, but there are periods when overseas sharemarkets outperform us. There are also times when certain international shares (particularly those in the USA) perform really well. When this occurs, you may feel you would like to get a slice of the action outside of Australia. If you want to do this, you must ensure your broker has the facility to arrange for you to be able to trade in the international market involved.

Tip

Trading internationally raises a heap of additional complications and costs, including greater difficulty in obtaining accurate information, increased fees and fluctuating currency exchange rates. You need to consider these complications carefully before you invest.

Initial public offerings (IPOs)

An IPO (initial public offering) or float occurs when a business enterprise or private company wants to convert to a public one. The company must prepare a document known as a prospectus, which outlines all relevant commercial and financial information about the business (including investing risks). Until the date at which the company floats, the shares aren't listed so cannot be traded on a securities exchange. You can find out which companies are in the IPO stage from various websites, and if you want to participate in the float you need to complete the application form in the prospectus and provide the required funds. There aren't usually any transaction costs involved. After listing, the shares are traded in the usual way and their price may rise above the application price or fall below it on the listing day.

I regard IPO investing as being rather risky because:

- There's no track record of the company as a public company.
- The performance of a company as a public company isn't necessarily going to be the same as its performance when the company was privately owned.
- You have no real idea of how the investing public will view the listing. Predictions regarding public perception are often wrong.

Tip

It's possible to make fast profits if the price rises above the listing price on listing day; traders who participate in the float and then sell on listing day for a profit are known as 'stags'.

Listed managed investments

A listed managed investment is an entity that's listed with the ASX that invests in a variety of securities. It trades as units of the overall entity so as to maximise profits.

A listed managed investment has two main features:

1. It is listed, which means that the security is listed on a stock exchange and can be traded (bought or sold) by an investor in the same way as ordinary shares. Each listed managed investment is identified with a unique code, just as with shares, and once you have this you can place a trade order with your broker. Market forces determine the trading price on the exchange, so you may be able to trade at a discount or a premium in relation to the listed managed investment's net asset value (NAV).
2. There is no 'product' as such. For example, the business does not produce a saleable product or perform a needed service, such as a retailer does. Rather, the business invests in shares here or overseas

or in some commodity (such as gold or silver) or another type of investment product according to the purpose for which the listed managed investment has been set up.

Tip

Buying a listed managed investment at a discount to its NAV appears to be a bargain—for example, if the trading price is $1.20 and the NAV is $1.30, effectively you can buy $1.30 worth of assets for only $1.20. However, in my experience the trading price can often stay below the NAV for a long time.

There are four different types of listed managed investments, namely:

- listed investment companies (LICs)
- listed managed funds
- listed investment trusts (LITs)
- exchange-traded funds (ETFs).

The primary difference between them is their business structure and taxation treatment, but from an investor's viewpoint these are generally not that significant.

The main advantages of listed managed investments include:

- Because they are listed, they are transparent—that is, all their business operations are fully disclosed to everyone as they have to comply with the listing rules of the exchange.
- They are easy to trade.
- A single investment can give you exposure to a wide range of securities, or the opportunity to diversify your investment across different asset classes and market sectors.
- You have access to investments such as international shares, currency or precious metals that are usually more difficult for you to directly invest in.

- Your investment is managed by one or more specialists who have expertise in the field.
- You are free of the necessity (or worry) of trying to shuffle your investments in the most profitable manner, as this is done for you.

The main downsides of these types of investments include:

- As you would expect, you have to pay for the service provided. This takes the form of a management fee—known as the management expense ratio (MER). This is the management fee expressed as a ratio of the asset value. You really don't need to concern yourself too much with this—as I said previously, the bottom line for you as an investor is the profitability after all expenses have been taken out, so a high MER isn't a downside if the profitability is high.
- You lose control over the investment mix.

Tip

Listed managed investments are a good way to diversify your portfolio and spread the risk, so I recommend you consider including one or more of them in your portfolio. They are especially useful as a starting off investment when first setting up an investment portfolio.

Listed investment companies (LICs)

Listed investment companies are set up with a public company structure and are subject to the same rules and regulations and taxation structure as any other listed company. Trading shares in an LIC is no different from trading any other listed shares, as you can buy and sell them as you wish and you will receive any dividends and franking credits that are issued.

Some LICs, such as Argo (ARG) or the Australian Financial Investments Company (AFI), concentrate on Australian shares and have a long, proven record of profitability.

Tip

I regard investments in a well-known listed investment company with a proven track record of operation and profitability as one of the safest blue-chip types of investments you can make. They are therefore ideal for risk-averse, longer-term investors.

Listed managed funds

A managed fund is a pool of capital provided by investors in the fund that is managed by professional fund managers. Managed funds issue units (rather than shares), but from an investor's viewpoint this really makes no difference. Each unit represents an equal portion of the fund's value. Investors may receive regular payments from the fund—called dividends or distributions—based on the profit or income received from the underlying investments. The management style of the fund can be active or passive. With an active fund, the managers aim to outperform the market by selectively choosing the securities they will trade or hold. Passive funds, such as index funds, are managed so they will closely match the index they are tracking.

Some managed funds are diversified and invest in a broad range of asset classes such as shares, bonds, property and infrastructure assets, whereas others have a narrower investment profile and concentrate on specific investments, such as property. Other funds (index funds) aim to track a specific market index, and the fund managers aim to invest in shares in proportions such that the overall performance of the fund will (hopefully) closely match the index they are tracking.

Tip

Experience shows that it is very difficult to outperform the market so, over the longer term, active funds seldom outperform the more passive ones.

Listed investment trusts (LITs)

A listed investment trust is a business that is set up using a trust structure. (Please refer to chapter 1 where I discuss the various business structures in Australia.)

From an investor's viewpoint, the fact that a trust structure is used really makes little difference. The trust itself doesn't own the assets and therefore doesn't pay tax on the earnings; rather, the beneficiaries need to include income from the trust (earnings and realised capital gains) in their personal income assessment and are taxed accordingly at personal income rates.

Exchange-traded funds (ETFs)

An exchange-traded fund is another type of listed managed investment that you can trade in the same way as you would ordinary shares. They are similar to LICs, though there are some key differences between ETFs and LICs:

- LICs are closed-ended—that is, like any listed company, they issue only a certain number of shares. ETFs are open-ended, meaning the number of units on issue can vary at the discretion of directors and according to demand.
- LICs, like any listed company, can make dividend payments to shareholders according to profitability and at the discretion of the directors, whereas with ETFs all net income (after expenses) is distributed back to the unit holders.

As an investor, these differences aren't really important—the main significance to you is that the management expenses with ETFs are usually lower than they are with LICs, and could be as low as 0.1%, whereas with LICs they are typically in the range 1–2%.

Various ETFs crop up over the years and may have a more specialised investment mix that includes securities other than shares. You may find these attractive if you want to concentrate on a specific niche in the investment market.

Tip

Although you pay management fees for the administration of managed investments like ETFs, this doesn't necessarily imply that your return would be less than if you invested directly and thus avoided the management fee. You're unlikely to have the same expertise or time as fund managers as, for many of them, it's a full-time occupation.

Company-issued options

Company-issued options give the holder the right to acquire a certain number of fully paid shares at a stipulated price at any time in the future up to a date limit known as the expiry date. There's no obligation on the option-holder to take up the option, but options not taken up (exercised) by the expiry date become worthless. If the option is exercised, the holder needs to pay the stipulated amount. The advantage of options from the company's viewpoint is that at any time up to the expiry date additional capital flows into the company as options are taken up. This also means that more shares will be issued and the market cap of the company will increase. In some cases, when a company floats (that is, has an initial public offering or IPO), options are issued as well as shares; in other cases, a listed company may issue options to existing shareholders.

These types of options are usually given an identification code and quoted on a securities exchange, and they can be traded just as shares are traded. An option holder can decide to sell the options rather than take them up. This is common practice with directors when options are included as part of their salary package. Sometimes options will trade for only a few cents, in which case, if the option holder has only a small allocation of options, it may not be worth selling them, taking into account the trading cost.

> **Tip**
>
> While options provide additional capital for the business when they are taken up, it does mean that more shares are on issue, which potentially dilutes the benefits (such as dividends) to existing shareholders. However, the company may be able to use the additional capital to create proportionally more profit, such as by expanding, increasing efficiencies or investing in new technology.

Exchange-traded options (ETOs)

Exchange-traded options are very similar to company-issued options as they are essentially a contract between two parties to trade an underlying instrument at an agreed price at some time in the future up to the expiry date. One difference is that it is not necessary for a company to issue the options;

they may be issued by anyone (known as the writer) and purchased by anyone (known as the taker). They can be written over shares or indices—usually only the larger market cap types of shares. Options are a form of 'derivative' in that their value derives from some other instrument.

There are two main types of ETOs: call and put. Call options give the holder the right to buy at a certain price, whereas put options give the holder the right to sell at a certain price. Writing or taking options has several potential advantages:

- You can profit from price falls as well as price rises. For example, if you take a put option that gives you the right to sell certain shares at a price of $1 and the share price subsequently falls to 80 cents, you can profit from the price fall because you can buy the shares for 80 cents then sell them to the option writer for $1.
- Options can provide protection from a fall in value of shares in your portfolio. This is also known as hedging—for example, by taking put options over the shares (as illustrated in the preceding example).
- Options provide leverage (or gearing) and thus may give you 'more bang for your buck'. This is because they are much lower in price than the underlying instrument, but the price of the option tends to change in step with (or is almost the same as) the price of the underlying instrument changes. For example, if you believe the price of a share (or a market index) will rise, you could buy call options. If you are correct and the price does rise, when you exercise the option you will make a profit. But you will make a greater percentage profit than if you had purchased the underlying share, because the option was much cheaper.
- You can earn additional income with shares you own. For example, if you write call options over shares you own you will receive the premium as income, and this will be an additional profit if the options aren't exercised.

The disadvantages of options are:

- Trading costs are higher.
- Not all online brokers have the facility to trade them (although most of the larger brokers will be able to do so).

- Options have a limited life span.
- Options usually apply to high market cap shares (or indices) only and aren't relevant to low market cap or speculative shares.
- Losses will be magnified if the trade goes against you. The leverage of options is a two-edged sword as profits will be magnified but losses will also be magnified.
- You can also incur unlimited losses if you write uncovered calls and the market moves against you. An uncovered call is also known as a naked position, because you do not own the underlying shares and if the option is exercised you will have to buy them regardless of the price.
- If you take up an option and the market moves in the wrong direction, the option can expire worthless and so you lose whatever you paid for it.

Tip

Option trading has many advantages and can be profitable, but it is fraught with traps for the unwary. I don't recommend it unless you are an experienced trader and are fully conversant with the possible pitfalls and how to minimise potential losses.

Warrants

Warrants are financial instruments issued by banks and financial institutions and traded on the ASX. Warrants are similar to ETOs in some respects but there are also many differences. Like ETOs, warrants are a form of derivative—that is, they derive their value from another 'thing' (the underlying instrument). They provide leverage and allow you to gain exposure to an underlying instrument at a lower price than market price without actually owning it.

Warrants can be broadly classed into investment-style and trading-style warrants, but within these classifications there are many different types, including instalment warrants, trading warrants, MINIs, barrier warrants, commodity warrants, currency warrants, structured investment products and endowment warrants. Warrants can be written over shares, ETFs, a basket of different securities, a share price index, debt, currencies or commodities. The terms of different warrants can vary widely and are not standardised. Some warrants give you the right to buy, others to sell the underlying security (such as a share) to the warrant issuer for a particular price according to the terms of the warrant. Others may entitle you to receive a cash payment relating to the value of the underlying security at a particular time (for example, index warrants).

The main differences between warrants and ETOs are:

- The terms of ETOs are standardised and are set by the ASX, whereas the terms of different warrants are set by the issuer and can be quite diverse.
- There are many different types of warrants tailored to suit the needs of investors.
- Unlike ETOs, you cannot write warrants and there are no margin payments associated with them.
- Whereas ETOs usually have a relatively short time period before expiry, warrants may have a longer period, which can be as much as several years.

Each warrant has a unique code and is listed on the ASX and therefore can be traded using your online broker.

Tip

Because there are so many different warrants with so many different terms, I suggest you don't consider them unless you have first sought financial advice from an adviser with relevant experience in them or thoroughly researched the relevant terms and conditions and fully understand their implications.

Futures

A futures contract is an agreement you enter into with a third party to buy or sell an asset such as a commodity or financial instrument at a specified time in the future for an agreed price. The financial instrument could be a market index or sector index and the commodity could be gold, crude oil, natural gas, wheat or a similar commodity with a market value and price. If you think the demand and price of the instrument or commodity will rise, you could agree to purchase at current prices and sell at a higher price on expiry of the contract. If you judged the market movement correctly, you will make a profit on the contract; however, if you were incorrect, you will incur a loss.

It is important to note that a futures contract does not transfer ownership of the underlying instrument or commodity. For example, a futures contract to buy gold will not deliver any gold to you; rather, it gives you the right to purchase a certain amount of gold at a certain price at some time in the future.

If you wish to enter into a futures contract, you need a broker who acts as an intermediary and arranges the financial terms and conditions, and also arranges settlement. Of course, the broker will charge a fee for the service provided and this will reduce your profit (or increase your loss).

Tip

Futures are trading contracts that are really not relevant to most investors. They are considered risky, so I suggest you avoid trading futures unless you have special reasons to do so.

Contracts for difference (CFDs)

A popular way of gearing your share trades is by trading CFDs over shares rather than trading the actual shares. CFD trading is similar to futures trading except you don't enter into the contract with an unknown third party; rather, you arrange the trade with a CFD provider. When you trade a CFD, you don't actually buy or sell shares or securities; rather, you enter (or open) a contract with a CFD provider and sometime later you close the contract. Another difference between CFD trading and futures trading is that CFDs don't have an expiry date. When you close a CFD contract with a contra-transaction, the difference between the opening and closing value of the contract (less fees and charges) is your profit or loss on the deal—hence the name contract for difference.

A great advantage of CFD trading is that most CFD providers allow a level of gearing that's usually as high as 10:1 but can be as high as 20:1. A 10:1 gearing level allows you to trade shares with a value up to $100 000 with only $10 000 of your own capital! Another significant advantage of CFD trading is that you can profit in falling markets as well as rising ones. For example, if you think a share price will fall you can open a CFD contract to sell those shares, even though you don't actually own them. Then you close the contract sometime later with a contract to buy those shares. If you are correct in your judgement and the share price has fallen between the contract opening and closing periods, you'll make a profit from the fall.

While all this sounds like a great deal, you need to be aware that the risk of CFD trading is magnified by the same amount as the extent of your gearing. That's great if you get it right but can be disastrous if you get it wrong! Also, CFD providers charge interest daily on the full value of outstanding buy contracts, and there may also be a significantly higher trading cost.

Tip

Because of the higher costs and level of risk with CFD trading, it's usually not recommended for anyone other than experienced traders.

Forex (currencies)

Forex (an abbreviation of foreign exchange) is a field of trading in which currencies are traded. As every overseas traveller knows, different currencies throughout the world have a value relative to one another and that relative value is known as the exchange rate, which is constantly changing. For example, if the Australian dollar is quoted as having a value of 70 cents relative to the US dollar, it means that one Australian dollar will be exchanged for 70 US cents. Looked at the other way, it means that US$1.00 will be exchanged for A$1.43. This is good for exporters to America because a product costing, say, A$100 will cost Americans only US$70. On the other hand, if we want to buy a product that costs $100 in the USA it will cost us A$143. American travellers to Australia will find things cheaper in Australia, whereas Australian travellers to the USA will find things more expensive.

Because exchange rates constantly change, it's possible to make profits by trading currency if you can predict the direction of the exchange rate correctly. If you want to try this form of trading, many online share brokers have the facility to allow trading in foreign currencies. As this book is devoted to share investing, however, I won't delve into forex trading any further.

> **Tip**
>
> Forex trading can be a risky proposition because it is very difficult to predict how exchange rates will change in the future, so I suggest you avoid this type of trading unless you have special expertise.

Cryptocurrencies

A cryptocurrency is a digital asset that can be used in place of the normal currency of a nation as a medium of exchange in financial transactions and the transfer of assets. Cryptocurrencies originated in 2009 with Bitcoin, and Bitcoin remains the most popular cryptocurrency, although many other cryptocurrencies have sprung up since. You can look on a cryptocurrency as similar to chips in a casino. When you go to a casino, you exchange cash for chips. You can then use the chips rather than cash to place bets and receive winnings, and when you leave the casino you can cash out any chips in your possession.

In the same way as currency values between nations in the world fluctuate, so the value of a cryptocurrency also fluctuates and can be traded. Surprisingly, although cryptocurrencies have no legal status, quite a few online brokers provide a facility to trade them. However, while forex trading is risky, cryptocurrency trading is several levels higher in risk, and I suggest you avoid trading them unless you have special expertise.

Setting up to trade online

I'll now walk you through the process of setting up to trade using your chosen online broker. I'll use CommSec, the most popular online broker in Australia, as my vehicle. If you don't use or intend to use CommSec the information will still be relevant, as most online brokers in Australia have very similar arrangements.

Tip

Although CommSec is affiliated with the Commonwealth Bank, it has separate divisions with little customer interfacing. So, a branch of the bank usually won't be able to help you a great deal with any CommSec-related queries.

Becoming a client

You can apply online or request an application form from CommSec. CommSec offers a Commonwealth Direct Investment Account (CDIA), which you can use as your online trading account if you wish, otherwise you need to use another nominated account of your choice. If you decide to open a CDIA account, then you can use the account as you would any other account (such as an online banking account).

Tip

If you're planning to trade with CommSec, I suggest it's worthwhile opening a CDIA account for your share trades, especially if you are a longer-term investor.

Brokerage

At the time of writing, CommSec brokerage for Australian share trades is as shown in table 5.1. For international shares and other types of trades, please consult the CommSec site.

Interest

Unless you keep a substantial balance in the CDIA account, the interest rate is minimal; for example, at the time of writing, only 0.1% interest was earned on balances up to $50 000.

Table 5.1: CommSec brokerage rates for online share trades

Trade execution	Brokerage fee amount by
Trade online and settle your trade to a CDIA or CommSec Margin Loan	$5.00 (up to and including $1000)
	$10 (over $1000 and up to and including $3000)
	$19.95 (over $3000 up to $10 000 inclusive)
	$29.95 (over $10 000 up to $25 000 inclusive)
	0.12% (over $25 000)
Trade online and settle into a bank account of your choice	$29.95 (up to and including $9999.99)
	0.31% ($10 000 and above)
Trades over the phone and deceased estates	$59.95 (up to and including $10 000)
	0.52% (over $10 000 up to $25 000 inclusive)
	0.49% (over $25 000 up to $1 000 000 inclusive)
	0.11% (over $1 000 000)

Source: CommSec

Tip

Interest rates on online trading account balances (both with CommSec and other online brokers) are generally lower than on traditional bank accounts, so I suggest you keep a minimum balance in your trading account and transfer funds into and out of your trading account from other accounts when funds are required.

Securities you can trade

CommSec provides trading in all listed Australian securities. CommSec also provides the facility for trading exchange-traded options (ETOs). You can buy options (take them) or sell options (write them) in both types of options—namely, call options and put options. To do so you need to be a CommSec customer with a CommSec CDIA. You will also need to open an options trading account. CommSec has the facility to enable you to trade warrants, and the procedure for doing so is very similar to that for trading options.

If you want to trade international shares or other international securities you can do so with CommSec, which has the facility to trade US equities as well as equities listed on many other international trading exchanges. You will need to open a CommSec International Shares Account, and once you do so you can trade on international exchanges by contacting their international trading desk. The brokerage and fees charged depends on the international exchange and varies with each exchange and the equities being traded. You can find a list of these fees and charges on the CommSec site.

Other types of trades

Besides providing conventional online trading platforms, CommSec offers additional trading facilities, including:

- phone orders
- trading shares from deceased estates
- one-off trades
- off-market share transfers (such as from one family member to another or from privately owned shares into a self managed superannuation fund).

Special fees and conditions apply for these types of trades and these are listed on the CommSec site.

Margin loan

A margin loan is a loan specifically for the purpose of share trading and investing. The main difference between a margin loan and any other type of loan is that some of the existing shares you own can be used as security (collateral) for the margin loan. The shares that can be used are so-called 'approved' ones and are mainly blue- and green-chip type shares; most speculative-type shares will not be accepted. The amount of the loan will be a percentage of the value of your approved shares. This is known as the loan security ratio (LSR), and you must ensure you do not exceed it. The trap you need to be aware of is that you may exceed the approved LSR not because you have borrowed more but because there has been a fall in value of the shares in your portfolio. If you do exceed the LSR you will be issued a 'margin call', which means you need to pump more cash into your loan or sell some shares to obtain the cash. If you do not take the necessary action within the time period allowed, CommSec can sell some of your shares without requiring your approval to do so. It is therefore prudent to maintain a safe margin at all times and not borrow to the maximum amount allowed, so if there is a fall in the value of your portfolio you will not exceed your approved LSR.

If your application is approved, you'll be allocated a margin loan customer account number, a trading account number and an HIN with CHESS. You then transfer your existing shares, managed funds or cash into it as collateral. You are charged interest on the daily loan balance; this interest can be found on the CommSec website and varies from time to time.

Tip

Margin loans boost returns when the market is in a bull phase but increase the level of risk and generally increase losses in a bear phase. In order to improve your level of safety, ensure your gearing is well below the allowable so if the market falls you avoid a margin call. As risks and costs are higher, I suggest you don't consider taking out a margin loan unless you're an experienced investor with a good track record of success.

Self managed superannuation fund

Another method of investing in shares online is by means of a self managed superannuation fund (SMSF). If you set up an SMSF, your shares will be owned by the fund (that is, by the fund members). Under current legislation, an SMSF can have up to six members and each member is also a trustee. Rather strangely, even in single-member SMSFs, there must be at least two trustees (but only one human trustee is required if the second trustee is a corporation).

The members own the fund's assets and (just as with any other managed fund or superannuation fund) an SMSF is controlled by the trustees (of which you'll be one). As a trustee you have control over the management and financial decisions of the fund. Apart from shares, you may be able to include other assets (such as property) in the cash pool available for your SMSF, but special statutory requirements apply and you need to check these out.

SMSFs are very popular in Australia, and there are a number of online and offline providers who can help you set up and manage an SMSF. Naturally, the fees charged by an online provider will be less than those charged by an offline provider. The economics of having your own SMSF depend on your choice of provider and the fund balance in your super account. Because of the fees involved in setting up and running an SMSF, it's generally not worthwhile setting one up unless you have at least $200 000 to invest.

There's a capped limit to the amount you can deposit into the fund each year, and after you reach a certain age you can no longer add to your SMSF. Profit made by the investments in your SMSF receives a far more favourable tax treatment than shares held outside super (unless you're a low-income earner). In fact, it's possible for your SMSF (when in pension mode) not to pay any tax but rather to receive a rebate from the ATO for franking credits.

If you set up an SMSF, it's a good idea to ensure it reverts to pension mode as soon as legally possible because of the beneficial tax treatment. This requires you to take a pension from the fund that must be at least equal to the minimum amount stipulated by legislation and that increases as you age. The pension may be taken in instalments during the financial year or as a single payment.

Tip

Taking a pension from an SMSF means effectively withdrawing funds from the SMSF and paying them into a personal account. Nowadays, you are required to take your pension in cash, so if your assets in the fund include shares, you may need to sell your shares in the SMSF and then buy them back later, using the cash from your personal account, if you want to keep investing in these shares. In the old days you were able to simply transfer the shares from your SMSF account to your personal shares account, which was a lot less complicated!

Like most things in life, the benefits of an SMSF need to be balanced against the costs and additional hassles. The main drawback to consider is that investments in a super fund can't be cashed in or used until you reach a statutory retirement age (unless certain exceptional circumstances apply). This can greatly increase your nest egg when you reach this age but can be very frustrating if you want to access some of these assets prior to this age. In addition, there are a number of statutory requirements involved (including annual auditing), and these involve fees. Super legislation is constantly changing as governments tinker with the super system, so you need to keep abreast of the changes in order to maintain compliance, otherwise penalties may be incurred. To avoid the hassles involved, you can use an accountant or financial adviser with expertise in SMSFs to advise you or even manage the fund on your behalf. Naturally, the fees charged by them for doing this will erode some of the benefits.

All in all, it's not an easy decision and you need to carefully consider whether the benefits of an SMSF make it a worthwhile investment. If you want to set one up, CommSec provides an SMSF account facility, and if you are interested you can obtain the information you need from them.

There are also a number of other online SMSFs, and if you set up and manage your SMSF online it will be cheaper to run. One of the largest online funds is Esuperfund, and if you set this up online then there is zero set-up fee, while the annual fee is currently about $1500. Esuperfund won't directly trade shares but it links to Ebroking, which is a low-cost trading platform.

Tip

Over a number of years the power of compounding really kicks in, and in the longer term the favourable taxation treatment from having your investments in an SMSF can boost your after-tax return. Many investors set up an SMSF in order to provide a retirement nest egg, and the favourable taxation treatment can make a significant difference to your retirement.

Key points

- Once you've chosen the online broker (or brokers) you wish to use for your online trading and investing, you'll need to apply to become a client. To do this you need to provide all the details required by the broker, including personal ID. If you can do this online, the whole process speeds up considerably.
- When you apply to become a client with an online broker, you'll be asked if you want CHESS sponsorship. I suggest that you join CHESS as it's free and has significant benefits.
- You can transfer any shares you acquired prior to joining CHESS to your online trading account at any time. This will simplify your account-keeping and make it easier to keep track of your portfolio. It's simple and free.
- It may be beneficial to open a dedicated bank account with your online broker at the time of your application. Otherwise you'll need to nominate a personal account where funds can be withdrawn or deposited for your trades.
- After you've set up to trade online, you could have four or more important numbers to keep track of. I suggest you keep them in some secure and accessible fashion, as you'll often need to use them. You also need to consider making them available to executors of your estate—whether or not you have a will.
- Adequate funds need to be available in your trading account to pay for the net value of any purchases at settlement day (T+2, or two business days after the trade).
- Interest rates on online trading account balances are usually lower than on other bank accounts, so I suggest you keep a minimum balance in your online trading account. You can transfer funds in and out of your trading account from other accounts that pay a higher rate of interest on an as-needed basis.
- Apart from plain-vanilla shares, there are many other securities you can trade online. If you are interested in these, you should check with your broker to find out the types of securities you can trade.
- Most online brokers will provide the facility to trade a listed investment product, such as LICs, listed managed funds, LITs or ETFs, and I strongly advise you to consider one or more of these in your investment mix.

- There are various ways you can increase your gearing—that is, increase the amount of capital available to you for trading. But remember that increasing your gearing increases your profitability if you get it right, but it also magnifies your losses if you get it wrong.
- One method of increasing your gearing is by means of CFDs (contracts for difference). With this method, you don't trade shares as such but rather set up contracts to buy or sell shares (or other securities). At settlement you receive the difference in value between the buy and sell transactions—hence the name contracts for difference.
- An SMSF can be a very effective vehicle for share investing as dividends and capital gains profits receive very favourable tax treatment. Under normal circumstances, however, assets in an SMSF can't be accessed until you reach statutory retirement age.
- Over the years the tax benefits from having an SMSF can really kick in due to the power of compounding, so on retirement you'll have a much larger nest egg.
- Managing your share investments using an SMSF involves some fees and charges as well as complying with additional statutory requirements, so you need to consider carefully whether the benefits justify the additional cost and effort involved. Generally speaking, you need an appreciable investment balance to make the exercise worthwhile.
- I strongly suggest you resist the temptation to trade online until you've read through this book in its entirety. This should help you to avoid possible errors and pitfalls that otherwise could prove costly.

Chapter 6
Planning, monitoring and reviewing

Now you've investigated the online broking facilities available in Australia, made your choice of the one (or ones) you'll use and organised all the details, you'll no doubt be itching to start trading. Before you do so I strongly recommend you develop a trading plan. In this chapter I discuss how you might go about this and what factors you need to cover in your plan. I'll also outline how you can monitor (or keep tabs on) your trades and the performance of your portfolio.

Impulse and planned trading

There are essentially two methods of online trading, which may be termed 'impulse' and 'planned'.

Impulse trading

The impulse (or ad hoc) trading method is as follows:

1. You receive a trading stimulus that may come from a number of sources, such as an article you've read online or in a paper or

magazine; the advice of an adviser, friend or associate; a tweet, newsletter or message (from a forum or social media); or a media news report.

2. You consider this stimulus to decide whether or not you'll act on it. The amount of consideration you give the stimulus could vary from almost none to a more thorough investigation (perhaps using fundamental or technical analysis).

3. If you decide to act on the stimulus, you place a trade order with your online broker.

4. You check the profit or loss of the trade at random intervals and take subsequent action (such as buying more shares, selling them or just holding on) when you have time and the mood takes you.

Planned trading

In the planned method of trading (known also as the systematic method), you have a plan that you've thought about and prepared in advance. The plan has a number of aspects, and you evaluate each one before you place an order. When you receive a trading stimulus, you incorporate it into your plan and act on it only if the stimulus conforms with the criteria outlined in your plan. You monitor your trades regularly and initiate any subsequent action in accordance with the plan.

Which method is best?

I suspect most online trades made by people rather than computers follow the impulse method because it's simple and fast. The planned method requires some forethought and time, and in the busy world of today most people have limited time to devote to share trading. Nowadays, online trading is so convenient and rapid that there's a real temptation to 'just do it' without much forethought. To emphasise the point I'm making, I'll share with you a true-life experience of mine.

Some years ago when I was living in Sydney, I bought a cruising yacht. I moored it in a bay that was very crowded with other moored boats. One day when leaving my mooring, an adverse combination of wind and tide caught me unawares and very nearly resulted in disaster. When I told an experienced yachtsman friend about the near miss, he explained that there is a right and a wrong way of leaving a mooring and he outlined the right way. I realised that the method he outlined was logical and indeed obvious, and I didn't understand why I hadn't followed it. His reply has stayed with me ever since and is something I often think about. He said:

> ***'You didn't do it because you hadn't thought about it'.***

In other words, if I had thought about it and planned a strategy before I actually acted, I would have devised a safe procedure that I could have followed and thereby avoided any trouble.

The lesson I learned that day applies to so many situations in life, and certainly to online trading. When I left my mooring without following a planned method, I was like a trader initiating a trade on impulse and without a plan.

I'm not suggesting that if you don't have a plan, you can't trade successfully. Before I adopted a planned method of leaving my mooring, I had successfully left it many times. No doubt there are many traders who make profitable impulse trades. But profitable impulse trading over the long run requires a special talent most of us don't have. We might have a particularly fortuitous run of good luck, but that can't be relied on.

Tip

If you want to swing the probabilities in your favour and make worthwhile profit from share trading without relying on luck, you need a plan that you follow.

Planning your trades

It's best to write a plan for online trading, whether in hard copy or digital form, before you begin to trade. A written plan makes it less likely you'll ignore or omit some important considerations along the way, helping you to develop a strategy for each trade.

I suggest you planning should happen in two stages:

- *Master plan.* This is the outline of the headings you are going to consider when planning a trade. This plan will seldom change (if at all) and will act as your template for planning each trade.

- *Trading plan*. You fill in the details for each planned trade in accordance with your master plan. This plan will be different for each trade according to the type of trade involved.

Tip

I suggest you write a trading plan and refer to it every time (no exceptions) before you initiate any online trade.

Your master plan can be written at any convenient time (perhaps after reading this chapter). Your trading plan should be finalised when you are contemplating each order you place, as the details in your plan may be different for each trade. Indeed, in some cases your trading decisions may be influenced by current market action and therefore can't be planned a long way in advance (or sometimes even a relatively short way in advance) as the market can change significantly in a short period of time.

Tip

I recommend that you convert your master plan into a pro-forma you can fill in later for each trade you contemplate, so come up with your detailed trading plan for each trade.

Main considerations

There are three main factors you need to consider before you write your plans: entry, monitoring and reviewing, and exit.

Entry

These are the conditions that must be satisfied before you initiate a trade.

Monitoring and reviewing

After you've purchased shares and started a share portfolio you need to 'keep an eye on them', a process known as monitoring and reviewing. You need to plan how you will monitor and review your shares to ensure that you manage your share portfolio wisely.

Exit

It's tempting to ignore exit conditions while planning your trades, with the vague idea that you'll think about an exit strategy at some time in the future. I suspect many share purchases are made with a thought such as: 'I'll buy these shares because [insert reason] and I'll see how they go. If they do well I'll keep them, but if the price falls I'll sell'. This approach is too vague and indefinite, too 'rubbery'. If you don't have a well-defined exit strategy, it's really difficult to maintain a disciplined approach as the future unfolds, particularly if the price rises for a while and then enters a gradual and intermittent downtrend. In these circumstances it's really tempting to think that you'll hold them a bit longer... and a bit longer... and... Often the price drops way below the limit you would have placed had you planned your exit in advance, so you incur a big loss that wouldn't have happened had you planned and followed your exit strategy.

Note: If you've already bought shares without a plan, it's not too late to put a plan in place. Simply skip the entry conditions and move on to the monitoring and exit phases.

> **Tip**
>
> A monitoring and exit strategy is very important, even for blue-chip shares you intend to hold for the longer term. It's especially important for more speculative shares.

Headings to consider in your master plan

I suggest you include the following headings in your master plan:

- intention
- reasoning
- entry strategy
- exit strategy
- timing
- duration

- profit target
- parcel value
- quantity (number of shares)
- order type
- monitoring and reviewing (discussed later in this chapter).

Intention

This is where you outline what you want to do. For example:

- Buy some XYZ shares.
- Increase my existing holding of XYZ shares.
- Sell all of my XYZ shares.
- Sell some of my XYZ shares.

Reasoning

This is probably the most important aspect of your planning, where you ask yourself, 'Why am I contemplating this trade?' There could be many reasons why you want to buy or sell shares.

Typical reasons for wanting to buy include:

- I have some spare cash I would like to invest so as to get a better return than I receive from the bank.
- My friend (who knows a lot about shares) suggested these shares could be a good buy at present prices.
- I read a good report about these shares.
- I read a report by a financial adviser indicating that these shares are now a good buy.
- I already have some of these shares and they've been good performers, so I would like to buy some more.
- I read a thread on a forum where a number of people liked these shares.

- I like the products the company produces and I think the sector is in a growth phase.
- The shares pay a good dividend and I would like the additional income from the spare cash I have saved.
- The shares have good fundamentals that conform to my criteria, so they look to be worth purchasing as a long-term investment (more on fundamental analysis in chapter 8).
- The chart of these shares indicates the price is in an uptrend that looks likely to continue (more on charting in chapter 9).

Typical reasons for wanting to sell include:

- I need cash because I have some upcoming expenses.
- The shares have been poor performers and I can see better opportunities elsewhere.
- I've held these shares for some years now and they haven't done much, so I'm getting disenchanted with them.
- I'm making a profit on these shares but I'm worried that the price may fall shortly and I want to cash in the profits before this happens.
- I read a report by a financial adviser indicating that it is now time to sell these shares.
- The company cut its dividend, so I want to sell them and buy some higher-yielding shares.
- The company has fallen on hard times and doesn't look like recovering any time soon.
- There's been a downturn in the fundamentals of the business, so it no longer has sound fundamentals.
- The chart indicates the price is entering a downtrend mode.

Combining intention and reasoning

It's important to consider your reasoning in conjunction with your intention. For example, if the reason why you want to buy particular shares is because they were recommended on a forum or on social media, it will focus your mind on the validity of your reasoning. If you consider it dispassionately, you can ask yourself: is the suggestion of a friend or total stranger (who may or may not have any financial expertise) really a good reason for me to initiate a trade? Even if the shares were recommended by one or more brokers or financial advisers, you need to think, 'Are their recommendations always correct? Can anyone really predict the future? Are there other reasons I need to consider?'

Tip

It's not uncommon to find one or more brokers recommending certain shares as a buy when at the same time one or more others are recommending a sell. This demonstrates that no person or computer can predict the future with any degree of certainty, which is why you should always carry out your own research before acting on advice you receive from any source.

Entry strategy (purchase)

The entry strategy is the strategy you plan to use to initiate a purchase trade. Some examples are:

- Buy at market—that is, the lowest price offered by a seller.
- Buy when the price rises to $x.
- Buy when the price falls to $x.
- Buy at no more than $x.
- Buy at market when the market is rising and the share price is rising.

Each of these strategies has advantages and disadvantages that will become clearer in later chapters when I discuss the various orders you can place online.

Exit strategy (selling)

The exit strategy is the strategy you plan to use to exit a purchase trade (or trades) you made previously. Unless you're a short-term trader, there's a great temptation to ignore the exit strategy in your trading plan and regard it as something you'll think about later after you see how the shares perform. The exit decision is usually the most difficult one to make because if you've bought shares that are profitable, you won't want to sell them. On the other hand, if you've bought shares that have proved to be unprofitable it's really tempting to hang on to them in the hope that there'll be a change in fortunes and your loss will eventually turn into a profit.

Tip

Psychological experiments conducted over the years indicate that the pain of a loss is far greater than the joy of a gain. This tempts you to hang on to a losing share so as to avoid the pain of the loss. The benefit of an exit strategy is that it makes the selling decision less emotional and so it is easier to make, especially when making a loss trade.

Some examples of an exit strategy include:

- Hold the shares indefinitely provided the price rises over time (or at least remains stable) and the dividend yield remains above 3%. Sell if the price starts to trend down and reaches $6.20 or the dividend yield falls below 2%. (This is fundamentally a modified buy-and-hold strategy.)
- Sell shares if the price falls to $6.20 (loss-minimisation strategy).
- Sell half the shares if the price falls to $6.20 and the other half if the price falls further to $6.00 (averaging with a two-tiered loss-minimisation strategy).
- Sell all the shares if the price rises to $6.50 (profit-taking strategy).
- Sell half the shares if the price rises to $6.50 and the other half if the price rises further to $6.70 (averaging with a two-tiered profit-taking strategy).
- Place a stop-loss order at 10% below the purchase price and adjust it upward if the price rises so as to maintain it at 10% below the end-of-day market price (but don't adjust it downward if the price falls).

- Place a profit stop order at 10% above the purchase price.
- Hold the shares for three months and if the price doesn't rise to a target profit level of $6.50 by this time, sell.

Tip

It's generally not a good idea to initiate a trade regardless of current price movements. It's usually best to consider how the market and the shares are performing before initiating a trade. In particular, avoid placing a buy order when the market as a whole is falling and/or the price of the shares you intend to buy is falling. (I'll discuss this in more detail in later chapters.)

Timing

After you've written down what you intend to do and why you intend to do it in your trading plan, you need to consider when you'll act; that is, turn your plans into reality. For example, if you're keen to buy shares so as to get the next dividend, you need to time your purchase so the transaction takes place before the ex-dividend date. On the other hand, if you want to sell shares but still get the dividend, you need to time your sell order so it transacts after the shares have gone ex-dividend. Your timing can be somewhat flexible; in fact, in many cases it's a good idea that it is. For example, you might plan to act next Monday provided your trigger conditions are satisfied (more on trigger conditions follows). If your trigger conditions aren't satisfied on Monday, you'll wait until the next day, and so on.

If you specify a share price you can place your order almost anytime with an online broker, as most will accept the order on a 24/7 basis, even when the market is closed. For example, you could place an order with your online broker on Sunday afternoon, but your order won't transact until trading commences on Monday morning. I suggest you avoid placing orders outside of market trading hours unless exceptional circumstances apply. There are two reasons for this:

- I believe it's wise to get an idea of general market direction and share price movements before you trade, and that means not trading until the market has been open for some time.

- The trading screen you access at, say, 7 pm on a Sunday evening may be very different from the screen that appears when trading commences at 10 am on the following Monday (even though the Australian market has been closed during the intervening period). If you act on the information available on Sunday evening, you could enter into a trade at an unfavourable price or perhaps make a trade you would not have made had you seen the screen after the market had opened.

There can even be situations when you look at the market depth screen when the market is closed and see apparent nonsense, like bids that are higher than offers. This means that buyers are prepared to pay more than the price at which sellers are willing to sell! This type of anomaly can occur during non-trading periods as a result of unfulfilled orders in the system or international trading in Australian shares while our market is closed, which can occur due to time differences.

It's possible for unscrupulous traders to place 'dummy' orders when the market is closed, knowing full well that the orders won't transact. Then, just before the market opens, they cancel the orders. Dummy buy orders give the false impression of high demand for the shares and tend to drive opening bids up, whereas dummy sell orders have the opposite effect.

Assuming you intend to place an order during a time when the market is open, when is the best time to do so? During the opening period there's usually a great deal of volatility, but after an hour or so the market settles down and clearer trends become established. After the initial jostling is over you can get a much better impression of the tone of the market and how prices are moving. For this reason, I generally avoid placing orders during the first hour or so of trading. The downside to this strategy is that the market could move against you during this period and you might have traded at a better price if your order had transacted during the early period. However, I have found that, on balance, it is usually safer to wait until sometime after market opening before placing orders.

As a small investor, I have found that it's very difficult to get a jump on the rest of the market in the hope of pre-empting a significant price move by placing an order before the market opens. The market is informed, and generally by the time my order transacts any major price change in the offing will have already taken place.

Tip

Unless you're desperate to sell, I suggest you don't place orders outside of market opening hours or immediately after the market opens because there's too much initial volatility; it's usually better to wait until the jostling is over and the market settles down.

Duration

In your planning, you should consider the duration of the trade; that is, the time between entry and exit. This could vary from just one day or even less for short-term day trades to indefinitely if you're planning what is essentially a buy-and-hold strategy. The duration will also depend on the type of shares involved in the trade. If you're planning to make a fast dollar from price movements in speculative shares your planned duration could be very short, whereas if you're looking at blue-chip or green-chip shares you'll usually be planning a long-term investment that will hopefully produce good annual returns over a number of years.

Profit target

No doubt everyone trades shares with the vague intention of making as much profit as possible in the shortest possible time, but that's not a good enough target for a plan. You really need to have some concrete idea of what profit you're hoping to make from the trade over what period of time.

If you're buying shares with the idea of making a fast dollar, you might aim to make a capital gain of at least 10% within a week or a month, whereas if you're buying shares as a long-term investment, your aim might be to make a combined dividend and capital gain profit of 10% per year for the indefinite future.

Tip

Many studies have shown that humans perform best when striving to achieve a concrete goal that's challenging but at the same time realistic; that is, not too easy but also not too hard. Bear this in mind when setting your profit target by considering realistic future price movements and dividend payments of the shares involved in the context of the market as a whole.

Parcel value

You need to consider the funds you plan to allocate to the trade, making sure you include brokerage. This will depend on:

- your available funds (if you're planning a purchase)
- minimum brokerage for small parcels (if you're considering a small parcel value trade)
- your level of confidence; that is, the riskiness of the trade and how much you are prepared to lose if the trade goes against you. I suggest you maintain an inverse relationship between parcel value and riskiness: the riskier the trade, the lower the parcel value. This enables you to 'test the water' so you can purchase more shares later if the price rises, or sell them and take a small loss if the price falls. Of course, this involves more brokerage than a single trade, but if you trade online it's of less importance.

Tip

When considering parcel value, I suggest you use the 1% rule; that is, you should limit the downside risk to no more than 1% of your available capital. (This is discussed in greater detail in chapter 11.)

As previously indicated in table 5.1, online brokers (indeed all brokers) usually have a minimum charge for orders regardless of their value. Once you exceed the minimum value, brokerage is usually on a stepped or tiered scale. When there is a tiered scale you may want to take this into account when deciding on the parcel value of your planned trade. For example, if you are considering a parcel value of about $3000 and the brokerage is $10 for orders below $3000 and $20 for orders above $3000, it makes sense to make your parcel value just below $3000 rather than just above it.

With brokerage of only $5 for a parcel of value up to $1000 (as shown in table 5.1), this represents only 0.5%, which is very small compared to your planned profit on the trade that could be possibly 20% or more.

Nowadays, the low cost of online trading makes it feasible to trade small parcels. This is a great advantage if you're a small investor with limited trading capital, or if you wish to dabble in some speculative trading or test a trading system without committing yourself to large amounts of money.

Quantity

When placing a trade, you need to specify exactly how many shares you intend to trade. In the old days the number of shares needed to be a round number such as 1000 or 1200, but nowadays you can place an order for any number of shares you like, such as 1362. For sell orders, the number of shares depends on the number you own and how many of them you plan to sell (your broker will usually tell you how many you own as part of the selling process, so you don't inadvertently try to sell more than you have). For buy orders, the number of shares you can buy depends on the share price, your planned parcel value and the brokerage.

Tip

On many online sites you aren't required to calculate the number of shares you can buy; rather, you enter the price and your planned parcel value and you will be told the number of shares you can buy, as well as the total cost to you (including brokerage) for buy orders or the total net revenue for sell orders. You should always check this before finalising the order. When placing 'at market' orders, you need to exercise some caution, as the actual transaction price may not be precisely certain when you place the order. (I explain different types of orders in chapter 7.)

Example

You intend to buy a $5000 parcel of shares currently trading at $2.26, so you specify this price as your price limit. If brokerage is $19.95 for the trade, how many shares can you buy?

Solution

Because of the brokerage, you can buy $4980 worth of shares, so at a price of $2.26 you can buy 4980/2.26 = **2203** shares.

Note: You can check to make sure your calculation is correct:

The total cost of the trade is: 2203 × 2.26 + 19.95 = $4998.73

This checks out because it is just below your stipulated maximum parcel value.

Order type

There are three different types of online orders you can place:

- market order
- limit order
- conditional order.

I'll discuss these orders in greater detail in the next chapter, but in every case your trading plan should consider the type of order you want to place for each parcel of shares you intend to trade.

Monitoring your investments

Monitoring is the process of keeping up to date with your portfolio and how your investments are performing. You also need to keep abreast of changes to both your investments and the market as a whole so you can get a feel for likely developments. Reviewing should go hand in hand with monitoring and is the process of comparing how things have panned out in comparison with your plans and deciding whether you need to tinker with your portfolio. I discuss about the specifics of reviewing later in this chapter.

Tip

Even if you've sold all your shares in a stock, it's still a good idea to monitor at periods after the trade so you can see if your decision to sell was a good one and the success (or otherwise) of your trading plan.

Monitoring frequency

How often you should monitor depends a great deal on the volatility of the shares. If they're volatile and speculative, you may need to monitor several times a day, but if they're defensive and blue chip, once a week should be fine. Some share investors adopt a 'bottom drawer' approach after they've bought blue- or green-chip shares. The name derives from the idea that the shares are virtually filed in the bottom drawer of a storage chest where they're out of sight and out of mind. This approach tends to minimise stress and worry and over the long term and can be effective if you're a long-term investor and are confident about these shares.

Tip

I recommend you have a good monitoring system for all the shares in your portfolio, regardless of their nature. Even your long-term, blue-chip investments are worth checking regularly just to ensure they are performing as expected.

Monitoring plan

Some plans for monitoring share performance include:

- Check prices and announcements after the market closes every business day.
- Check the prices and announcements once a week (say, on Saturday mornings).
- Check the prices and announcements once a week on Saturday mornings and also look at the share price chart.
- Arrange an alert to your mobile device or by email if the share price rises to $x or falls to $y.
- Arrange to receive an alert each time the company makes an announcement.

Monitoring your portfolio online

Your online broker will maintain a portfolio for the shares you hold and have purchased with them and they should automatically update your portfolio with current prices and values. When you sell shares, they will be deleted from your portfolio. If you've joined the DRP (dividend reinvestment plan) and receive shares in lieu of cash dividends, the portfolio will be updated to show your new shareholding as soon as the allocation is made. Your portfolio will usually show purchase costs and profit or loss, but if it doesn't you'll need to work this out for yourself. In any case, if you've joined the DRP, the online portfolio won't provide a true reflection of actual profit or loss.

The format of a typical online portfolio is shown in table 6.1 (overleaf).

Note: Only two rows are shown here as it is an example, but an actual portfolio would have as many rows as there are different shares in the portfolio.

Notes:

- In your online portfolio, colour coding (such as green and red) is often used, as are symbols, such as up and down arrows to differentiate between rises and falls and profits and losses.
- The shares are listed in alphabetic code order.

Moving from left to right, the columns are:

1. *Code:* the unique distinguishing code for the shares—in the first row AAB, the second BCD and so on until XYZ in the lowest row.
2. *Available units:* the number of shares available for you to sell (should you wish to). This is equal to the number of shares you own unless you have an open sale order for shares (that is, an order placed but not transacted) or you've traded shares in the last two days. (Remember, settlement takes two business days.) The term 'units' is used rather than 'shares' because, strictly speaking, trusts and managed funds issue 'units' rather than shares, and the term 'unit' covers both.

Table 6.1: Typical online portfolio (hypothetical)

Code	Avail units	Purch price $	Last $	Change $	Change %	P/L $	P/L %	Market value $	Weight %	Market value change $
AAB	6039	2.58	2.55	–0.05	–1.96	–181	–1.16	15 399	8.83	–302
BCD	373	35.56	83.15	0.85	1.02	17 751	133.8	31 015	17.8	317
XYZ										
Total						20 278	11.6	174 267	100	1167

3. *Purchase price \$:* the price you paid for the shares when you bought them. This price won't be accurate if you have owned these shares for some time and joined the DRP (because each parcel you receive is at a different allocation price). It also won't be accurate if your total shareholding consists of different parcels purchased at different times and at different prices.

4. *Last \$:* the last sale price. If you check your portfolio after the market is closed in the evening, this price will be today's closing price and if you check on the weekend, this price will be the last sale price before the market closed on Friday night.

5. *Change \$:* the change in price so far today; that is, the difference between yesterday's closing price and the last sale price today. You can see that today AAB's price dropped 5¢ whereas BCD's rose 85¢.

6. *Change %:* the change in price as a percentage of the last sale price. Today AAB dropped 1.96% (0.05/2.55 = 0.0196 = 1.96%), whereas BCD rose 1.02% (0.85/83.15 = 0.0102 = 1.02%).

7. *P/L \$:* the total capital gains profit or loss on these shares; that is, the difference between the last sale price and the purchase price multiplied by the number of units.

   - For AAB, the profit or loss in dollars is (2.55 – 2.58) × 6039 = –\$181 (loss).
   - For BCD, the profit or loss in dollars is (83.15 – 35.56) × 373 = \$17 751 (profit).

   Note: The P/L figure will understate your true profit on dividend-paying shares, as dividends are not included. Also, the P/L is not strictly accurate as the brokerage cost on the original purchase is not included.

8. *P/L %:* the capital gains profit/loss on these shares expressed as a percentage of the original cost.

   - For AAB, the percentage profit or loss is ((2.55 – 2.58)/2.58) × 100 = 1.16% (loss).
   - For BCD, the percentage profit or loss is ((83.15 – 35.56)/35.56) × 100 = 133.8% (profit).

Note: You can also work out the capital gains P/L using the original value and current value.

- For AAB, original value = 6039 × 2.58 = $15 581.
  Their current value is $15 399 so the percentage loss is (181/15 581) × 100 = 1.16%.
- For BCD, original value = 373 × 35.56 = $13 264 and the percentage profit is (17 751/13 264) × 100 = 133.8%.

Comment: You can see that BCD shares have been very profitable whereas AAB are underwhelming and showing a small loss.

9. *Market value $:* the market value of these shares, namely the last sale price multiplied by the number of units. Of course, if you sell some shares you need to deduct brokerage to get the actual dollars you'll receive.

   - For AAB, the value is 6039 × 2.55 = $15 399.
   - For BCD, the value is 373 × 83.15 = $31 015.

10. *Weight %:* the weighting of these shares in your portfolio; that is, their value expressed as a percentage of the total portfolio value.

    - For AAB, the weighting is (15 399/174 267) × 100 = 8.83%.
    - For BCD, the weighting is (31 015/174 267) × 100 = 17.8%.

    Comment: You can see that there is approximately twice as much value in BCD shares as in AAB, and this has most likely occurred because BCD shares have gone up in value so much since purchase.

11. *Market value change $:* The change in value of these shares so far today; that is, the price change multiplied by the number of units.

    - For AAB it is –0.05 × 6039 = –$302.
    - For BCD it is 0.85 × 373 = $317.

    Comment: Today so far there has been little difference in value change and both are about the same in dollar terms, except that AAB went down in value whereas BCD went up.

Tip

The profit/loss figure shown in your portfolio may not be accurate enough for income tax purposes should you decide to dispose of any shares during the financial year, as it may not take into account brokerage or the cost of shares received through a DRP or differing prices if you have bought shares in a stock in more than one parcel at different times when the price was different.

Portfolio spreadsheet

I like to keep my own portfolio information, so I've set up a portfolio spreadsheet on my computer. Each time I monitor my portfolio in this way, I compare my portfolio with the portfolio shown on my broker's website. This enables me to obtain my true profit or loss for each of my shares and gives me the accurate information I need each year for my tax return. It also allows me to double check the accuracy of the information I have for my portfolio and ensures I haven't made any errors. If I find any discrepancies, I check them immediately to discover the reason and correct any mistakes or omissions I've made.

The format I use is shown in table 6.2 (overleaf).

Notes:

- Table 6.2 is hypothetical to give you an idea of the format.
- As with table 6.1, I've only completed two rows as an example. In practice, my table contains many rows because I have more than two stocks in my portfolio.
- I've programmed the spreadsheet to perform any calculations necessary, and I input changes as needed.

The information I include in each column is as follows:

1. *Date:* the date of the review.
2. *Name:* the name of the security.
3. *Code:* the code of the security.

Table 6.2: My portfolio spreadsheet—example

Date												Cap	
Name	**Code**	**Qty**	**Pr**	**Value**	**Div**	**EPS**	**PE**	**DPS**	**Y**	**GUY**	**TC**	**Gain**	**Strategy**
Andrew Invest	AAB	6039	2.55	15 399	uf	10	25.5	12	4.7	4.7	15 581	−181	Sell <2.40
Balan Ent	BCD	373	83.15	31 015	ff	245	34	205	2.47	3.52	13 264	17 751	Hold >80
CDIA				762									
Total	This week			83 542	XAO	9939						37 648	
	Last week			82 978	1%	9035	1%						

4. *Qty:* the number of shares or units held.
5. *Pr:* the latest price.
6. *Value:* the value, which is calculated by multiplying the price by the quantity.
7. *Div:* the type of dividend (uf = unfranked; ff = fully franked; pf = partly franked; drp = there's a dividend reinvestment plan that I joined; drpff = dividend reinvestment plan plus fully franked).
8. *EPS:* earnings in cents per share, updated periodically when a new earnings announcement is made (usually twice a year).
9. *PE:* price to earnings ratio, which is price in cents divided by EPS.
10. *DPS:* dividend per share in cents, updated periodically when a new dividend is declared (usually twice a year).
11. *Y:* yield as a percentage, which is calculated by dividing the earnings in cents by the price in dollars.
12. *GUY:* grossed-up yield, which is calculated by multiplying the yield by the grossing-up factor.
13. *TC:* total accounting cost of the shares in dollars, which includes the cost of shares allocated in lieu of dividends.
14. *Cap gain:* the capital gain or loss in dollars.
15. *Strategy:* a summary of my strategy for these shares according to my plan.
16. *CDIA:* the cash balance in my investment account.
17. *Total:* total value of all shares held, plus the dollars in my account this week as compared to last week and the percentage change.
18. *XAO:* I use the All Ords index (code: XAO) and I compare the change in the index compared to the change in my portfolio (in this case they both increased by about the same amount—1%).

Reviewing your trades and investments

If you want to improve your performance and maximise profits, you need to review and not just monitor your trades and your portfolio. It's all very well knowing what happened, but you also need to understand why it happened if you want to continually improve. Ideally you should review each trade a short time after the transaction was finalised but also each time you monitor your portfolio.

Reviewing a trade

I hope by now I've convinced you that each of your trades should have been made in accordance with a trading plan. If you review a trade and your review shows that the trade was in accordance with your plan, give yourself a pat on the back. If the trade wasn't in accordance with your plan, you need to ask yourself why. If you are really honest with yourself, you might come up with reasons such as these:

- I panicked.
- I acted on impulse because I was feeling particularly optimistic (or pessimistic).
- I received a 'hot tip' that I wanted to act on immediately before the market wised up to it.
- I acted quickly because the market was very volatile and I wanted to get the best price.
- Because of other commitments, I didn't have enough time to carry out the necessary research first.
- I engaged in wishful thinking and decided to continue holding the shares even though their price had fallen.
- I believed I was right and the market was wrong (again, wishful thinking).

Being honest with yourself about why you made a trade or didn't make a trade that you should have made if you were following your plan will help you to avoid making the same mistake in the future. Let's face it, if you have a plan and you haven't stuck to it, you have erred. Most likely you've acted impulsively for some reason or other. As I've said before, it's best to try and keep emotion out of the equation when you contemplate trading (or not trading) shares.

Reviewing your investments

Reviewing should go hand in hand with monitoring as a combined process. There's really not much point in just knowing what happened unless you can also explain why it happened. Likewise, in our day-to-day lives, when an accident happens, it's obvious that something went wrong—but the question is, 'What?' Clearly, if the performance of your portfolio is below your planned targets, you need to consider the reason (or reasons) and how you might do better in the future. If you're achieving or surpassing your targets, you may still wish to consider whether your strategies could be finetuned for even better performance because it's possible that your good performance was simply down to good luck.

When you are reviewing, try to be dispassionate and, in effect, become a self-auditor. A good way of reviewing your portfolio is to ask yourself several questions.

For your share portfolio as a whole:

> ***'If I owned no shares but had this amount of investment capital available, what would my ideal portfolio be?'***

For each parcel of shares in your portfolio:

> ***'If I didn't already own these shares, would I buy them today?' If the answer to this question is 'No', then ask:***
>
> ***'If I sold these shares and had this amount of cash, what shares would I buy instead?'***

Asking and answering these questions honestly will help you to review your portfolio realistically and so continuously improve your profitability.

If your portfolio performance has been below expectations, self-flagellation is pointless, and regret over poor decisions can't alter them. Instead, try to learn from each experience and, if you have made a mistake, try to avoid repeating the same mistake in the future. An excellent way of doing this is to work out how you can avoid the mistake and incorporate the improved strategy into your trading plan.

There are a few well-known share trading sayings that can be helpful to keep in mind:

- 'Anyone can make money on the stock market with the wisdom of hindsight'.
- 'Not every trade will be a profitable one'.
- 'Without the wisdom of hindsight, it's virtually impossible to get your timing just right when you trade'.

Tip

As long as you are making decisions that are in accordance with your plans, accept that not all your online trades will be as profitable as they might have been and just move on without ruminating over what might have been. The reality is that most markets go through down periods as well as up periods, and you really have no control over this. The trick is to maximise your profits in the ups and minimise your losses in the downs.

Using a watchlist

If there are a number of different shares (or other securities) on your radar, you can set up an online watchlist. A watchlist enables you to keep tabs on securities you're interested in without committing to a purchase. An online watchlist enables you to keep track of the securities you nominate in one place rather than by checking each one by one. This is a time-saving facility that is usually available on online broking sites and also on some public-access sites. There may be a limit to the number securities you can include in a watchlist. You may be able to set up several watchlists by giving each one a different name. You can then edit each list whenever you want to, adding and removing securities as required.

For example, on the CommSec site there's a 'Watchlist' tab that you click on. You'll be asked to give it a name and a blank watchlist screen will appear. You then click the 'Add stock' button and you can include the codes of the securities you wish to keep tabs on.

An example watchlist is shown in table 6.3. The bell symbol indicates a recent market-sensitive announcement. The rest of the watchlist should be self-explanatory.

Table 6.3: An example of a watchlist

Code	Last	Change	Chg %	Bid	Offer	Open	High	Low	Volume	🔔	Announce		
■ AGH	**0.028**	**0.00**	**0**	0.027	0.028	0.028	0.028	0.027	1 088 932			Buy	Sell
▼ ALI	**2.31**	–0.01	–0.43	2.31	2.33	2.33	2.33	2.31	41 144		(2)	Buy	Sell
▲ DJW	**3.19**	0.01	0.31	3.18	3.20	3.18	3.19	3.17	80 227	🔔	(2)	Buy	Sell
■ PTX	**0.045**	–	–	0.044	0.045	–	–	–	–	🔔	(2)	Buy	Sell
▼ VGS	**145.65**	–0.17	–0.12	145.64	145.65	145.65	145.79	145.45	92 063		(1)	Buy	Sell

Source: CommSec

Note: In table 6.3, you will see that at the time this watchlist was sampled there had been no trading in PTX shares on that day. The reason for this could be found in the announcement indicated by the bell symbol—namely, the shares were in a self-imposed trading halt pending the release of some new information that had the potential to substantially impact the share price.

Tip

Table 6.3 shows a short list; however, the watchlist option is more useful if you have a reasonably large number of securities you wish to keep tabs on.

Trading frequency

Your trading frequency is the number of times you trade in a given time period. There are three possibilities for your trading frequency:

- undertrading
- overtrading
- optimum trading.

Undertrading

You undertrade when you don't trade often enough. This is usually for two main reasons:

- You hang on to unprofitable investments for too long. It's a classic trap you can fall into when you indulge in wishful thinking, hoping that a loss will turn into a profit if you only exercise patience and wait long enough.
- You hang on to profitable investments for too long. It's another trap you can fall into when you have some good securities that have been profitable for you and you 'fall in love' with them. You think because they have been good performers in the past they will continue to be so into the future, so you don't heed the warning signs and tend to focus on good news only and ignore or brush over the bad stuff.

Tip

An extreme case of undertrading is a buy-and-hold strategy where you enter trades but never exit them. This strategy is often criticised as an extreme case of undertrading, yet in certain circumstances it can be successful. After all, if an investment is performing well and there's no imminent change on the horizon, then there's no logical reason to sell. Nevertheless, you should have a good monitoring system in place so you're alerted should circumstances change significantly and holding on is no longer appropriate.

Overtrading

You overtrade when you switch in and out of trades too often. If you are like many other traders, you might believe that in order to maximise profits you need to trade frequently. In fact, in the vast majority of cases the net result from overtrading is that you pay a lot more in brokerage and end up making less profit. This is the main reason why women tend to be more successful investors than men—because women tend to be more conservative and don't trade as often.

Tip

Avoid the temptation of trading online too often simply because it's so cheap and convenient. A useful pointer to indicate you're overtrading is if you're making a lot of trades but underperforming the market; that is, your overall market performance is significantly below that of the market as a whole.

Optimum trading

If you can find a balance between undertrading and overtrading, you will make the optimum number of trades, as shown in figure 6.1 (overleaf). In practice, it's very difficult to determine the optimum point, as it's not static and varies with volatility and market movements. Endeavour to find a good balance point that suits your investing style and optimises your profit.

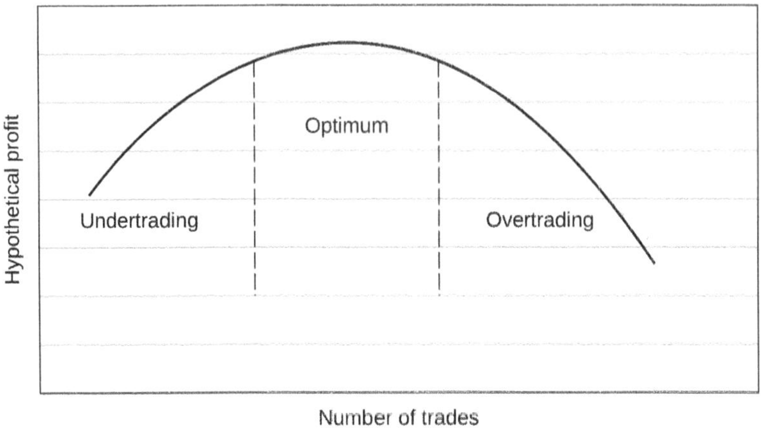

Figure 6.1: Optimum trading frequency

Tip

Keep figure 6.1 in mind when planning your online trades and try to strike a balance between undertrading and overtrading. Apply a disciplined approach to avoid the temptation to trade too often or, on the other hand, becoming apathetic or indulging in wishful thinking so you trade too seldom.

Following your plan

I suspect that the majority of investors don't have a plan. Even when there is a plan, it isn't necessarily followed. You could say that planning is the easy part; the hard part is being disciplined enough to follow the plan through thick and thin.

There's very often a conflict between rational and emotional considerations, and all too frequently emotion overrides rationality. For example, you might trade in the expectation of making a short-term profit, but instead the trade goes pear-shaped and before long it's showing a loss. If you have a considered plan you'll have considered this possibility and have an exit strategy you can use to minimise losses. However, all the planning in the world won't help if your emotions override rationality and you fail to exit as planned.

You may justify abandoning your plan with thoughts such as:

- 'If I sell now I'll make a loss, but if I hold on for just a bit longer the price could rise again—and if this happens, I'll make a profit'.
- 'The price drop is probably a temporary one and I reckon it will reverse'.
- 'I think the current price is the lowest that will be reached, and I don't want to be a mug and sell at the bottom of the market'.

When you look at it dispassionately, you'll realise that these thoughts are nothing more than wishful thinking. From personal experience, I've found out that markets have a way of ignoring my wishful thinking; they go on their own merry way, regardless of what I believe (or hope) may occur.

Tip

The hardest part of planning your online trades is sticking to your plan. The less emotional you are about your trades, the more successful you're likely to be.

Key points

- You can trade online using either the impulse method or the planned method. The impulse method is probably the most widely used by most traders but is not the most reliable way to trade. In the long run, you'll do better if you follow a plan you've thought about in advance.
- You really need a master plan, in which you consider the various headings you will include in your plan, as well as a trading plan, where you fill in those headings for each individual trade.
- Ideally you should write down your plans so you have a hard copy or digital version you can access at any time. A written plan turns your research into strategies rather than just ideas in your mind.
- A plan to buy new shares (or other securities) that you don't already own should consider three aspects: entry, monitoring and exit.
- The entry aspect of a plan to buy new shares (or other securities) is where you decide what you intend to invest in and the reasons why you intend to invest. This should include a minimum profit target for the trade.
- Your profit target should be realistic and take into account overall market performance. It's counterproductive to set unrealistically high targets that most likely won't be achieved, or to set targets that are too low so you miss out on the great profits you could have made.
- The monitoring aspect of your plan should state how you will 'keep tabs' on the trade. You need to plan the method and frequency of your monitoring process. If you have a relatively stable, longer-term portfolio you may be able to check prices and announcements each weekend. For more speculative trades, you may wish to monitor more often and also consider arranging to receive relevant notifications by email or text message, or as a notification in your trading app.
- As well as monitoring, you should also review your trades and your portfolio. This is the process of evaluating performance in an effort to discover what (if anything) can be improved.

- You should plan an exit strategy for all purchase trades before you initiate the trade. The exit aspect of your plan should state how you will close off the trade, considering the duration of the trade and the profit target you want to achieve.
- In some cases (particularly for low-risk blue- or green-chip shares), you might plan a buy-and-hold strategy, but it's still a good idea to plan an exit strategy in case of an unforeseen development.
- You can place a number of different types of online orders. Your plan needs to consider which of these is the most suitable for the trade you're contemplating and whether or not you intend to use conditional (or deferred execution) type orders.
- If you are planning a purchase trade, the maximum parcel value depends on the funds you have available. Parcel value dictates the number of shares you can purchase at the price you'll be paying.
- With a purchase trade, the parcel value should be inversely proportional to the riskiness of the trade; that is, the higher the risk, the lower the parcel value.
- If you're planning a low parcel value trade, you need to take into account the minimum brokerage charge and how this affects the cost per share.
- Using the 'watchlist' option is a very convenient way of keeping tabs on securities you may be contemplating for your portfolio. The more securities you wish to keep tabs on, the more convenient it is to set up a watchlist because with one click you can view the latest action.
- Because online trading is so easy, there's a temptation to overtrade in the belief that more trades will result in higher profits. This belief isn't substantiated in practice, and overtrading usually results in less profit.
- There's a happy medium between undertrading (holding on for too long) and overtrading (trading too often), and you should try to find this optimum trading frequency.
- Preparing a plan is relatively easy; sticking to the plan is the hard part. Above all, try to be rational rather than emotional when you trade and don't allow wishful thinking or other emotions to override your planned strategies.

Chapter 7
Trading shares

In this chapter I discuss the nuts and bolts of online trading; that is, the types of orders you can place online and how to do so. I'll look at online trading ASX-listed shares using CommSec for my examples, but the same principles apply to the trading of any instrument with most online brokers.

Buying and selling

When share trading began in eighteenth-century England, buyers and sellers met at a common location (usually a London coffee shop) and negotiated the trade as a private treaty (contract) between them. Later, share trading exchanges developed where agents (brokers), acting for the buyers or sellers, met and negotiated the trades. This took place on a very noisy, busy trading floor. With the advent of online technology, trading floors became obsolete, and most trading now takes place using exchange trading software platforms that match buyers and sellers.

Whether in a coffee shop in eighteenth-century England or online today, the principle of share trading remains the same. Trading is essentially an auction between competing buyers and sellers, and trades occur when there's agreement between a buyer and a seller on price and quantity.

Tip

Any person or organisation can legally enter into a private treaty with another person or organisation to exchange or trade a security such as shares. In particular, high-value traders may bypass brokers and negotiate trades by private treaty, thus saving on brokerage.

Bids and offers

The price a buyer is prepared to pay is known as the *bid* and the price a seller is prepared to accept is known as the *offer*. Interestingly, this terminology isn't necessarily the same as in everyday life, where a potential buyer might say, 'I'll offer you $x'. In share trading the buyer's offer is always known as a bid.

The difference between the closest bids and offers is known as the *spread*. It can be as little as a fraction of a cent or as much as 20 cents or more for certain types of shares.

Liquidity

For most shares there are many buyers and sellers, with bids and offers in the system at all times, so many trades occur each trading day; that is, there's a high volume of trades. Shares that trade frequently are said to have high liquidity; indeed, most shares listed with the ASX have high liquidity. However, sometimes there are few or even no trades for a particular share for a day or two (or even longer). This may occur when the shares are in a trading halt (usually because of some impending significant announcement). If there is no trading halt to explain the inactivity, few or no trades indicates low liquidity, and such shares are considered to be illiquid. These shares are usually the less well-known ones or those where almost all the shares are owned by a small number of shareholders (or other companies).

As you might expect, with liquid shares there's usually a low spread, whereas with illiquid shares the spread can be quite high.

Tip

Unless you have particular reason to trade them, I suggest you avoid illiquid shares. They are too difficult to trade at the price you may want when you want to do so.

Trading orders

The two most common types of orders are purchase (buy) orders and disposal (sell) orders.

Within the two broad categories of buy and sell orders there are two different and common types of online orders: market orders and limit orders. So, in fact, most orders are one of four different types:

- market buy order
- market sell order
- limit buy order
- limit sell order.

Market order

You place a market order (known also as an 'at market' order) when you agree to trade at the current market price; that is, if you want to buy, you accept the lowest offer at market, and if you want to sell you accept the highest bid. The advantage of a market order is that the trade will usually transact very quickly (literally within a second for liquid shares), so there's no dilly-dallying and you can be sure of the trade. The disadvantage of a market order is that you won't necessarily trade at the best price because you're accepting the current market price. It's analogous to buying or selling without haggling, where as a buyer you agree to the seller's offer and if you're a seller you agree on the buyer's bid.

As everyone knows when you're in the market for any commodity, be it real estate, motor vehicles or whatever, the buyer usually bids a lower price than the seller wants and the seller is usually optimistic in the price they ask, knowing full well they will usually get bids at prices below this.

However, with shares there can be circumstances where a market order gives you the best trade price of the day. This occurs when you want to buy shares in a rising market or sell them in a falling one. In these circumstances a market order is most appropriate as it places you at the top of the list of traders so your order will transact quickly and at the best price.

Tip

Unless the price is in a strong uptrend or downtrend mode, the premium you need to pay when you place a market order for a liquid share is usually small, and it's usually not worth missing a trade by holding out for a small price difference.

If the price is falling, it's generally prudent to wait before placing a market buy order—unless you have good reason to believe that the falling price is only a temporary aberration. If you wish to sell, all the opposite conditions apply. A market sell order in a rising market is generally unwise, whereas it's the best strategy in a falling market, as you can offload quickly before the price falls further.

Tip

You need to be aware of the way the market is moving for the trade you want to make so you can decide whether or not a market order will ensure you trade at a good price. It's generally best to avoid placing a market buy order in a falling market or a market sell order in a rising one.

Limit order

A limit order is one where you specify a price limit, which is the highest price you're prepared to pay if you're buying and the lowest price you'll accept if you're selling. In a sense, you're ignoring market movements and taking the attitude, 'It doesn't really matter what other traders are doing; I'm setting my price and if I can't get my price I won't trade'. The advantage of a limit order is that you're setting your price, so you know what price you'll get if the trade transacts and the exact total value of the trade. You'll buy at a lower price than you'd get with a market order if the price falls to your limit. Also, you'll sell at a higher price than you'd get with a market order if the price rises to your limit.

The main disadvantage of a limit order is that you're not assured of the trade. This means you need to keep monitoring the market and checking your order status for some period after placing the order. It also means you could miss out on the trade if the price moves away from your limit and doesn't return to it. In this situation, if you still want to trade you have to amend your order and specify a new price, which will most likely be a less favourable one than you could have received in the first place with a market order.

Tip

Be aware that if your price is too far away from the current price action, your broker may reject the order (as it will be regarded as unreasonable), or if the order does go to market it will be way down in the queue and may not show up on the market trading screen.

Example 1

You want to buy shares, and trades for these shares are taking place at around \$1.20, so you bid \$1.15, hoping to pick up the shares at a good price. Instead of weakening, the price rises during the day and closes at \$1.22. Next day, the price gaps up and the shares open at \$1.25 and trade all day at around this price. Now what are you going to do? You have to decide if you'll amend your bid or leave your order as is. If you don't amend your order and the price continues to rise, you'll miss out on the benefits of the uptrend you could have been participating in had you initially placed a market order and bought the shares for \$1.20 or maybe \$1.21.

Tip

If you place a limit order, you need to monitor the market closely and be prepared to amend your order quickly if the price moves away from your limit.

Time limit

As well as a price limit, you'll generally be asked to specify a time limit when you place an online order. This is the time you want your order to be left at market (that is, how long you want the order to remain active) if it doesn't trade quickly. Generally speaking, you shouldn't allow an order to remain in the market for too long; if it doesn't transact quickly, you would be wise to rescind the order and reconsider your strategy.

> **Tip**
>
> If you place a market order, it's a good idea to specify a time limit of one day. In the vast majority of cases, a market order will trade very quickly.

Parcel value

You can calculate the parcel value of an online order by multiplying the number of securities (such as shares) by the price and including brokerage. For a buy order, brokerage adds to the cost, whereas for a sell order, brokerage reduces the revenue (the funds you obtain). Before you place an order, your broker should provide an estimated parcel value and you can compare this to your calculated value. This will highlight any errors and help you prevent them.

With market orders, the parcel value will be only an estimate because share prices usually vary with each transaction, and the exact value of your order cannot be determined until the exact trade price is known.

If you place a limit order, you will know the exact parcel value when you place the order (unless the order transacts over a number of days and additional brokerage is involved).

Small parcels

Most brokers specify a minimum parcel value, which is a factor you need to consider if you want to trade a small parcel. If you want to place a sell order you can do so for any number of shares you own, whatever the parcel value. However, if you want to sell some low-value shares (or options)—that last traded for, say, 1.5¢—you need to consider the proceeds from the sale in comparison with the brokerage. If you want to buy some more shares in a stock you already own, you can buy any number for any parcel value, but remember that the smaller the parcel value the greater the effect brokerage has on increasing the actual cost per share. For example, if you want to buy some shares in a stock you don't already own, CommSec sets a minimum parcel value of $500; the order won't be accepted if the parcel value is lower than this.

Tip

Small parcel value shares are a nuisance and the brokerage can make the trade a counterproductive exercise. Also, small parcel value shares are a nuisance in your portfolio and for the share registry.

Tick

Tick is the smallest price increment allowed by the securities trading system for bids or offers, and it varies according to the share price. At the time of writing, tick sizes for ASX-listed securities are:

- 0.1¢ for prices up to 10¢
- 0.5¢ for prices from 10¢ to $2.00
- 1¢ for prices over $2.00.

For example, you can bid or offer 51.5¢, but you can't bid or offer 51.6¢ or 51.8¢ because for prices between 10¢ and $2.00 the tick increment is 0.5¢.

Trading data

Most online brokers provide real-time trading data, which means that data is automatically updated after each trade and you'll see the screen change after each trade is made.

Tip

You may need to refresh the screen periodically in order to keep tabs on the latest trades.

Trading hours

ASX trading hours are 10 am to 4 pm Sydney time on business days. Three hours before the market opens brokers can enter orders in the system, but these won't transact until the market opens. There's also a short period of ten minutes after the market closes when brokers can adjust or cancel orders. Remember that most brokers will accept your order at any time subject to certain conditions, but the order won't transact if the market is closed.

> **Tip**
>
> I recommend you don't place orders outside of normal trading hours (refer to chapter 6 for more information on timing your trades).

Order processing

The ASX trading system matches buyers and sellers, and trades occur when there's agreement between them about quantity and price. If there is more than one buyer or seller at a certain price, orders are transacted on a first-in, first-out (FIFO) basis. When there's no agreement on price but instead there's a difference (spread) between the closest bids and offers, orders are listed in price order sequence.

> **Tip**
>
> If you want your order to transact quickly, you can place a market order. If you wish to use a limit order, you can jump the queue by specifying a price that's a minimum tick amount above the top bid (if you are purchasing) or below the lowest offer (if you are selling). This will ensure your order goes to the front of the queue.

Order confirmation

You should be able to arrange to receive an email or text after you place your order to confirm that your order has been received and placed by your online broker. It also ensures there's no miscommunication and that you're both in complete agreement about all the order details.

Tip

Your broking website should contain details of all the orders you have in place or that have transacted over a time period that you specify.

Contract note

When a share trade occurs, it's regarded as a legal contract and your broker will provide a contract note as documentary proof of the contract. With online brokers this is usually in electronic form, so if you want a hard copy you'll have to print it yourself. Usually after the order transacts, you'll receive email or notification with the contract note attached.

Tip

I suggest you keep a file of all your contract notes, preferably in date order. You can keep them in hard copy form, but if you opt for the electronic version, make sure you have a backup on a separate storage device that won't be corrupted. I also keep a summary file of all transacted orders so I can quickly check the details at a glance if I need to do so for any reason.

Multiple-parcel order transacting

Usually your order will transact as a single parcel, but that's not always the case. For example, suppose you place an order to buy 10 000 shares at a certain price. Let's say there was a seller for 4600 shares at this price. In this case your order will partially transact and you'll buy 4600 shares.

The balance of your order for 5400 shares will remain open (and might not transact) unless another seller enters the market willing to sell the shares at your specified purchase price. If this seller has 5400 or more shares for sale, the balance of your order will transact. In this case you've bought 10 000 shares in two parcels. However, if the seller has only 4000 shares to sell, you'll buy another parcel of this size, leaving a balance of 1400 shares. If another seller enters the market willing to accept your bid, the balance of your order will transact, thus fulfilling your order in three parcels.

When a single order transacts in more than one parcel, each parcel is regarded as a different transaction so each will be listed separately on the contract note. If the trades occur on different days, there'll be separate contract notes for each transaction. In such cases, there'll be different dates of acquisition (for buy trades) or disposal (for sell trades), and this could possibly have capital gains tax implications.

The system will automatically amalgamate parcels in the same shares so your CHESS statement or SRN statement will show your total shareholding. With most online brokers you won't pay additional brokerage (compared with buying the shares in a single parcel), provided you haven't changed any details (prices or quantities) from those in your original order.

Tip

In rare cases, brokerage may be charged on a 'daily transaction' basis rather than on a 'per transacted order' basis. Additional brokerage will apply when a single order transacts in separate parcels over separate days, so it's a good idea to obtain an up-to-date fee structure if you are using a broker who's not using a conventional fee structure.

Order status

You can check the status of your orders at any time on your broking website. If your order hasn't transacted, most likely you've specified a price too far away from the current action.

Tip

As previously stated, 'at market' orders normally transact very quickly. If you check market order status shortly after placing the order, you should find that the order status is 'complete' and you will know the precise purchase cost or sales revenue.

Amending or cancelling your order

If your order doesn't transact you can amend or cancel it. I know of no broker (online or offline) who charges a fee for amending or cancelling an order not transacted. However, if you amend an order by changing the price or quantity after partial transaction, the amended order will be treated as a new order and will incur additional brokerage.

For example, suppose you place an order to buy 10000 XYZ shares at $1.00. You obtain 5000 shares at this price but then the price rises to $1.10 and shows no indication of dropping back. You now feel there is little chance of obtaining the additional 5000 shares at $1.00 so you raise your bid to $1.10. Your order now transacts, but now you'll have to pay full brokerage for each parcel.

Order purging

When you place an online order that doesn't transact, it won't stay in the market indefinitely and may be purged (either by your online broker or by the exchange). Expiry periods for orders vary with the type of order and with each online broker, so you need to check this if you don't specify a relatively short duration with your order. Orders can be purged for other reasons, such as trading halts, takeovers or the shares going ex-dividend during the period when your order is at market but hasn't transacted. Automatic purging will also occur if you're trading contributing shares or options that pass the expiry date before your order transacts.

Tip

If you're unsure about the status of any order, check the 'Order status' (or similar) tab on your online broking website.

Unfulfilled trades

If your order doesn't transact quickly, three things could occur in the future:

- Your order will transact at some time in the future as prices change and become more favourable.
- Your order will be cancelled because it passes the time-lapse date.
- Your order will be cancelled (purged) because of a status change in the shares.

If your order doesn't transact and you leave your order at market, the consequences can be unfavourable. For example, you place a limit buy order but the price rises and your order doesn't transact, so you leave your order at market. A few days later the price reaches a peak, then starts to fall and enters a downtrend. The price falls to your initial bid price and your order now transacts. The result is that you've bought in a falling market and this is generally not a good strategy. If the price continues to fall, you'll note with dismay that you're already losing money on your purchase and your losses are mounting! On the other hand, if you had withdrawn your order when it didn't transact quickly, you could have sat on the sidelines until the price bottomed. If the price later started to rise, you could then place a buy order secure in the knowledge that you were buying at a good price and into an uptrend—a good strategy. Of course, the same type of scenario can occur with a sell order if it doesn't transact and you leave it in the market.

Tip

In your trading plan, it's a good idea to include a strategy in case your limit order doesn't transact within a reasonable time. It's best to specify a duration and if your order doesn't transact within this time, cancel it and rethink your strategy.

Trade price

Buyers can bid whatever price they feel is a good buy price and sellers can offer whatever price they feel is the best price they can get. A trade won't occur unless agreement is reached between them, and the agreement can be reached in two basic ways:

- The buyers increase their bid price or decide to accept the seller's offer price (at market buy order).
- The sellers reduce their offer price or decide to accept the buyer's bid price (at market sell order).

Which of these scenarios will occur depends on the competition between buyers and sellers. The number of bids determines the demand and the number of offers determines the supply. According to traditional economic theory, the price will rise when demand (bids) exceeds supply and the price will fall when supply (offers) exceeds demand. This is illustrated in figure 7.1.

This theory is borne out in practice every day in the sharemarket and explains why share prices rise and fall. The market is dynamic and buyers and sellers frequently change their bids and offers or may enter or leave the market, so supply and demand can be constantly changing. So the share price often moves continually (even during the course of a day), rising or falling as supply and demand change.

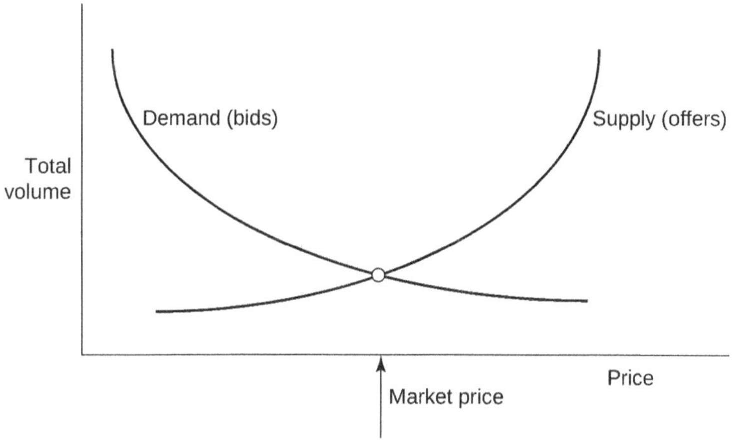

Figure 7.1: Market price

Tip

It's a good idea to check market action and the movement in share price of any shares you are thinking of trading before you place an order. Check the bids and offers at market and their relative proportions to gauge supply and demand and so get an idea of likely price movement.

Trading transparency

Trading using a securities exchange is transparent; that is, anyone can access the trading platform and view the bids and offers in the system. You can also see the last trade price and how trade prices have moved throughout the day; that is, the trading history (also known as the course of sales or course of trades).

Just as in a public auction, transparency is a very important factor in share trading as it allows everyone to see what everyone else is bidding or offering.

Tip

Just as in an auction, share traders are influenced by other traders, so trade prices don't necessarily change in a way that's consistent with the intrinsic worth of a given security but rather according to the mood of the market.

Key prices

There are five key prices of importance to share traders, namely:

- opening price: the price of the first trade of the day
- last sale price: the price of the most recent trade today
- high price: the highest price of a trade so far today
- low price: the lowest price of a trade today
- closing price: the price of the last trade for the day.

Tip

Apart from the opening and closing price, share prices can change constantly and sometimes dramatically during a day's trading. Naturally, the closing price won't be available until after the market has closed for the day.

Price variations

During the course of a day's trading there are many possible price change scenarios, including:

1. the price rises all day, so the closing price is the highest price
2. the price falls all day, so the closing price is the lowest price
3. the price rises, then falls
4. the price falls, then rises

5. the price rises, falls then rises again
6. the price falls, rises then falls again.

And so on … These scenarios are illustrated in figure 7.2.

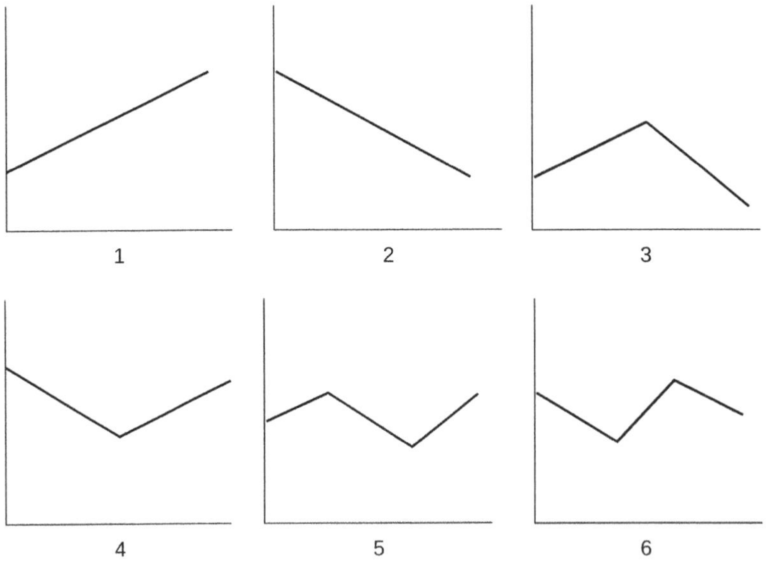

Figure 7.2: Some daily price scenarios

Tip

You might expect that the price moving in one direction all day (scenarios 1 and 2) is common, but prices often move both up and down during the course of a day's trading. As well as prices changing in various ways during the course of a day's trading, they can also change in these ways (or others) over the longer term. A continual price movement either up or down is known as a trend (I discuss trends in more detail in chapter 9).

Volume

When you look at daily price variations, it's a good idea to check volume as it can be an important factor. To see why, consider the following example.

Example 2

Trader A has 10 000 shares to sell and Trader B has 500 of the same shares to sell. Buyers are in the market but the price they're offering is 5¢ below the last sale price. If Trader A accepts the buyer's bid, this will cause a revenue drop of $500. On the other hand, for Trader B, accepting the buyer's bid will cause a revenue drop of only $25, and that isn't much in the total scheme of things.

Consequently, while Trader A will probably baulk at selling at a price of 5¢ below the last sale price, Trader B will probably accept the lower price.

The point of this example is that traders with relatively small numbers of shares to trade will often trade at prices significantly away from the last sale price because there's not much money involved, a decision that can cause a relatively large share price change. Consequently, small-volume share trades can result in price movements that aren't really significant because the volume and trade value are relatively small.

Tip

When checking trade price movements, it's a good idea to consider volume in conjunction with price. Price movements on low volumes aren't nearly as significant as those that occur with high volumes.

Gaps

It would seem reasonable that yesterday's closing price would be today's opening price but that's not always the case—in fact, it seldom is. Today's opening price is usually higher or lower than yesterday's close, particularly if the weekend has intervened (or even more a long weekend) when traders and investors have adequate time to rethink strategies.

When there's a difference between yesterday's close and today's opening price this is known as a gap, which may be either up or down.

I illustrate up and down gaps in figure 7.3, where Y is yesterday's closing price and T is today's opening price.

Gaps may have a number of causes, which may include the following:

- A change (or rumour of a change) becomes more well known after the market has closed.
- Today is the ex-dividend day—shares will almost always gap down by the amount of the dividend and usually also the value of any franking credits.
- Trading takes place on overseas exchanges while our market is closed. In particular, we tend to follow the trend set by the US market. Also, remember that some Australian companies have shares listed on overseas exchanges as well as in Australia and these shares can trade while our market is closed.
- While our market is closed, world events influence global markets and affect our market when it reopens.

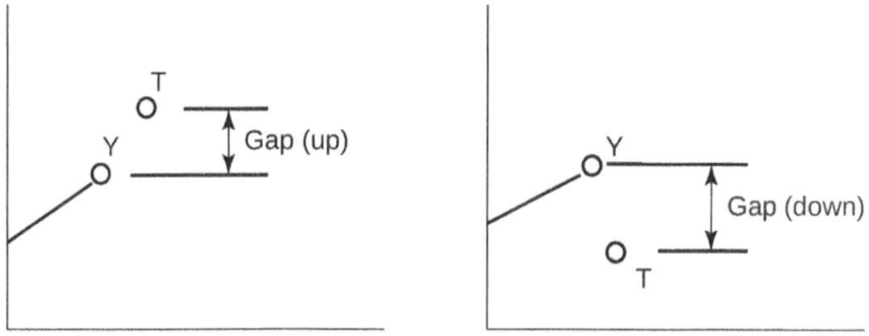

Figure 7.3: Up and down gaps

Tip

Small gaps aren't usually significant and are caused by normal fluctuating supply and demand in the market, but large gaps are usually significant and it's a good idea to try and ascertain the reason for the gap. Company announcements may help here, but it's often a frustrating exercise to try to ascertain the reason for a gap when it's not supported by any accessible news. Something is obviously going on…but what?

Price spikes

Sometimes a share price will spike up or down dramatically during a day's trading, as shown in figure 7.4 (overleaf).

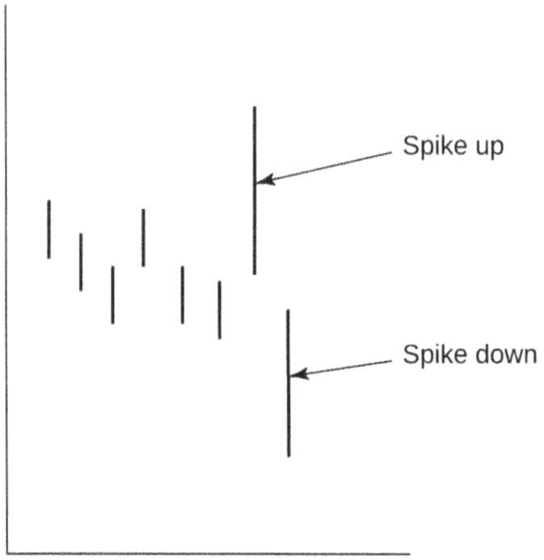

Figure 7.4: Price spikes

Tip

Beware of dramatic price spikes or gaps—they're danger signals for the inexperienced and it's usually best to stay away until the price stabilises.

Price spikes are usually triggered by an announcement of a major impending change or rumour of such a change. Very often there's irrational optimism or pessimism about the change. In such cases, after the price spikes (either up or down) there is a subsequent correction as traders realise that prices have gone too far one way or the other. If it spiked up, profit taking inevitably occurs as sellers scramble to cash in quick profits before the price falls; if it spikes down, buyers often scramble to buy at bargain prices before the price bounces upward again.

Tip

When looking at a share price chart, spikes and gaps won't be evident on a line chart. To see them you need to use a bar chart (or a variant such as a candle chart). The various types of chart are discussed in chapter 9.

Conditional orders

I've already discussed market and limit orders, but there's a third type of order that's common—namely, a conditional (or deferred execution) order. As the name suggests, a conditional order is one that goes to market not when you place it but at some later time, and only if certain conditions you've specified are met. These conditions are known as 'trigger' conditions, because your order won't 'fire' unless the trigger activates. If the trigger conditions aren't met, your order will remain dormant until it activates or lapses. For most types of conditional orders, you can't place a conditional market order but only a conditional limit order. This is because market orders usually transact without delay, whereas conditional orders don't do this and their execution depends on future movements in the market.

With a conditional order you need to specify two prices—a trigger price and a limit price (or trail value). The trigger price is the activating price; the limit price is, as usual, the price limit you set; and the trail value is a value used with trailing orders. (I will explain the different types of conditional orders in the upcoming sections.)

On the CommSec site, with conditional orders you can select a trading period during the day at which your order will be active, but it will remain dormant outside this period. This allows you to avoid the flurry of trading activity around market opening trading and closing periods when prices can be very volatile. You can also specify a trigger volume if you wish to ensure that your order won't be triggered on small volumes.

Tip

Conditional orders are particularly useful when you don't have the time (or inclination) to keep continually checking the market.

Example 3

You would like to sell some shares but the price seems to be rising, so you decide to wait and get a better price if possible. The current market price is $2.24 and you believe a resistance level could be $2.30. So, you place a conditional sell order with a trigger price of $2.30 and a limit price of $2.28.

Scenario 1: The price rises to $2.30 and continues to rise. Your order will go to market and the shares will be sold at the highest bid price achievable above $2.30.

Scenario 2: The price rises to $2.30 and then starts to fall. Your shares will be sold at the highest bid price above $2.28.

Scenario 3: The price rises to $2.28 and then starts to fall. None of your shares will be sold.

Common types of conditional order

The six most common (and simplest) types of conditional order are:

- rising buy
- falling buy
- rising sell
- falling sell
- trailing buy
- trailing sell.

Rising buy

A rising buy order will activate only if the price rises to your trigger price, which is above the current trade price. The purpose of this order is to ensure you buy in a rising market.

Example 4

The price of some shares you are interested in has been in uptrend mode and is currently $1.20. If the uptrend continues you would like to purchase. So, you could place a rising buy order with a trigger price of $1.25 and a limit of $1.27. If the price rises to $1.25 your order will go to market and you will buy the shares at a price no greater than $1.27.

Falling buy

A falling buy order will activate only if the price falls to your trigger price, which is below the current trade price. The purpose of this order is to buy shares at a lower price than the current market price.

Example 5

Some shares you are interested in have been in downtrend mode and are currently trading for $1.30. You believe the downtrend is only temporary and the price will rise again. You place a falling buy trigger of $1.22 with a limit of $1.25. If the price falls to $1.22 your order will activate and you will buy at a price no greater than $1.25.

Note: This type of order violates the principle of not buying in a falling market so is not one I recommend unless you are very confident that the current downtrend is only a temporary aberration.

Rising sell

This is also known as a profit stop order. Your sell order will activate only if the price rises to your trigger price, which is above the current trade price. The purpose of this order is to take profits when a profit target is reached.

Example 6

Some shares you own have been in uptrend mode for a while and the price has risen to $1.50. You place a rising sell order with a trigger price of $1.65 and a limit of $1.62. If the price rises to $1.65, your order will go to market and your shares will be sold at a price no lower than $1.62.

Note: This type of order violates the principle of not selling in a rising market so is not one I recommend unless you are very confident that the current uptrend won't be sustained.

Falling sell

Also known as a stop-loss order, this is the most common type of conditional order. It's a sell order that will activate only if the price falls to your trigger price which is below the current trade price. The purpose of this order (as the name suggests) is to stop further losses (or protect profits) should the price fall. It is sometimes described as being like an insurance policy for your shares, because you are protecting yourself from a major loss.

Example 7

You have some shares that you are jittery about because you feel the price could fall. Currently the shares are trading for $1.25. You place a falling sell order with a trigger of $1.20 and a limit of $1.18. Your idea is that should the price fall to $1.20, your order will activate and the shares will be sold at a price no lower than $1.18.

All this seems very logical, but suppose the price suddenly gaps down to $1.17. Your stop-loss order won't transact and you haven't protected yourself against the price fall you feared. So you can see that when share prices are volatile, stop-loss orders won't always protect you from sudden price falls.

Tip

In practice, stop-loss orders don't always guarantee profits will be locked in or losses will be limited.

Trailing buy

As already noted in relation to a falling buy, I don't consider it a good strategy to buy shares in a falling market. However, you can mitigate the disadvantage somewhat by using another type of conditional order—namely, a trailing buy. You use this type of order when you want to buy shares but not while the price is falling. So, you can place a trailing buy order with a trigger price and a trailing limit that can be specified as a dollar amount or as a percentage of the price. The shares will not be purchased unless the price falls to your trigger value but rises again by at least the amount of the trail value you have set.

Tip

You can also set a trail value as a percentage of the price. For example, instead of using 10¢ you might use 10%. This means the trail value will automatically be reduced as the price falls. If the price is $1.00 the trail amount is 10¢, but if the price falls to 80¢ the trail value will be 8¢.

Example 8

Some shares you are interested in are currently trading for $1.50. However, the price has been trending down, and you don't want to place a buy order in a falling market. So, you place a trailing buy order with a trigger price of $1.30 and a trail value of 10¢. This means that if the share price falls to $1.30 your buy order will be triggered but not activated unless the price rises back up to $1.40. If the price doesn't rise but continues to fall, the buy price will be revised down.

(continued)

For example, if the price falls to $1.20 your order remains triggered but still doesn't activate unless the price rises to $1.30, and so on. If the price continues to fall without rising, your order will remain triggered but dormant until the price rises by your trail value.

Note: If your trailing buy order activates, the shares will be bought at market. You cannot set a limit because the price depends on previous prices and you cannot place more than two restrictions on the price.

Trailing sell

One of the principles of good profit making with shares is to stop your losses but let your profits run. A trailing sell order is designed around this principle as it is essentially a stop-loss order where you specify an initial trail starting price and a trail stop value as a certain dollar value or percentage. Normally the starting price you specify will be the current market price. The stop-loss trigger will then be below this price by the amount of the trail stop value. If the market price of the shares rises the stop trigger rises accordingly, but if the price falls the stop-loss trigger price doesn't change, and the order activates only if the price falls to this value. This allows you to set a limit to the maximum possible loss, without setting a limit to your maximum possible gain.

Note: Like the trailing buy order, if your trailing sell order activates the shares will be sold at market, as you cannot set a limit because the price depends on previous prices and you cannot place more than two restrictions on the price.

Example 9

Some shares you are interested in are currently trading at $1.50. However, the price has been choppy and you want some insurance in case the price falls. You place a trailing sell order with a trail starting price of $1.50 and a trail value of 20¢. This means that if the share price falls to $1.30 your stop-loss sell order will activate. If instead the price rises, say to $1.60, your trigger stop will be reset at $1.40, (20¢ below the market price). In this way, if the price continues to rise your stop-loss trigger is continually revised upward, but if the price falls it isn't reduced. Say the price rises to $1.65, your stop-loss trigger is reset to $1.45, but now the price starts to fall and continues to do so until eventually it reaches $1.45. At this point your stop-loss order is triggered. Note that your loss has been only 5¢ per share, whereas if you had placed a fixed stop order at 20¢ below the price when the shares were $1.50, your shares would not have been sold until the price dropped to $1.30 and your loss would have been 20¢ per share.

You can also set a trail value as a percentage of the price. For example, instead of using 20¢ you might use a percentage in the range 10–20%. This means the trail value will automatically be reduced as the price falls and increased if the price rises. So, if the price is $1.50 and you set a 10% trail value, the trail amount will be 15¢, but if the price rises to $1.60, the trail amount will be 16¢.

Tip

If you aren't comfortable with conditional orders, you can achieve virtually the same result with market or limit orders. However, to do this effectively you need to keep a close watch on the market and be very disciplined in your trading. For example, you buy some speculative-type shares for $1.00 hoping for a quick capital gain, but you also want to limit your loss to 10¢ per share should the price fall. So, you monitor the market and if the price drops to 90¢ you sell. On the other hand, if the price rises you continue to hold the shares, and you don't place a sell order unless the price falls from the peak by an amount you decide on or when you have achieved your profit target.

Specifying a conditional order

As we have seen, conditional orders are more complex than conventional market or limit orders because you need to specify additional conditions. You need to consider the trigger price carefully in relation to the current market price, because if your trigger price is too close to the current market price (last trade), your order could be rejected by the broker or it could be triggered by small price variations that aren't really significant.

Many different systems for setting conditional orders have been devised, with varying degrees of complexity and each with some claimed superiority. I've seen no factual evidence that a more complex system produces better results than a simple one. For example, with a stop-loss order I've found that a simple 10–15% down from the current price or a 10–15% trail value usually works as well as some of the more complex systems I've tried.

Tip

If you plan to use conditional orders, start out with a simple system and increase complexity after you have had more experience, if you feel there might be an advantage to doing so.

More advanced conditional orders

In addition to the types of conditional orders I've specified, there are many other types of advanced conditional orders that can become quite complex. Many variations can be tailored to sophisticated trading strategies, which can differ widely between different investors.

Tip

Don't place more sophisticated conditional orders until you become experienced with the simpler types.

Pros and cons of conditional orders

Conditional orders have both advantages and disadvantages.

Advantages:

- Conditional orders provide additional flexibility compared with ordinary limit or market orders and allow you to use more sophisticated trading strategies.
- Conditional orders such as stop-loss orders or profit stops allow you to minimise losses or crystallise paper profits (in most situations).

- In most situations, conditional orders allow you to 'set and forget' your trading orders. This is very useful if you have a busy job, or if there are times when it is impractical for you to keep close tabs on the market.
- After you place a conditional order, the emotion tends to be taken out of the decision. You don't need to agonise over it because market forces will determine whether or not the trade occurs. As previously discussed, the less emotional and the more disciplined you are about your trading decisions, the better your likelihood of success.

Disadvantages:

- Not all brokers accept all types of conditional orders and some charge an additional fee for them.
- In times of rapid market movement (particularly when prices gap unexpectedly), conditional orders may be ineffectual as prices can shoot above or below the trigger point without the order activating.
- Conditional orders can result in you selling at a low price or buying at a high price that isn't subsequently sustained. This can occur when there's a significant price rise or fall that's only temporary but sufficient to trigger your order. The result is that you end up trading at a much less favourable price than you might otherwise have done.
- Considerable research and testing of the various types of conditional orders indicates that these orders aren't necessarily a panacea for improved share trading profitability. In other words, their use won't necessarily guarantee that your trades will be more profitable in the long run.

Deciding if conditional orders are for you

Conditional orders seem a logical way to reduce losses or lock in profits, but there's no factual evidence that they actually increase overall trading profitability. If you aren't an active trader or you simply can't (or don't want to) monitor the market continually, conditional orders can be useful, especially if you're trading speculative securities. If you're an investor following a disciplined trading plan and you're regularly monitoring the sharemarket and your trades (or proposed trades), you may be better off placing ordinary limit or market orders. However, most of us tend to be more emotional and less dispassionate in our decision making than we think we are, and conditional orders certainly help to maintain a more disciplined approach to trading.

To indicate how emotions may adversely affect your share trading conditions, consider the following example (which illustrates the benefit of a stop-loss order).

Example 10

You bought some shares for $2.51, and since your purchase the price has been rising and is currently $2.72. You think of selling and taking profits but wait to see if the price rises higher. When trading opens one day the price gaps down and opens at $2.48. You consider selling but decide to wait, because after all the price was rising and has been a lot higher. However, the price continues to fall and in several days is $2.37. You still agonise over the sell decision and decide to 'wait just a little longer'. Finally when the price reaches $2.28 you place a sell order and lose 23¢ per share.

You can see from this example that had you placed a 10% stop-loss order when the price was $2.72, your shares would have been sold when the price fell to $2.45 and you would have lost only 6¢ per share, rather than the 23¢ you lost by not using a stop-loss order and procrastinating over the sell decision.

If you're not short-term trading and have some blue-chip or green-chip shares in your portfolio, there may be no point in setting conditional sell orders. After all, you don't want to sell good shares just because the market is going through a jittery phase unless some significant adverse change occurs that causes you to re-evaluate the investment.

Tip

If you're unsure whether to use conditional orders, it might be a good strategy to try them with speculative shares and monitor the results. That is, after a trade, review it and consider whether you believe that setting the conditional order improved your profitability. As time goes on, you'll be in a better position to decide whether or not you want to use conditional orders on a regular basis.

Placing an online order

I will now step through the process of placing online orders for shares using the CommSec site. All online brokers follow essentially the same procedure, but there may be variations in access details, the amount of data available and how it is presented.

Tip

Some online broking sites (including CommSec) have a default time disconnect, so if you take no action within a reasonable time period you may be disconnected and you'll have to log back in again.

First, you need to sign into the site with your account number and password. You will then enter the default home screen.

Quotes screen

It is generally a good idea to look at the Quotes screen and get an idea of current market action. You can do this by entering the identifying code for one of the securities you're interested in and you will progress to the Quotes screen. You can also enter the Quotes screen from the home page without entering a securities code by clicking on the 'Quotes and Research' tab at the top of the home page then selecting 'Quotes'.

Tip

If you want to trade and are certain about the details, you can bypass the Quotes screen and progress directly to the Trading screen by clicking on the 'Trading' tab. However, unless you have a very good idea of current market action, I suggest you visit the Quotes screen before placing any orders.

A typical Quotes screen from the CommSec site is shown in figure 7.5.

In this case the Quotes screen is for ANZ Bank (code ANZ). The screen shows the last trade price and whether the price has risen or fallen from the previous day's close as a dollar amount and also as a percentage. The screen also summarises current bids and offers and the number of them, as well as key trading data including opening price, high and low prices for this day, trading volume so far, and the value of the shares traded. This screen also shows the 52-week high and low prices.

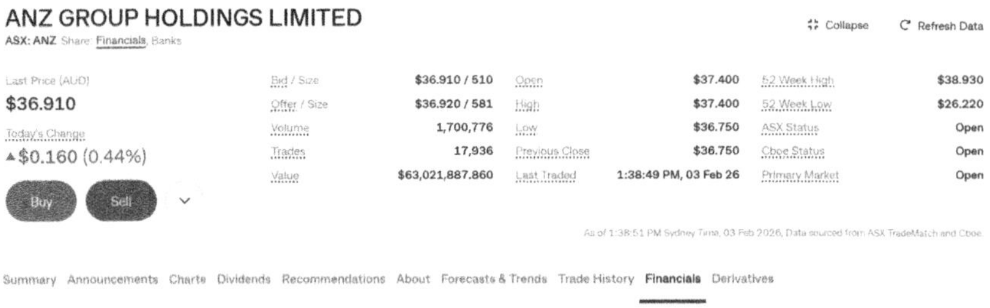

Figure 7.5: Typical Quotes screen
Source: CommSec

Below this quotes data, several links are provided if you want more detailed information. These are (from left to right):

- Summary—prices, orders in the system for these shares and some other info.
- Announcements—announcements released over the past month, but you can also specify a different period if you want. Below this is a one-month closing price chart.
- Charts—the default charts are a price chart with a trendline, and a volume chart for the past six months. You can customise the charts as discussed in chapter 9.

- Dividends—dividends that have been paid over the past ten years, both in chart and table form.
- Recommendations—analyst's recommendations, shown in table and chart form. The chart indicates changes in the consensus recommendation.
- About—basic information about the company, directors and contact details, and whether a DRP is operating.
- Forecasts and trends—dividend and earnings forecasts and trends.
- Trade history—summary of close of trade data going back in time.
- Financials—summary of financial statistics in table and chart form. These fundamentals are discussed in detail in chapter 8.
- Derivatives—the various call and put options that are operating over the stock.

Tip

As you can see, CommSec provides heaps of information on its website (as will any reputable broker). Actually, there's so much to consider that it can be rather overwhelming. When planning a trade, be selective in the data you consider, otherwise you can get bogged down in detail (paralysis by analysis).

Trading screen

After you have investigated the information you are interested in from the Quotes screen, you can progress to the Trading screen, where you actually place orders. You can do this by clicking the green 'Buy' or red 'Sell' tab on the Quotes screen according to the type of trade you are planning. If you bypassed the Quotes screen, you can get to the Trading screen simply by choosing the 'Trading' tab provided.

When the Trading screen appears you need to make a choice from the tabs at the top of the screen; that is, you need to select from:

- Shares
- Conditional orders

- Options
- International
- IPOs
- CommSec Iress.

CommSec Iress is the name of an advanced trading platform that you need to subscribe to and pay for if you want to use it.

Tip

If you first check your portfolio you can progress to the trading screen by simply clicking on the 'trade' option shown on this screen.

Assuming you are planning a share trade, a screen such as the one shown in figure 7.6 will appear (in this case, the trade is a buy for ANZ shares).

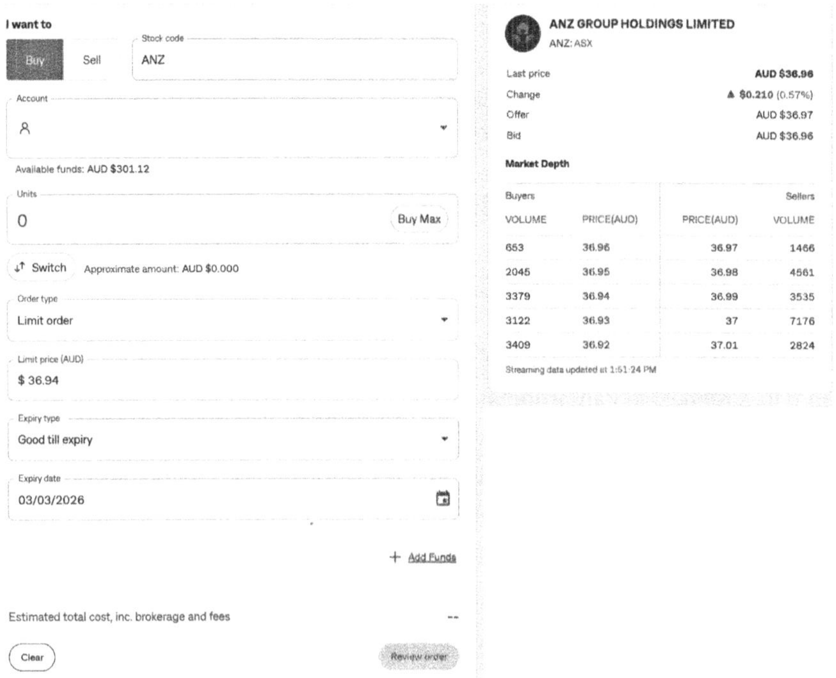

Figure 7.6: Trading screen
Source: CommSec

You can now insert the details of your planned order:

- *Your planned trade:* Click 'buy' or 'sell' as appropriate. (In this case, the trade is a buy order.)
- *Stock code:* This is the code of the securities you want to trade (in this case ANZ). If you aren't sure of the code, you can click on the magnifying glass image (search function) and you will be taken to a screen that allows you to name the security and determine the code. *Note:* the ASX site has a comprehensive list of all securities listed with the exchange.
- *Units (quantity):* Enter the number of shares (units) you wish to trade. If you're planning a sell order, the screen will show the number of available units you have to trade, which you should double check against your own records. Clearly the two must agree; if not, you will need to check the discrepancy before continuing further.
- *Switch button:* By clicking this button you can switch from specifying the number of units you wish to trade to specifying the dollar value of the trade. If you specify the value, the platform calculates the number of units you can buy to keep the trade value to a maximum of the amount you specify. This can be a particularly useful feature if you're placing a buy order and you want to keep the trade value just below a threshold, so you don't move into a higher brokerage rate. It also enables you to make sure that you're committing only the funds you have available for your planned buy trade.
- *Order type:* Here, you can specify whether you want to place a limit order or market order.
- *Limit price:* If you're placing a limit order, you need to state your maximum buy price or minimum sell price. If you're placing a market order, you leave this blank and instead click on the down arrow to the right, which allows you to choose a market order. The site will determine the most probable best price obtainable at the current time.
- *Expiry type and date:* You can specify an expiry date for the order, but you can also specify that you want the order to be good only for the day.

Tip

The term 'units' is sometimes used rather than shares because with some types of investments (such as listed funds) units rather than shares are issued and traded.

Order estimate

After you've entered your order details, an order estimate will be displayed at the bottom of the screen showing the dollar value of the parcel, the brokerage fee and the total net parcel value. As I've explained, if you place a buy order, brokerage is added to the cost, and if you place a sell order, brokerage is deducted from the proceeds.

Tip

I suggest you always check the estimated order value prior to confirming the order as this provides an additional safeguard against error.

Order transaction

The final step is to click the 'proceed' button at the bottom of the page and you are taken to the next screen, where you need to confirm your order and ensure that all details are correct before the order is sent to market. This screen gives you the opportunity to review all details of your order, and outlines the contract you're about to enter into with your broker. If you confirm your order it will go to market, but if you're not completely satisfied this is your last opportunity to amend or cancel the order. If you confirm a market order it should transact quickly. If you've placed a limit order it will go to market, and if your price limit is close to the current market price your order should show up on the market screen, which will change to reflect your order. Whether or not your order transacts quickly (or at all) depends on how close your specified price is to the latest trade price and how quickly the market is moving.

Tip

Some brokers require an additional trading password before they'll accept your order.

Placing conditional orders

To place conditional orders, you follow the same initial procedure, except you select 'Conditional orders' from the order options available on the Trading screen and are taken to a screen such as that shown in figure 7.7.

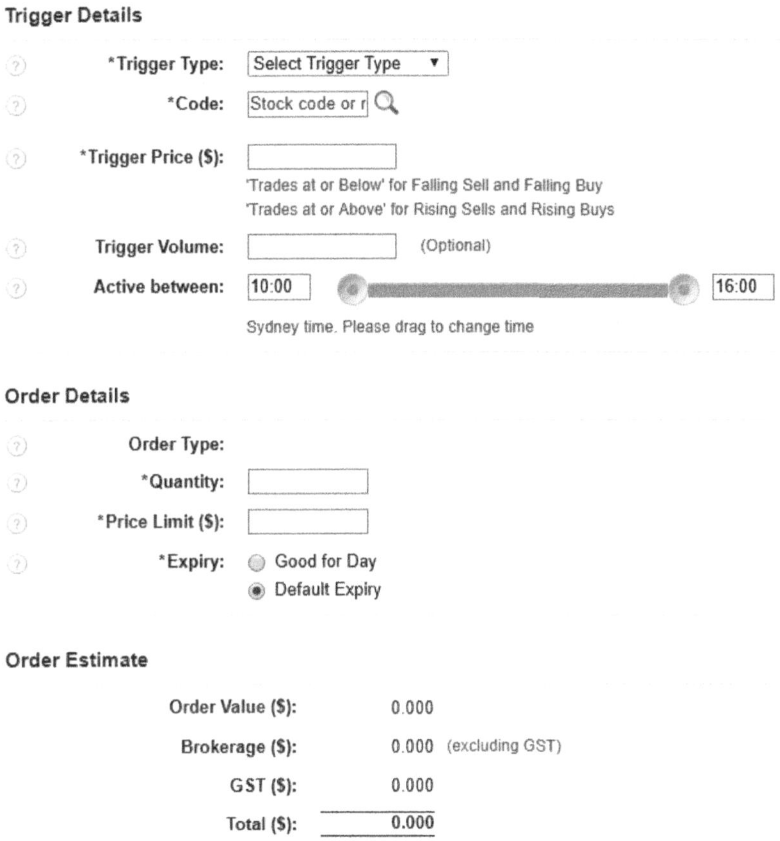

Figure 7.7: Conditional order screen
Source: CommSec

You now need to enter the required details as follows:

- *Trigger type:* Select from the six types available on the site as previously described: rising buy, falling buy, rising sell, falling sell, trailing buy or trailing sell.
- *Code:* Enter the code of the securities you want to trade.

- *Trigger price:* Specify your trigger price.
- *Trigger volume:* This is an optional condition that allows you to prevent your order from triggering on low volumes. You can specify a minimum cumulative trading volume for that day that must be reached before your order triggers.
- *Active between:* This is an optional condition that allows you to select the time period during the day in which your order will be active (and so avoid volatile periods, such as those that often occur at market opening and closing times).
- *Quantity:* This is the number of securities you wish to trade.
- *Price limit:* Enter the maximum purchase price or minimum selling price of the securities you want to trade. Note that if you place a trailing buy or sell order you can't specify this, because your order will transact at market price.
- *Expiry:* You can choose whether you want the order to be good for the day only or you can choose the default expiry (20 trading days for standard orders or five days for orders made with a margin loan account). Note that with trailing orders you do not have this choice (for obvious reasons) and the default expiry will apply.

After you've completed these details, you'll be given the chance to review your order by clicking on the 'Review' tab. After that, if you're satisfied that everything is correct you can place the order. If after reviewing the details you aren't completely satisfied, you can clear the order or adjust it as you wish before it's sent to market.

Amending a conditional order at a later time

If your conditional order has been sent to the market but it doesn't transact within a reasonable time, you can amend or cancel the order at some later time it if you wish to do so. It won't cost you anything to make such amendments provided no transactions have taken place. With conditional orders, you're most likely to want to amend your trigger conditions if the market moves in a direction contrary to your expectations. In particular, you can reset a stop-loss trigger higher should the share price rise rather than fall. Alternatively, you can use a trailing sell order so this will be done for you by your broker.

Tip

It's a good strategy to reset a stop-loss order upward if the price rises, but you shouldn't revise it downward if the price falls. There's no point in using a stop-loss order if you don't stick to your original intention if the price falls.

Price trends

If you want to trade on a particular day, you'd like an idea of how prices are trending so you can decide whether or not to place your order. It's a good idea to first check the market as a whole using an index like XAO or XJO, which captures most of the sharemarket action, and then look at the price movements of the shares (or other securities) you're thinking of trading.

The best way to look at this data is by means of a chart. To do this, you look at the chart of the share price for a time period of one day. This is known as an intraday chart (also known as a course of sales or course of trades chart), and a typical chart of this type is shown in figure 7.8.

Figure 7.8: Typical intraday chart

Source: CommSec

In this case, the chart was accessed at around 2.30 pm, so it shows most of the day's price action. As well as the price, this chart has a trend line that enables you to better see the trend. Normally you would access this chart at the time you were thinking of placing the trade, but the later in the day you access it, the better you are able to see the trend. In this case, you can see that there was a flurry of selling action just after the market opened, with a steep initial price rise, and then the price fell shortly after and settled down.

Note: The early price fall is typical of a market reaction—as I've mentioned previously, there's usually a flurry of activity just after the market opens that sets the tone of the market for the day.

Market and price trends

Various trend scenarios are outlined in table 7.1.

Table 7.1: Daily price trend scenarios

Market price trend	Security price trend
Up	Up
Up	Down
Down	Up
Down	Down
Sideways	Up or down
Up or down	Sideways

When both the market and the security price are trending in the same direction, you have a clear indication of the action. When they are both trending up, it is generally a good indication of a price uptrend and a time to buy. When they are both trending down, it indicates a good time to sell (or at least to avoid purchase). If the price is trending up or down and the market is side trending, you can generally be reasonably confident of the price trend. If the price is trending up and the market is moving down (bucking the trend), this can be a strong signal indicating a good price uptrend is in place.

Tip

Regardless of market action, I suggest you avoid buying securities when the price is trending down or selling them when the price is trending up.

Possible errors

Errors can occur with any method of trading, but they're more likely when you trade online on your own. If you don't have a broker or share adviser with whom you can discuss your proposed trade, you don't have someone who can check that the details are correct and conform with your established investing and trading preferences.

Possible trading errors include:

- incorrect code
- incorrect quantity
- price error
- unfavourable timing
- the order doesn't transmit
- insufficient funds.

Incorrect code

The code identifies the security and it's possible to use an incorrect code when you place an order. This error is most likely to occur if you jot down the code from a report you've read or from some verbal source. This error should be readily detectable because when you enter the code on the order screen, either the name of the security will appear different than expected or you will get an error message.

Incorrect quantity

It's possible to inadvertently make an error with the number of securities you intend to trade—for example, you could accidentally add or omit a zero in the order quantity. This error isn't difficult to make if you're trading a large quantity of low-value shares (such as 250 000 shares at a few cents each). Also, it's a very common human error to write down a number with some digits in the wrong order—for example, 2463 instead of 2643.

You can't rely on the trading platform to detect this error unless you're trying to sell more units that you own. The best way to avoid this error is by checking the parcel value after you have inserted the price and volume.

The trading platform will estimate the parcel value and you can (and should) always check this. For example, if you plan to trade about $5000 worth of securities and the estimated parcel value comes out to be $50 000 or $500, you will know immediately that you have made an error.

When you place a sell order, you can make an error with the number of shares or other securities you actually own. If you try to place a sell order for more shares than you hold (or are entitled to), your broking site should detect this error and notify you before acting on your order. You might also want to sell all the shares you hold (or are entitled to) but place a sell order for fewer shares than this when you actually wish to sell them all. This might be due to an error in your records, or you might have failed to include some shares you received in lieu of cash from a DRP allocation. If you participate in a DRP and have some shares due to you in lieu of a dividend, the records of these shares won't be received by you until sometime in the future when you receive your dividend statement or CHESS statement. It's easy to overlook these additional shares when placing a sell order. In this case, you'll receive a small parcel of shares sometime in the future, and selling them will incur extra brokerage and may not even be worthwhile. Therefore, when you participate in a DRP and place a sell order, you need to be aware of the ex-dividend date and the number of shares you will be allocated.

Tip

Before placing a sell order for shares that pay a dividend, check the ex-dividend date and also confirm your shareholding by checking your online portfolio, so you know the precise number of shares you hold (or are entitled to).

Price error

If you place a market order, the price is determined by market forces as the broker will attempt to buy at the lowest possible offer price and sell at the highest possible bid price at market at the time. When you place a limit order, you need to specify your limit price, and it's possible to make an error when doing so. If you do happen to make a favourable mistake (such as too high a sell price, or too low a buy price), the only effect will be that your order won't transact unless the market moves significantly in a favourable direction, in which case your mistake could end up producing a profitable windfall. On the other hand, if your order doesn't transact it could mean you miss out on a trade you might really want to make.

> **Tip**
>
> Before you send a limit order to market, you should check the price you have specified with regard to current market action.

Unfavourable timing

All details of your order may be correct, but the timing of your order can be unfortunate. For example, you buy shares and then the price falls, or you sell shares and then the price rises. Although you'll no doubt tell yourself that you've made a mistake, it isn't necessarily a mistake, because no matter how careful you are it's actually impossible to get the timing right all (or even most of) the time. Be content if you buy in an uptrend and sell in a downtrend, even if you could have made a lot more profit (or reduced losses) had your timing been more favourable. Remember: it's impossible to predict the top or bottom of any price movement.

A common timing error can occur with dividend-paying shares when you place the order at around the ex-dividend date. If you make an error, you might miss a dividend you want or receive a lower price for a sell order. Naturally, the way to avoid this error is always to check the ex-dividend date for dividend-paying shares.

Another timing error can occur with a limit order or conditional order if you leave your order in the system for too long (and you may even forget about it, if you get involved with other things). At some future date after the market moves significantly, your order might transact. In light of market action in the intervening period, you may realise that you didn't really want the order to transact and indeed you wouldn't have placed the order with your most recent knowledge.

> **Tip**
>
> Make sure you follow up all orders that don't transact within your planned time period. Amend or cancel the order—don't leave it in the system for any appreciable length of time.

Your order doesn't transmit

It's possible that your order doesn't actually go to the broker; that is, it doesn't transmit properly from your computer or mobile device. This could be because you inadvertently didn't press the 'send' (or similar) button, or because of a problem with your device, or a glitch in your internet connection, your online broker's system or the securities exchange system.

While this error can occur, it's most unlikely nowadays. Nevertheless, you need to be vigilant. Always check that your order has transmitted in exactly the way you intended. The best way of doing so is to ensure that you receive an email or text confirmation of your order as soon as you have placed it.

Tip

After you transmit your order, I suggest you check your text messages or emails immediately to ensure your order has been correctly received.

Insufficient funds

This error can occur with a purchase order should the total cost of your order (including brokerage) exceed your available funds. In some cases, your broker may ignore the order and send you an error message, but in other cases your order will process and you'll be required to quickly top up your funds. In the worst case, if you don't do so within a certain time the shares may be sold by the broker and you'll be liable for any cost deficit.

To avoid this mistake, you need to be aware of the broker's fee structure and carefully check the total parcel cost before you confirm the order. It can get tricky when you sell shares and use the proceeds to cover all (or some) of the cost of a buy order. Remember that the cash for the sell transaction will take two business days to go into your account, so you have to allow for that time delay. Also be aware of an additional time delay if you're transferring funds from one bank account to another.

Tip

When transferring funds into your trading account in order to buy shares, you need to exercise vigilance to ensure the transfer occurs in time to cover the total buy order cost on settlement day.

Minimising the risk of online trading mistakes

Online trading mistakes are most likely to occur when you're rushing because you have limited time, or because the market is moving rapidly and you want to trade quickly, or when you're distracted in some way. I suggest that before you trade online you set aside the time you need and that you sit down in a quiet place that's free from distracting background noise or other distractions. You should have a trading plan with you and know exactly what your intended strategies are. For example, you may be planning to purchase some shares you feel are a good buy, but when you check the market, you see that the price is trending down on that day. So, you decide to abort your intended order at this time and check again at a later date.

Tip

If possible, it's a good idea to get a drink (a hot drink will give you more thinking time) and sip slowly while mulling over your proposed trade. You might want to provide yourself with a pencil or pen, a sheet of paper and a calculator. And don't rush—a few minutes here or there is unlikely to make much difference!

Key points

- Before you place any online orders, have a copy of your trading plan with you, refer to it and stick to it.
- Obtain email confirmation of your order after you transmit it, and check it to ensure all details are correct.
- If your order doesn't transact within a reasonable time period, it could be purged automatically; however, if it remains at market, I suggest you review it and amend or withdraw it.
- You can amend or cancel an order at any time and you shouldn't be charged additional brokerage unless this is part of the brokerage fee structure, but that's uncommon.
- Avoid placing orders when the market is closed unless you have special reasons. It's also usually a good strategy to wait a while after market opening before placing orders, as this allows time for the market to settle and for you to get a feel for market and price trends.
- It's generally a good strategy to avoid buying when the price is trending down, or selling when it's trending up.
- A good way of getting an impression of price action is by looking at a price chart. On the day you intend to trade, an intraday chart can be helpful but I suggest you also have an idea of the longer-term price action. Charting is discussed in detail in chapter 9.
- Consider volume in addition to price movements, as price changes on small volumes are often unsustainable.
- The two most common types of orders are limit orders and market orders, and you're likely to use these for the majority of your trades. If you place a market order, your order will usually transact very quickly, but a limit order will transact only when the price reaches your limit.
- Conditional orders (particularly stop-loss orders) are a tool you may wish to use, but they have both advantages and disadvantages and you need to consider these carefully.
- Pay special attention to gaps and spikes in a price chart as they can be significant.

- When placing orders, it's certainly possible to make mistakes, so you need to exercise vigilance. Ensure your order is correct in all details before you confirm it, and that it transacts when you want it to.
- I've suggested several strategies for minimising the risk of mistakes. The best strategy of all is to ensure your orders are in accordance with your plan, and to allocate the time to place the order. Try to find a quiet environment where you can concentrate without distractions and it may be a good idea to have paper, a pen and a calculator handy.

Chapter 8
Benefiting from fundamental analysis

In this chapter I describe fundamental analysis, which is a useful approach to share investing. I'll discuss how to obtain fundamental data online and how to interpret and use this data to improve your online investing profitability.

Using fundamental analysis

Fundamental analysis is most useful when researching shares that are a medium- or long-term investment. As a shareholder, you're actually a part-owner of the business, and before you invest in any business for the longer term you should ensure it is built on a sound, solid base. This is where fundamental analysis helps, as it enables you to understand the basics of a business and gauge its longer-term prospects. There's little point in using fundamental analysis to select shares you want to trade in the short term, and it doesn't help you to choose the best time to enter or exit a trade. For these types of shares and trades, you need to use technical analysis, which is discussed in the next chapter.

Tip

Companies with a good history of sound fundamentals are the least risky and are usually best for longer-term investing.

Obtaining fundamental data

Imagine you are thinking of purchasing a business. You would no doubt conduct an on-site investigation—talking to the management, customers, staff and suppliers, examining the books and financial records, checking projected sales and earnings, and so on. From these investigations you could form a very good impression of how sound the foundations of the business are and therefore its likely prospects in the future. Clearly the average share investor can't use this approach, although large institutions, such as stockbrokers, banks or financial advisers, may be able to check the fundamentals of a business in this way.

Instead, your approach needs to be based on the published data you can access online. There are numerous websites that provide fundamental analysis data (I listed some of the most useful ones in chapter 3). Your online broker should also provide most of the fundamental information you need, and this will usually be the most convenient source for you.

Tip

If you want to delve deeper into the derivation and significance of fundamental data, please refer to my book *Teach Yourself about Shares*.

Types of fundamentals

When you are considering shares for investment, there are essentially two types of fundamentals you can consider:

- general fundamentals
- financial fundamentals.

General fundamentals

These are general features of a business:

- What size is the business: is it small, medium or large?
- Who are the directors and managers of the business, and what is their track record?
- How long has the business been in operation and how long has it been listed as a public company?
- What are the products of the business, and how well known and accepted are they in the marketplace?
- What are the business's future prospects—what does a SWOT analysis indicate? (SWOT represents strengths, weaknesses, opportunities and threats. Considering these areas helps you develop a deeper understanding of the future prospects of a business, including the challenges it might face.)

For some listed companies you won't need to research too deeply to understand the general details about the business, as they you will likely already recognise them. These businesses can be described as 'household names'. I imagine you would already have a very good idea about the general fundamentals of Australian businesses such as the major banks, BHP, Telstra, Qantas, Woolworths or Coles. But for many other less well-known businesses, particularly some of the smaller and newer companies, you might have little idea. In these cases, if you conduct an online search using the business's name, you should be able to obtain a reasonable amount of general information about it. Your online broker's website should also have general information about the business, but sometimes this may be only a short summary and you may need to delve deeper to get a better idea.

Tip

Warren Buffett (arguably the world's most successful long-term investor) once said that he never invests in any business he doesn't fully understand. I suggest this is a rule you should also apply to your share investing.

To access general fundamental data on a listed business (using CommSec as your broker for this example), you first enter the code of the stock then click 'Quotes'. Here, there is a 'Summary' page that gives you a snapshot of the business, the market action and broker recommendations. You can also access an 'About' page that further describes the company and provides some more information. For example, for BHP the following information is given:

> ***'BHP Group Limited (BHP) is a diversified natural resources company. It is engaged in mining of copper, silver, zinc, molybdenum, uranium and gold, iron ore, metallurgical coal and energy coal'.***

The 'About' page includes links to additional information such as 'Director's Interests' (the number of BHP shares held by the directors), 'Current and Previous Directors' and 'Shareholders' (which is a list of other major shareholders).

Tip

Changes to fundamental information can take time to filter through to online brokers such as CommSec, so your broker may not always be completely up to date with all fundamental information.

Financial fundamentals

The financial data about a business include:

- revenue (or turnover) from sales
- costs of operating the business
- earnings (profit) or loss
- amount of capital invested in the business
- assets and liabilities (what the business owns and what it owes).

You should be able to obtain the financial data you need from your online broker; however, the way the data is compiled and presented may vary from one broker to another.

Using CommSec's broking website as an example, if you enter the code of the shares you're interested in and then click on the 'Summary' link, you can see a snapshot of key financial data, as well as other information including recommendations. If you click on the 'Financials' link you'll find heaps of detailed financial statistics going back over ten years.

Tip

If your online broker doesn't have the financial data you want, I suggest you examine another site even if you don't use that site for trading. There's also plenty of free information available online (refer to chapter 3 for some ideas on where to start).

Reporting fundamental information

Exchange listing rules require a listed company to release certain financial information by specified dates. In addition, a company may release announcements to the exchange at any time the directors deem necessary—indeed, listing rules require that any key changes affecting a listed company are made available promptly for all to see.

Tip

Insider trading occurs when a select few seek to profit from information known only to them. It is illegal in Australia, which is why information affecting a listed company must first be released to the exchange so everyone can access the same information at the same time.

Facts and hype

We'd like to think that, most often, investors (including ourselves) make rational trading decisions based on sound data. There's even a theory, called the efficient market theory, proposing that the market works in this way. However, this theory has now been largely discredited, because it was found that sharemarket perceptions about the future are often based on rumour or hype and have little factual basis. Very often the price of a share changes before any official announcement is made, so clearly some rumour has swept into the market.

Despite all attempts to stamp out insider trading, it is inevitable that some people will have access to information that others don't have, and that this often filters down and affects the market well before the information is officially released. Subsequently, when an announcement is made and the information becomes official and is known to all, the market may react in the opposite way to what would appear logical. For example, a favourable announcement such as an increase in earnings may result in a share price fall, and vice versa! This usually occurs because the information has been pre-empted by investors and factored into the share price prior to the announcement.

Tip

If you're a longer-term investor rather than a short-term trader, I suggest you ignore rumours and try not to get caught up in market hype, but rather adopt a more rational and logical approach to your investing.

Reviewing financial fundamentals

In Australia there are strict controls over company accounting practices aimed at ensuring that published financial data has been compiled in a rigorous manner, and that it gives a true and accurate reflection of the financial health of a business. Naturally, the government has a direct interest in financial details, since taxes are based on profits.

Financial data must be compiled by an accredited accountant; in addition, businesses must have their financial data audited by an independent auditor.

However, despite this comprehensive financial regulation by both the government and securities exchanges, some companies have been found to have 'cooked the books' or 'massaged' financial results to make them look better through 'creative accounting'. In the past even highly esteemed businesses, including the large banks and retailers, have been found guilty of some shonky business practices, so the size or reputation of a business doesn't necessarily guarantee that all its business practices are strictly in accordance with all laws and regulations.

Tip

You can't always be sure that the published financial statistics are a true reflection of the current financial health of the business. Also remember that the financial information could be quite out of date when you access it so the business might be doing better or worse than indicated by the published information available at any given time.

Accounting periods

In Australia there are two official accounting periods for which all relevant financial data is compiled and published. These periods are:

- interim period: the first six months of the financial year
- final period: the last six months of the financial year.

Naturally, full-year data is the sum of the two and gives the financial performance for the total year. Most financial statistics will default to the full-year result unless stated otherwise.

Tip

Most Australian companies use a financial year ending 30 June, but this isn't always the case so you need to check.

Time delay

One of the problems with published financial data is that it can be quite out of date when you access it. The reason for this is that there's a lot of work involved in obtaining the data and arranging it in the form required by law and the listing exchange. For example, the company is required to produce an annual report, a comprehensive document that is expensive to produce and disseminate. As a result, there can be a time delay of a month or two after the cut-off date for the data before it is disseminated. Once disseminated, this data could remain in place unchanged until the next six months cut-off date. So, in fact, the financial data you access could be up to eight months old. Clearly, many changes to the finances of a business can occur in a time period of this length. This is one of the reasons why fundamental data isn't much help with short-term trading decisions and is more applicable to longer-term investing. This can also be the reason why a company (even a large one) suddenly announces financial difficulties seemingly 'out of the blue', as there is no evidence that something was amiss in the previously published financial information.

Tip

When the latest published financial data looks healthy but the shares are becoming unpopular with investors, the first thing you should consider is whether the financial data may be out of date. There is a good chance that adverse changes have occurred (or are anticipated) that aren't reflected in the published statistics.

Ways of presenting financial data

Financial data can be presented in a number of ways, including:

- total amount
- per-share basis
- ratio (or percentage)
- snapshot in time
- during a specified time period (historical)
- dynamic data (constantly updated)
- projected data (future).

Tip

When you examine financial data, ensure you know on which basis the data has been compiled.

Total amount

The total amount of financial data is simply the total dollar value. For example, a company may report earnings of $20 million for the financial year, or sales of $40 million.

> **Tip**
>
> 'Earnings' and 'profit' are key fundamental statistics—and they actually mean the same thing.

Per-share basis

The per-share basis is the total amount divided by the number of shares. For example, if the total earnings are divided by the number of shares on issue, the result is the earnings per share (EPS). You can see that this is a much more meaningful statistic than the total earnings, as it tells you how much profit each share is entitled to.

> **Tip**
>
> From a share investor's viewpoint, data calculated on a per-share basis is a more meaningful statistic than a total amount.

Ratio (or percentage)

Many financial statistics are expressed as ratios (or percentages) because a single value on its own doesn't provide a good basis for evaluation or comparison. For example, the total dollar profit doesn't allow you to make a good comparison of the profitability of one company compared with another because of size differences. A major factor that affects earnings is the size of the business—clearly, the larger a business, the more profit it should make (in dollar terms). A more meaningful earning statistic can be obtained by dividing the profit by the value of the assets or by the shareholders' equity, thus giving the return on assets or return on equity. These are usually converted to a percentage by multiplying by 100. The percentage return on assets or equity is a far more meaningful statistic than earnings itself as it allows you to make a fair comparison of the profitability between businesses of differing sizes.

> **Tip**
>
> You get a better comparison between businesses of different sizes when you examine statistics that are expressed as a percentage (or ratio).

Snapshot

As the name suggests, a snapshot statistic is one that applies at a given point in time only—usually at the end of an accounting period. For example, a balance sheet gives snapshot statistics such as assets and liabilities at a point in time. It's the same idea as a real estate valuation that estimates the value of a property at the time of the valuation.

> **Tip**
>
> Snapshot statistics on their own don't provide information on how these statistics may have changed in the past or could change in the future.

Historical

Historical data is data compiled over a number of periods in the past. Examination of historical data enables you to form an impression of trends; that is, how values have changed with time.

> **Tip**
>
> Historical data allows you to get an idea of trends, and these are usually much more significant than a single value. However, bear in mind this oft-quoted mantra: 'Past performance doesn't necessarily guarantee future performance'.

Dynamic

Dynamic data is data that's constantly changing. Each day a company operates, changes occur to its finances, but these won't be reflected in published financial statistics because the statistics are compiled at specific periods of time. Some statistics, such as the price/earnings ratio, are dynamic because they're based on the share price, which is constantly changing.

> **Tip**
>
> A dynamic statistic such as the price/earnings ratio changes with each trade; remember, though, that the change reflects the change in price but not necessarily any change in earnings.

Projected (future)

To help investors to get an idea of likely future performance, some websites publish financial analysts' forward estimates for financial statistics of importance. The most likely statistics to have forward estimates are sales, earnings, dividends and share price, and these may be projected for up to three years into the future.

> **Tip**
>
> Just because a forward estimate appears on a credible website, it doesn't mean that the estimate will be reliable. No one can predict the future reliably, and financial analysts are no exception.

Key financial fundamentals

While you can access a number of financial fundamentals online, if you try to access them all then you're likely to get bogged down by 'paralysis by analysis'. I suggest you focus on a few key financial fundamentals and, as your knowledge and expertise improve, you can include more data if you feel this will help. I won't attempt to describe and explain all the financial fundamentals you may encounter, otherwise this book would be taken up with nothing else.

Tip

Many websites (including CommSec's) have a facility where you can hover your cursor over the name of the statistic and a brief explanation will appear. This is a good way of increasing your financial acumen.

The key financial fundamentals I suggest you focus on (at least initially) are:

- market cap
- book value
- earnings per share (EPS)
- price to earnings ratio (PE, PER or P/E)
- dividend per share (DPS), dividend yield and grossed-up yield (GUY)
- depreciation
- return on capital (ROC)
- return on equity (ROE).

I also cover the following debt statistics later in this chapter, which I would add to this list of key financial fundamentals:

- debt to equity ratio (DE or D/E)
- interest cover (IC)
- current ratio
- quick ratio.

Tip

If you would like a more comprehensive treatment of financial fundamentals, I suggest you refer to my book *Teach Yourself about Shares*, which goes into them in greater depth and provides numerous worked examples and learning exercises with solutions provided.

Market cap

Market cap (market capitalisation) tells you how large or small a company is according to the number of dollars invested in it by its shareholders. Most of the larger companies in Australia, such as the big four banks, large miners or large investment companies, have very high market caps.

Tip

Companies with high market caps usually pay a reasonable dividend and are less risky.

Book value

This is the value of a company's assets after deducting its liabilities. Theoretically, book value per share is the amount each shareholder is entitled to if the company were to be liquidated.

Tip

Comparing the share price and the book value per share provides an idea of whether a company is undervalued or overvalued.

Earnings per share (EPS)

As the name suggests, EPS is the earnings (or profit) attributable to each issued share. It's the primary measure of company profitability and is obtained by dividing the total annual earnings (or profit) by the number of issued shares. As a simple example, if a company makes a profit of $2 million and there are 1 million issued shares, the EPS is $2.00.

While investors look at current and historical earnings, in reality these provide a guide only. What primarily drives a share price are perceptions of future EPS. Therefore, a vital principle underlying a share price is:

A share price is likely to rise when a change occurs to business activities that investors perceive could cause an increase in EPS, and it will fall when investors perceive the change may cause a decrease in EPS.

Tip

Today's investor can't profit from yesterday's earnings, so future earnings potential is far more important than current or past earnings.

Another aspect of importance to investors is how the EPS has been changing historically. Ideally, EPS should rise steadily over time, indicating that the business is constantly improving its profitability. A steady EPS is also usually satisfactory, as it indicates that the business is holding a profitable position and not losing ground. A falling EPS is undesirable, as it indicates the business is going backward. A 'jumpy' EPS also tends to be undesirable, as it indicates that the profitability of the business isn't stable and future profitability is uncertain.

Circumstances can arise where profitability takes an expected hit due to an Australia-wide issue, such as a pandemic outbreak (which may also be a global issue, as with COVID-19), or a major world event, such as a war or terrorist attack. These events affect almost all businesses and have a rational explanation and so don't reflect any major changes in company operations. Of course, future operations of a company may be affected—for example, if a business exports a substantial proportion of its sales, new tariffs by an overseas government on imports could impact future sales.

Tip

A steady or gradually rising EPS is most desirable, as it is a very good indication of a well-managed, profitable and stable business.

Price to earnings ratio (PE, PER or P/E)

This is the share price divided by the earnings per share. It provides a measure of price value or 'fairness'; that is, the higher the PE, the more 'expensive' the share, and the lower the PE, the 'cheaper' the share. In essence, PE is the number of years it would take to pay for a share from the earnings attributed to it.

For example, if a share price is $10 and the EPS is $1, the PE is 10; that is, it would take ten years to pay for the share from the earnings. However, if the EPS were 50¢ the PE would be 20 and it would take 20 years.

Traditionally in Australia, the average market PE sits in the band between 14 and 20. When the economy is doing well and investors feel optimistic, it tends to rise, but when conditions aren't so good and investors feel pessimistic, it tends to fall.

Tip

A company's PE that is significantly different to the average market value should be regarded with caution. A high PE indicates optimism, while a low PE indicates pessimism.

Dividend statistics

Most share traders aren't concerned with dividends because they trade shares in the shorter term and primarily for capital gains profits. However, for the longer-term investor, the dividend can be important as it provides a regular income stream. This is of special importance in times of low bank and bond interest rates, because after you have paid tax on interest-bearing investments, the net return may not even keep up with inflation. If this happens, your wealth (in terms of purchasing power) is actually decreasing.

Looking at it logically, if a business is making good profits, why shouldn't some of those profits flow back to the owners of the business? In a listed company, the owners are the shareholders, and I believe they are entitled to receive a share of the profits in the form of a dividend. However, some argue that if profits are ploughed back into the business it will grow at a faster rate and so shareholders can instead benefit from increased capital gains.

Tip

A regular worthwhile dividend indicates a company that is making a good regular profit and so can afford to share some of the profit with its shareholders.

There are three dividend statistics of importance to investors. They are:

- *dividend per share (DPS)*—the dividend allocated to each share in a year

- *dividend yield (or yield)*—the dividend per share divided by the share price and converted to a percentage. For example, if the dividend per share is 10¢ and the share price is $1.00, the dividend yield is 10%
- *grossed-up yield*—the yield adjusted upward to take into account the tax benefit of franking credits. If there are no franking credits available on the shares, this will be the same as the dividend yield.

Dividend per share and dividend yield

The dividend per share allows you to calculate the total income from dividends you will get per year. For example, if the dividend per share is 10¢ and you own 1000 shares your annual dividend income will be $100.

> **Tip**
>
> The dividend yield is equivalent to interest on your share investment. The grossed-up yield gives you the true value of the yield, taking into account taxation.

Grossed-up yield (franking)

Many dividends are franked, which means that the business has paid Australian company tax on its profits so dividends are paid out of after-tax profits. When the dividend is received by an investor, they don't need to pay tax again and will receive credit for the tax already paid by the company. These credits are known as franking credits or imputation credits, and when you declare the dividend on your tax return you receive these credits as tax offsets.

> **Tip**
>
> Under current legislation, if you pay no income tax or don't even submit a tax return you will still receive the tax offset as a cash payment. However, the government tinkers with the legislation relating to franking credits from time to time, so you need to keep up to date in case it changes.

For an investor, franked dividends are more valuable than unfranked ones. The additional value can be calculated by multiplying the yield by a 'grossing-up factor' so as to obtain the grossed-up yield (or GUY). Table 8.1 gives the grossing-up factor using the current company tax rate (for large companies) of 30%.

Table 8.1: Grossing-up factor for various levels of franking

Franking (%)	Grossing-up factors	Franking (%)	Grossing-up factor
0	1.000	60	1.220
10	1.031	70	1.266
20	1.064	80	1.316
30	1.099	90	1.370
40	1.136	100	1.429
50	1.176		

You can now get a fair comparison of yields for any level of franking by multiplying the yield by the grossing-up factor to obtain the grossed-up yield.

If a dividend is fully franked (100% franking), the factor is 1.429. So a fully franked yield of 3% is equivalent to an unfranked yield of 4.29% (3 × 1.429).

Tip

When considering yields from shares with different levels of franking, always compare the grossed-up yield so you can get a true comparison.

Depreciation

This is the loss in value of assets as time goes on. It's regarded as a business expense, so the business is allowed to depreciate assets each year. Depreciation is due to two factors:

- *Inflation.* Inflation goes on all the time and degrades the value of assets, including cash, and certainly the value of the assets of a business.

- *Wear and tear*. Assets are subject to wear and tear with use and over time. Even an asset such as a building is subject to wear due to the effects of weather. Assets such as equipment wear more because of their use.

Tip

A business should be making sufficient profit to more than cover depreciation, otherwise the business is going backward.

Return on capital (ROC)

Return on capital (also known as return on investment) is a more meaningful measure of the profitability of a business than profit alone. This is because it is a ratio that gives a true measure of how efficient a business is in utilising its capital to produce profits (regardless of its size).

The profit (or earnings) is the annual after-tax profit, and the ROC is calculated by dividing the after-tax profit by the capital invested and converting it to a percentage. For example, if a small company has an annual profit of $10 000 and the amount of capital invested is $100 000, the return on capital is 10%.

Tip

A high ROC indicates a productive business using its capital efficiently.

ROC is of little significance for the banking sector, because most of a bank's assets are in the form of loans and advances to customers and ROC is usually very low. ROC is most meaningful when comparing the profitability of companies in the same sector, because the nature of the business significantly affects the amount of capital needed to operate it. For example, a service-based business such as an employment agency may require a very low capital investment, whereas a manufacturing business may require a very high capital investment and accordingly have a low ROC.

Note: A similar statistic is return on assets (ROA), which is based on assets rather than capital invested but the principle is the same.

> **Tip**
>
> Don't confuse capital invested with market cap as they are entirely different. Market cap is determined by investors and fluctuates as the share price changes, but capital invested doesn't depend in any way on the share price.

Return on equity (ROE)

Return on equity (ROE) is very similar to return on capital and is calculated the same way except that shareholders' equity is used rather than capital invested. Shareholders' equity is also known as proprietorship and is the amount of capital contributed to the company by the owners (shareholders) plus accumulated reserves. Reserves are essentially retained profits—that is, profits that have been made in the past but instead of being distributed to the shareholders have been reinvested in the business.

> **Tip**
>
> Shareholders' equity is less than capital invested, so ROE will be higher than ROC.

Trends in financial statistics

If you can look at a chart of the statistics of importance you can get a better visual impression of how they have been varying with time. Unfortunately, these charts are not widely available, but on the CommSec site—in the 'Financials' section—you will find a bar chart showing both book value and earnings on a per share basis (EPS) over a 10-year period for any stock after you select the code. A typical chart is shown in figure 8.1 (overleaf). You can see at a glance that for these shares, the book value steadily increased (a good sign) but the EPS was rather choppy (not such a good sign, but it's still been reasonable). However, you will seldom find a company where all financial statistics conform to the ideal scenario!

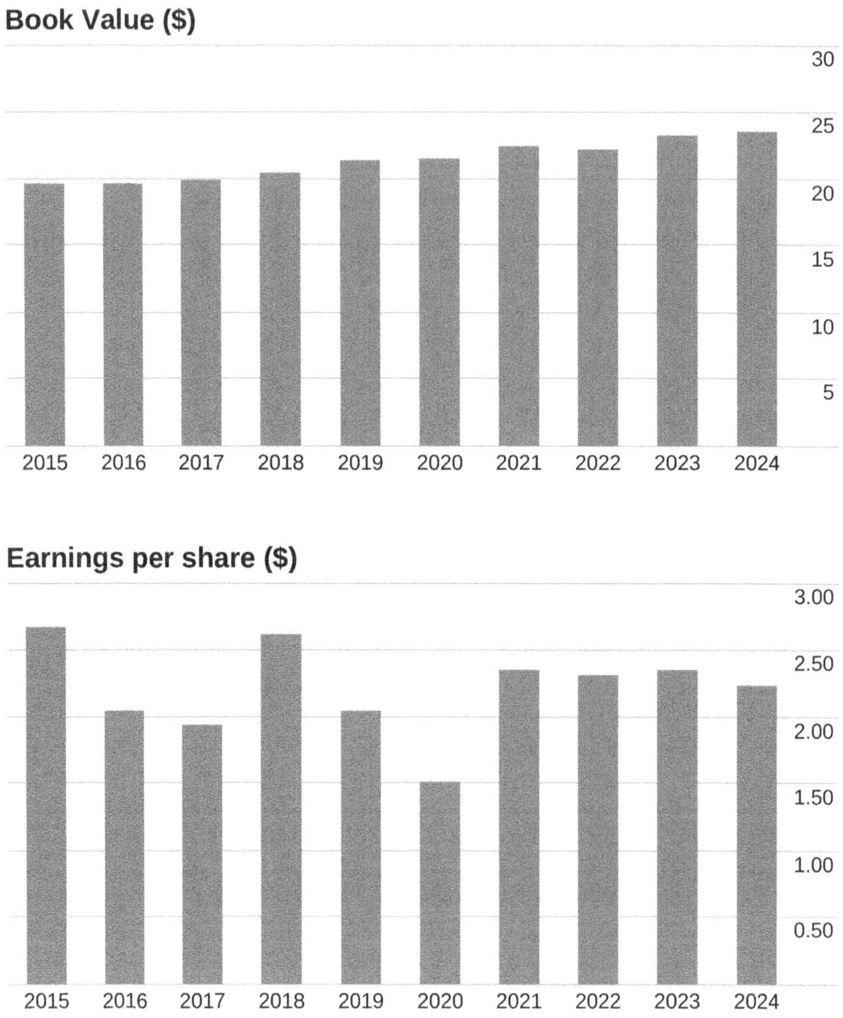

Figure 8.1: Book value and earnings per share

Source: CommSec

If you were interested in investing in these shares, it might be a good idea to you investigate the reasons for these fluctuations in the EPS before making your decision. However, it may be difficult to find a rational explanation for these fluctuations.

Debt statistics

Almost all businesses operate with some level of debt; for example, debt to suppliers for goods or services purchased but not paid for immediately, and debts to employees for wages, leave and superannuation accrued. In addition, many businesses use loan capital provided by banks or other financial institutions. A reasonable level of loan debt is actually beneficial for a business because it allows the business to improve its return on shareholders' capital. However, too much debt is generally not a good thing, because too much profit must be siphoned off to repay lenders and can't be reinvested in the business or returned to shareholders. Another factor to consider is that a business with a high level of debt is in a vulnerable position, because a downturn in profitability could leave the business unable to repay loan commitments, which could result in the business being declared insolvent.

As an investor, it is important to consider statistics that reflect the indebtedness of a business. The two most widely used statistics for this purpose are:

- debt to equity ratio (DE or D/E)
- interest cover (IC).

Debt to equity ratio

The debt to equity ratio is calculated by dividing long-term debt by shareholders' equity and converting to a percentage. It's also known as gearing and provides a measure of the indebtedness of the business. Companies with a high DE are said to be highly geared because much of their capital is derived from loans.

Interest cover

Interest cover is calculated by dividing the annual profit (before interest and tax) by the interest payable on interest-bearing loans. This debt doesn't include money owed to suppliers or other debtors where the debt is non-interest-bearing. IC is usually expressed as a percentage but may also be given as a ratio. For example, an IC of 5 is the same as an IC of 500%.

IC provides a measure of how well the business can meet its interest obligations from profits. For example, an IC of 5 means the business is making five times more profit than the interest on loans, and this would be a relatively comfortable situation. IC inversely correlates with DE; that is, a highly geared company (high DE) will have a low IC, and vice versa.

Tip

Experience shows that highly geared businesses are usually the first to go under in an economic downturn, and they take the longest to recover (if indeed they do). Therefore IC and DE provide a measure of one aspect of risk, as a low IC and high DE indicate a share that is more risky than one with a higher IC and lower DE (particularly in the same sector).

Short-term debt statistics

As well as DE and IC, there are two other statistics that give an indication of short-term debt. These are the current ratio and the quick ratio.

Current ratio

The current ratio measures the immediate financial viability of a business; that is, the ability of the business to repay its immediate debts. Current ratio is calculated by dividing current assets by current liabilities. Current assets are essentially short-term assets that can be readily converted into cash, as opposed to long-term assets—such as land and buildings—that aren't readily converted into cash. Similarly, current liabilities are liabilities or debts that need to be repaid in the short term. For example, a long-term loan is a liability but not a current liability, whereas the interest due on the loan each month is a current liability.

Tip

A current ratio of greater than two can be regarded as healthy, but the higher the better. A value less than one is decidedly unhealthy.

Quick ratio

The quick ratio is regarded as the acid test of short-term financial viability. It's similar to the current ratio except that it's calculated by excluding inventories from the value of current assets, the idea being that when the chips are down, inventories owned by a company may not readily be converted to cash as there mightn't be any buyers!

Tip

The quick ratio will always be less than the current ratio, but it should be greater than one.

Viewing financial fundamentals

As I have noted, there is no uniformity on broking websites with regard to which financial statistics are made available, and how the statistics are compiled and presented. Consequently, different websites often make different financial data available, and even when the same data is provided it may be compiled in different ways. You really need to review each site carefully to discover the data available, where it is located and how it's presented.

Tip

It's sometimes the case that the data you want isn't readily available and you have to perform some calculations yourself. For example, grossed-up yield isn't usually available and you will need to calculate it from the raw yield and the level of franking (using the grossing-up factor—see table 8.1).

The CommSec site has heaps of financial data in the 'Financials' section. After you enter the code for the share you are interested in, a bar chart showing book value and earnings per share going back ten years will appear (refer to the example chart in figure 8.1). This enables you to see these two key statistics and, more importantly, you can tell at a glance how they have been trending. Below these charts is a listing of the financial statistics for the share going back ten years. These statistics are organised under the following headings:

- **Historical statistics.** This includes sales, cash flow, earnings, dividends, franking, capital spending, book value and shares outstanding.
- **Performance.** This includes total return as a percentage (relative to the market and sector), average annual PE, and PE relative to the average market PE.

- **Capitalisation.** This includes long-term debt, shareholders' equity and market cap (all in millions of dollars), number of employees (in thousands) and $NTA (net tangible assets) per share.
- **Management and leverage.** This includes net interest cover, net gearing, return on equity and return on capital (all as percentages). However, for a bank, only the return on equity is meaningful and therefore shown.

Financial 'health test' for shares

In a similar way to getting a health check from a doctor, you can develop a financial 'health test' for shares to ascertain how 'healthy' the finances of a business are and therefore whether the business is likely to be able to continue operating profitably in the foreseeable future.

If you are considering buying shares (or adding to the shares you have), and you are comparing a number of prospective candidates, a basic financial health test is also most useful for preliminary screening a proposed investment. It enables you to scan quickly through your list of candidates and weed out those you consider unsuitable (or too risky).

Tip

You will probably find that a business you're investigating will satisfy some but not all of the criteria in your financial health test. You need to consider the shortfalls and the reason for them, and whether they're sufficiently important for you to eliminate the shares as candidates for your portfolio (or sell them if you already own them).

Compiling a financial health test

My suggested list of criteria you could consider in a financial health test are:

- earnings per share (EPS)
- price to earnings ratio (PE or PER or P/E)
- dividend yield

- grossed-up yield (GUY)
- return on capital (ROC)
- return on equity (ROE)
- debt to equity ratio (DE)
- interest cover (IC).

Tip

A health test for shares isn't applicable for short-term share trading, but it's very helpful for longer-term investing.

Earnings per share (EPS)

Ideally, the EPS should have been rising steadily, certainly within the past three years. A bar chart showing the EPS each year (such as is available on the CommSec broking site) is a very good way of quickly getting an impression of how the EPS is changing.

Price to earnings ratio (PE)

As I have mentioned, PE can vary widely according to the nature of the business. A high PE indicates that share investors value the shares highly and are prepared to buy the shares at a premium. The PE can also be high if there's a certain amount of 'blue sky' potential associated with earnings. For example, the business could be developing a new product or exploring some promising new region for a valuable resource. If no PE is given, it implies that the business isn't making a profit and is being bought by investors purely for its blue sky potential. Needless to say, if there is no turnaround in the future, the business will eventually run out of money and could become bankrupt.

A low PE indicates that investors are disenchanted with the business and it's out of favour, even though current profits could be reasonably healthy. This suggests that investors can't see much potential for increasing profitability in the future and may even believe that the business's current profitability cannot be maintained into the future, often due to increased competition or potential loss of customers.

Tip

A good rule of thumb for longer-term investing is to look for shares with a PE not too far away from the sector average.

Dividend yield

Whether or not you include the dividend yield in your health test depends on whether you value a regular income stream from your shares and not just capital gains. Ideally, dividend yield should keep pace with earnings. A falling yield is usually not a good sign, as it indicates the business is having profitability issues and needs to reduce the dividend paid out to shareholders to conserve its capital.

Tip

Even though profitability may be falling, some directors may decide to maintain a steady yield, probably in order to placate investors. While this seems to be good for investors, in the longer run it may not be good for the business as it may have to dip into its cash pool in order to maintain the dividend, meaning there's not as much cash available to reinvest in the business.

Grossed-up yield (GUY)

Grossed-up yield is more important than just the dividend yield because it is a measure of your investment's true benefit and it also allows you to compare yields on an apples-to-apples basis (despite possible differences in franking).

Tip

For my blue- or green-chip shares, I like a dividend yield of at least 3% fully franked, so in my health test the grossed-up yield for these shares should be at least 4%.

Return on capital (ROC)

A reasonably high return on capital indicates that a business is putting the available capital it has to good use to generate reasonable profits. As well as an adequate return on capital, it's important that ROC should be rising or at least steady and certainly not falling.

> **Tip**
>
> In my health test I like to see a return on capital of at least 8%. However, because much of the capital used by a bank is derived from loans to customers, this statistic is not meaningful for bank shares and is therefore not quoted.

Return on equity (ROE)

Return on equity should be higher than return on capital, so ideally I would like it to be at least 10%. Like ROC, ROE should be rising or at least steady but certainly not falling. Indeed, a continually rising ROE is an indicator of healthy profitability and a well-managed business.

Debt to equity ratio (DE)

As a rule of thumb, a DE less than 100% is comfortable, but a DE significantly higher than 100% indicates a highly geared company that's obtaining a large amount of its capital through loans. If business is booming, high gearing may not be a problem, but if there's a downturn in earnings a highly geared company is vulnerable if creditors get edgy (as they eventually will).

Interest cover (IC)

It's very desirable to have a safety margin for loans the business may have taken out. To achieve this, I would like the interest cover to be above 3 (and certainly above 2). This ensures that not too big a slice of the profits are going to creditors; rather, they are being reinvested in the business or paid out to shareholders as dividends.

Changes that could affect financial health

You may have shares in your portfolio that are essentially in good financial health, but there's no guarantee that this situation will continue indefinitely. The first warning you may get of an impending adverse change is when a stable or rising share price starts to fall and doesn't correct. On a price chart, this occurs when an uptrend falters or gaps down. This alert is detectable using technical analysis and will be discussed in the next chapter. Changes in fundamental criteria (such as those in the following list) are usually slower to appear, but there may be an alert or a company announcement. In many cases, by the time the change has been made public, the market has probably anticipated the change and has already reacted.

Tip

In my experience, share price is the most sensitive indicator of an impending change in fortunes for a listed company.

Adverse changes in fundamental criteria that could prompt you to consider selling include:

- a significant drop in earnings
- lower forecast earnings in the future
- the loss of a major customer
- a significant reduction in the dividend or level of franking
- abandoning the DRP (although this may have a rational explanation)
- significant pending litigation
- significant writedowns of assets
- the emergence of a new competitor
- changes to legislation or licensing arrangements that could have a major impact on profits.

Clearly, the opposite of these changes would be favourable and could prompt you to buy.

Tip

It's generally not a good idea to hold shares after a company experiences a significant downturn in fortunes, as reflected by a share price fall. However, you need to exercise some restraint to avoid a knee-jerk reaction, as investors often overreact and punish a share price unduly. If the fundamentals remain good, the downturn might only be a temporary one. In this case, a good strategy could be 'watch and see' and defer a decision until you are convinced that the downturn is likely to have an adverse long-term effect on profitability.

Key points

- Fundamental analysis is important for longer-term share investing rather than short-term trading.
- You can find heaps of fundamental data online. Your online broking website should provide much of the available data, but many public-access sites also provide such information.
- Fundamental data can be compiled in a number of ways, including the 'snapshot' method, which looks at the data at some point in time, and the 'historical' method, which shows historical data over a period of time (for example, the past ten years).
- Historical data allows you to form an idea of trends in important fundamentals such as earnings.
- It can be helpful to chart fundamental data so you can obtain a visual impression of the trend.
- The most important fundamentals are earnings per share (EPS), return on equity (ROE) and price to earnings ratio (PE). Dividend yield and grossed-up yield (GUY) are also important if you would like to receive a regular income from your share investment.
- Some fundamental statistics are based on share price, and because the share price constantly changes as trades occur, these statistics will also change constantly. For example, dividend yield and PE are based on share price, and a rising share price will reduce the dividend yield and increase the PE (and vice versa).
- Forecast financial statistics can be useful but can't be relied on.
- A 'health test' based on the key financial statistics of most importance to you may be worth compiling, especially when you need to choose between a number of prospective candidates you may be considering for your portfolio.
- If shares pass your health test in most areas but fail in some, you need to probe further to find a reason for these shortcomings so you can decide whether the shares are worth inclusion in your portfolio.

- Changes in fundamentals can be slow to appear as they're usually published only when the company releases an announcement or financial report. However, a significant change in a share price trend is usually a precursor of some impending change. This is because share prices react quickly, whereas it may take much longer before changes in fundamentals filter down and are published.
- An adverse change in fundamentals is usually not a good sign—especially if it could have a long-term effect on profitability. There are many reasons why this can occur, and it's a good idea to try to find the causes and decide whether or not you should dump the shares.
- Bear in mind that investors often overreact to some impending change and punish or lift the share price more than is rationally warranted. Be careful not to simply adopt a 'follow the herd' mentality; rather, conduct your own research to satisfy yourself whether or not the change in price is a true reflection of the change in fortunes.

Chapter 9
Benefiting from charting

Charts give an instant visual impression and are much easier to interpret than heaps of numbers. Analysing charts to detect trends and to predict likely future price movements is known as 'technical analysis' and it is a most important tool for any investor. In this chapter I outline the basics of technical analysis and how to use it to improve your profitability. If you'd like to expand your knowledge further, I suggest you refer to my book *Charting Made Simple.*

Note: In the examples I use shares as the investment vehicle, but the principles of charting apply in the same way to any type of investment.

Tip

If you're a longer-term investor, it's a good idea to use charting (technical analysis) in conjunction with fundamental analysis.

Why use charts?

There are two main benefits to using charts to analyse data:

- Trends and changes in trends are easier to spot. Keep in mind the saying ‘a picture is worth a thousand words’.
- Many tools are available to assist as you analyse charts. I’ll discuss some of the most important of these tools, also known as technical analysis tools or indicators, later in this chapter.

Tip

For technical analysis, it's beneficial to use a large screen as it makes charting analysis easier.

Obtaining charts online

You can obtain a variety of charts relevant to share investing online, such as charts from:

- your online broker’s website
- public-access sites with charts
- subscription charting sites.

Your online broker’s site

Online brokers usually provide charts on their sites and most also provide some technical analysis tools, the extent and number of which varies with each broker.

CommSec has a charting facility suitable for most of the analysis an investor will require. After you have entered the code of the stock you are interested in, here are two different methods by which you can access charts on the site:

- Method 1: Quotes & Research > Quotes > Charts
- Method 2: Quotes & Research > Tools > Interactive Charting

Both methods allow you to use analysis tools, but the charts available vary between the two methods. Method 2 is more comprehensive and has an interactive charting tool that allows you to set up and save a charting format so it becomes your default setting.

Tip

If you're accessing charts on the CommSec site, I recommend you start with Method 1 as it's easier to use. You can then try Method 2 when you're more confident using charting, as it allows greater depth of analysis.

Public-access sites

Many sites that contain information about shares have a charting facility—including the ASX site. The charting software on most of these sites may be rather basic and there's a limited amount of customisation available.

Subscription charting sites

Subscription charting sites provide a wide variety of tools for more sophisticated levels of analysis, but you have to pay a fee (usually monthly) to use the facility. Whether or not this is worthwhile for you depends on how deep you would like to go with technical analysis.

One site suitable for Australian investors is Incredible Charts (incrediblecharts.com). When you first access the site your default chart will be the All Ords index (XAO), but then you can call up any share or index you want by entering the appropriate code. You're able to customise charts for any time period you nominate and you can plot technical indicators of interest below the main chart. Once you customise the format of your chart, that format will be retained. You can also insert trendlines or support and resistance lines on your customised chart.

When you place the cursor over any point in a chart, the details of that day's trading (OHLC prices, which I explain in this chapter) appear at the bottom of the screen. This is a most useful way of quickly checking prices or market or sector index values at the close of trading at any date in the past.

There are three packages available, with current costs as shown:

- *Free*—the indicators are limited and there is a 30-day data delay, which is a serious disadvantage.
- *ASX Essentials ($20 per month)*—access to charts with no delay and unlimited indicators. You can also set up watchlists and stock screens. There is also a USA Essentials service if you're interested in the US market.
- *Premium ($30 per month)*—expands the service to cover overseas exchanges as well.

Tip

Full-time and serious traders often use subscription charting packages, but I suggest you don't get lured in by the promise of superior results that may be claimed, unless you're convinced that the free charts you can access don't provide all the metrics you want and in the form you want.

Types of chart

The most common types of chart used by investors are:

- price chart
- volume chart
- percent chart.

I will now discuss these charts in greater detail.

Price chart

By far the most widely used chart for investment research is the price chart. This chart shows price vertically (y axis) and time horizontally (x axis). If you're charting an index (such as the All Ords XAO), the chart shows the index's value rather than a price in dollars. You can't change the range on the y axis because it's automatically determined to fit in the available space. For example, if a price varied from a low of $1.10 to a high of $2.40, the y axis would probably vary from $1.00 to $2.50.

With the x axis (time), you can use the default time axis given or customise the time scale and the time period to create the chart you need.

Tip

If there's been a major change in the nature of a business, such as a major restructuring, a split or amalgamation, or a change in the share code, you may be able to chart back only to the time when the major change occurred. This is because the shares are now considered as basically different from what they were before the change. In most cases, charting software automatically compensates for splits or amalgamations.

Time scale

A time scale of one day is the default time scale on most charts. For longer-term charting, you may want to use a weekly time scale, because this produces a chart that's less cluttered. On the other hand, in a one-day chart (also known as an intraday, course of sales or course of trades chart), a time scale as small as one minute may be used.

Time period

The default time period is usually the most recent 12 months, but you can usually customise any time period you wish. You may choose as little as one day (for an intraday chart), one week, one month, six months, 1–10 years or even all data—as far back as data exists. This depends on how long the securities have been listed and whether or not a change in code or other major change has occurred in that period. Since charts can be created so quickly online, there's no reason why you can't look at more than one time period. If you're short-term trading or contemplating a trading decision, a suitable time period could be six months, but if you are a longer-term investor you would probably want to use a time period of ten years. If you're thinking of placing a trade order, an intraday (course of sales/trades) chart is most useful, as it gives you an idea of the price action trend on the day in question. A sample of this type of chart was given in chapter 7 (figure 7.8).

Tip

The time period you use for your chart should match your trading/investment timeframe. For longer-term investing, a good approach is to use a longish timeframe of several years with a weekly chart, then look at a daily chart with a medium timeframe of a year or two, and finally one over the past six months or less.

Types of price chart

The most common types of price chart are:

- line
- area
- bar
- OHLC
- candle.

Tip

On the CommSec site you can access these different types of chart by clicking on the 'Line' symbol at the top of the chart, whereby the various types will appear as options.

Line chart

A line chart is a chart where a continuous line is drawn through closing prices each day. These are the simplest and most easily interpreted charts and are usually the default option provided. However, significant data is omitted, because you can't see the range of prices each day and you can't detect any gaps or spikes.

Figure 9.1 shows a typical line chart taken from the CommSec site. A trendline is also shown. Volume is shown as a separate chart below the price chart (I talk more about volume charts later in this chapter).

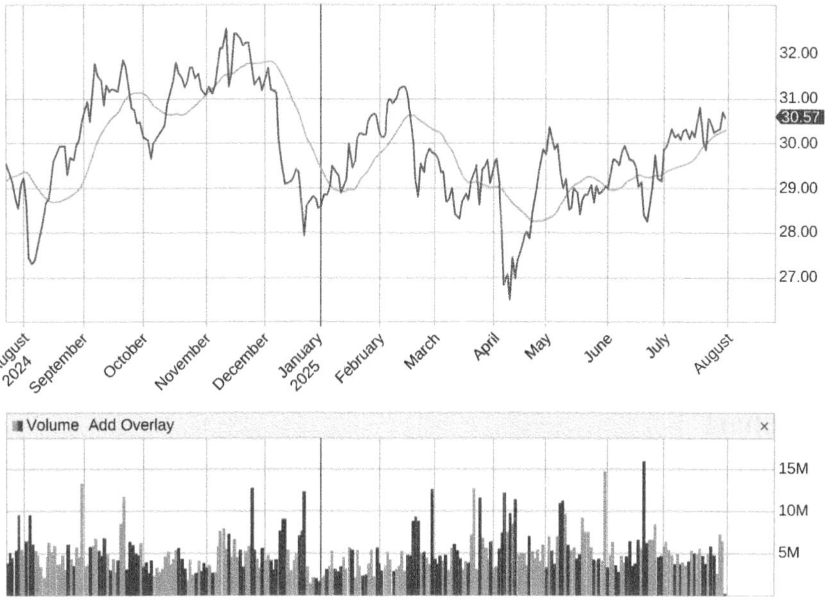

Figure 9.1: Line chart (with volume chart)
Source: CommSec

> **Tip**
>
> Line charts are simple but omit significant data, so I suggest you use other types of chart for more in-depth technical analysis.

Area chart

An area chart (also known as a mountain chart) is a line chart where the area below the line is shaded so the chart resembles a mountain. This makes the chart a little easier to interpret.

An area chart version of the chart shown in figure 9.1 is shown in figure 9.2 (overleaf).

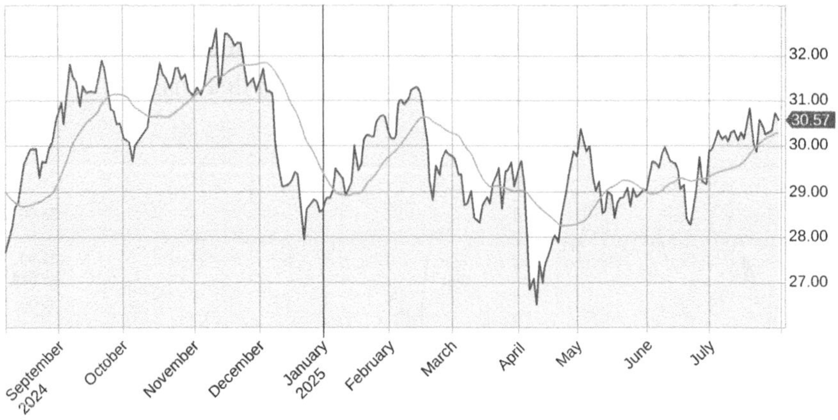

Figure 9.2: Area chart
Source: CommSec

Bar chart

On a bar chart, a vertical bar is shown for each day, where the length of the bar indicates the range prices from lowest to highest. This chart produces a series of vertical lines and allows you to see the range of prices over the course of a day rather than just the closing value each day and also to detect any gaps or spikes, so provides additional useful information when compared to a line or area chart. However, I seldom use a bar chart and prefer to use an OHLC chart.

OHLC chart

OHLC stands for open, high, low and close prices (I discussed these in chapter 7). An OHLC chart is a bar chart with an added refinement—namely, the two small horizontal lines that are superimposed on the vertical bar. The line to the left shows the opening price and the one to the right shows the closing price. A typical chart of this type is shown in figure 9.3.

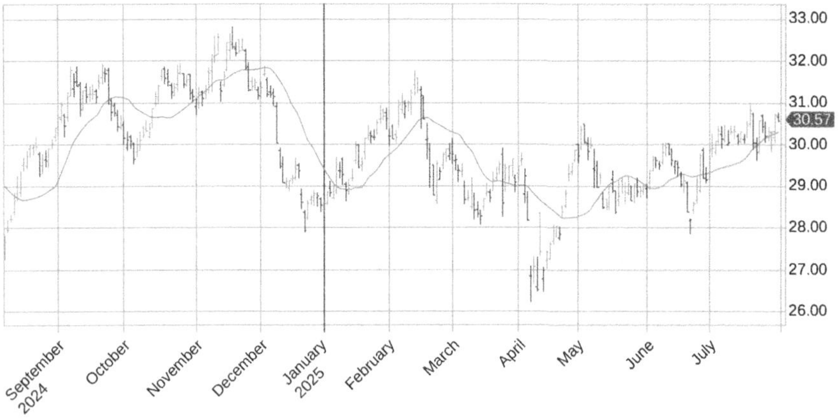

Figure 9.3: OHLC chart

Source: CommSec

Candle (or candlestick) chart

This chart provides the same information as an OHLC chart but in a pictorially different way, which makes the chart easier to read and interpret, as shown in figure 9.4. The range between lowest and highest prices is shown as a thin line. A wider bar is superimposed on this line, showing the range between opening and closing prices. If the closing price is higher than the opening one (an up day), the wide bar is usually shown in white, and if the closing price is lower than the opening one (a down day), the

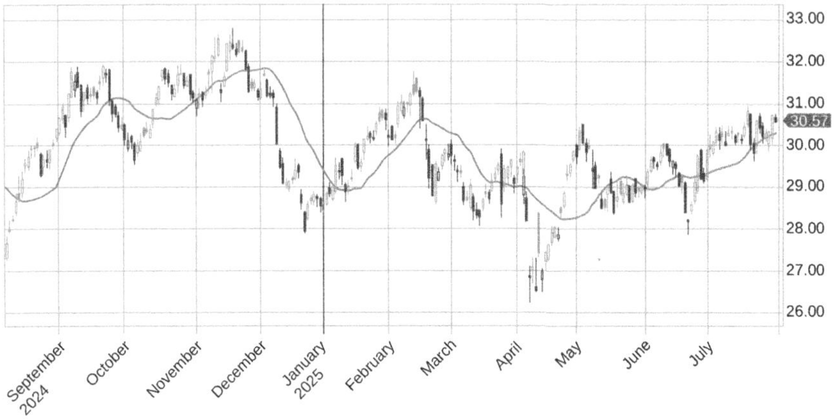

Figure 9.4: Candle chart

Source: CommSec

wide bar is usually black. Some charting packages use other colours, such as green and red, to indicate up days and down days.

Tip

The interpretation of candle charts is a study in itself. Devotees use a special vocabulary to identify common features such as 'hammer', 'doji', 'dark cloud cover', 'evening star' and 'morning star'. However, these refinements won't be necessary for you to understand unless you become a more advanced chartist.

Volume chart

The volume—that is, the number of trades made each day—can be significant. High volume indicates plenty of interest and trading activity, whereas low volume indicates a lack of interest and few trades. Volume is conventionally shown as a bar chart and usually appears by default as a smaller chart below the main chart. Colours are usually used in volume charts to distinguish between up days and down days; conventionally on an up day, the volume bar is green, whereas on a down day it is red. A typical volume chart can be seen below the price chart in figure 9.1.

Tip

Blue- and green-chip shares usually have a fairly steady volume because most shareholders hold them long term. For these shares, analysing volume isn't really of much significance unless there has been a sudden change that could result in a surge in trading volume.

Percent chart

This chart is different from all the others in that it doesn't show actual values but rather the change in value as a percentage (up or down) from an initial one. This provides an instant picture of gains or losses in percentage terms over the time period chosen. The initial value depends on the starting point of the chart and is automatically determined.

Another benefit of a percent chart is that you can usually draw several lines on the same chart and thus compare the performance of one stock to another or to an index of your choice. When various lines are drawn on the same chart, different colours are used to distinguish each of them.

Figure 9.5 shows a percent chart comparing the performance of the Commonwealth Bank (CBA) to the ANZ bank (ANZ) over a one-year period (differences indicated here by the dotted versus dashed lines).

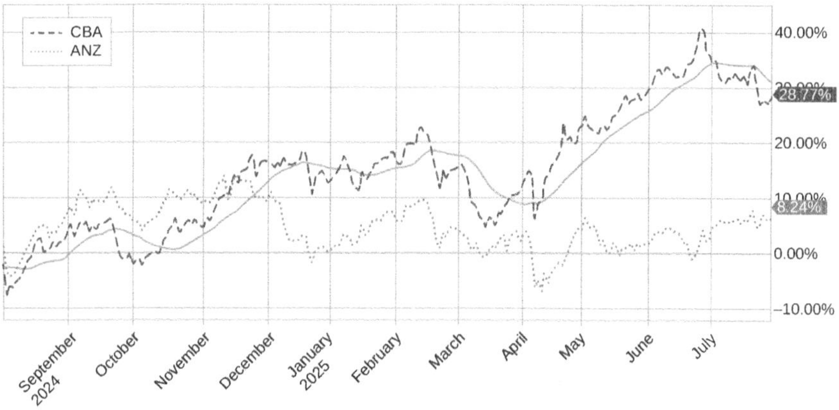

Figure 9.5: Percent chart
Source: CommSec

You can see that in the initial months, ANZ outperformed CBA, and in November they were both showing a gain of about 12%. After that, CBA steadily outperformed ANZ. At the time this chart was accessed (beginning of September 2025), CBA showed a gain of 28.77%, whereas ANZ tracked more or less sideways and finished with a gain of only 8.24% over the one-year period.

> **Tip**
>
> If you use Method 1 to obtain a percent chart in CommSec, you need to compare at least two shares or indicators as you can't get the percent format for only one.

Effect of a dividend

As discussed in chapter 1, for dividend-paying shares the price will invariably fall when the shares go ex-dividend.

The amount of the fall at opening on the ex-dividend day will usually be the same as the dividend per share, or somewhat greater to reflect the benefit of franking credits (if any). However, if there's negative sentiment about the shares, the fall could be more significant; if the sentiment is positive, it could be less. The price drop due to the dividend should appear as a noticeable downward gap in the price chart between one day and the next. You are often able to have the ex-dividend date marked on the chart as shown in figure 9.6. On the CommSec site, you do this by clicking on 'Event' and choosing 'Dividend'.

Tip

If you detect a downward gap in a share price chart, check the ex-dividend date and the amount of the dividend, as the gap could be due to the dividend and therefore not indicative of any significant change in investor sentiment.

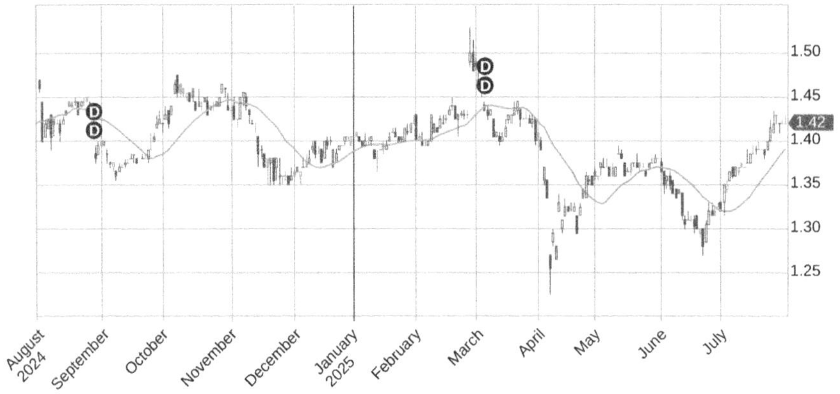

Figure 9.6: Candle chart with dividends marked
Source: CommSec

You can see at a glance that when the shares went ex-dividend in August and March, the share price dropped accordingly. In this case, the dividend was 30 cents—which was the extent of the fall.

Which type of chart is best?

Of the charts I've mentioned, you're probably wondering which type to use. A line chart is the most common as it's easy to interpret, but it omits significant data because you can't see the range of prices nor detect any gaps that might have occurred.

I usually use a candle chart as it provides the best pictorial representation. However, a candle chart is not suitable for longer time periods because the candles tend to merge and become difficult to separate visually. For longer timeframes, an OHLC or bar chart is a better option.

Tip

A wonderful advantage of online charting is that you can experiment to your heart's content, so it's a good idea to try the various chart types available to decide which of them you find most useful.

Trends

The primary purpose of charting is to identify trends; that is, the general direction in which prices are moving. I use the word 'general' because the market doesn't move in a smooth way but rather exhibits volatility; that is, it tends to jump about in a series of steps. Short-term traders can use these steps to make fast but small profits, but longer-term investors look for the general trend over the longer term.

The benefit of identifying trends is expressed in the well-known saying:

> ***The trend is your friend.***

That's to say, it's usually better to trade with a trend rather than against it. Those who don't follow trends are known as 'contrarians'. They don't 'go with the flow'; instead, they swim against the current. In some cases this may outperform the market, but it's a risky strategy and one I suggest you don't adopt unless you have very good reasons. While I don't advocate a 'follow the herd' mentality, when a trend becomes established it can continue for a long time before faltering.

Tip

Trends seldom continue indefinitely. They generally falter at some stage and may even reverse and form a new trend. If you can identify trends and pick up changes in trends promptly, you can trade with minimum delay and maximise profits.

Basic trends

Despite the complexities of technical analysis, there are really only three basic trends:

- *Sidetrend*. This is a trend where the shorter-term up and down moves balance over the longer term. You can think of it as moving along a flat field with a few small hills and gullies. On a chart, this trend is a horizontal line.
- *Uptrend*. This is a generally rising trend where the up moves are greater than the down moves. You can think of it as ascending a hill: there may be some small hills and gullies along the track, but as you progress you rise upward. On a chart, this trend is an upward-sloping line.
- *Downtrend*. This is a generally falling trend where the down moves are greater than the up moves. You can think of it as descending a hill: there may be some small hills and gullies along the track, but as you progress you gradually lose height. On a chart, this trend is a downward-sloping line.

Over a period of time, these basic trends can combine in many ways to form more complex patterns.

Figure 9.7 illustrates these three basic trends.

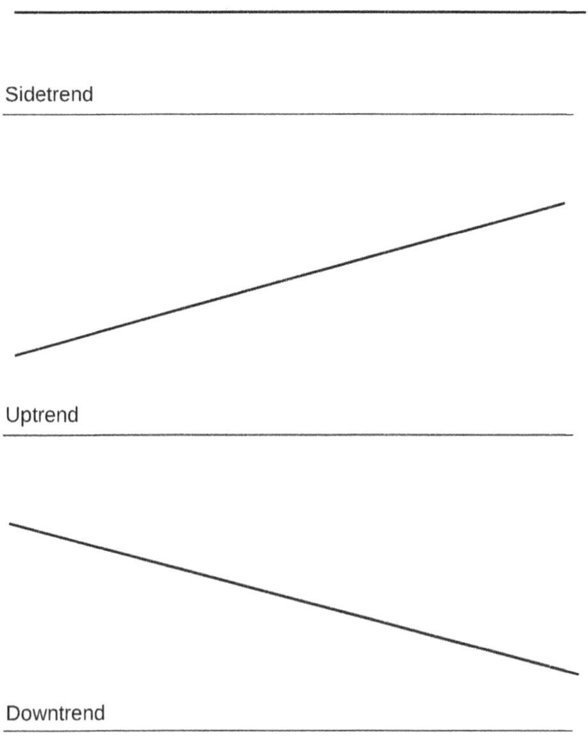

Figure 9.7: The three basic trends

As you would expect, the greater the slope of the uptrend or downtrend line, the more significant the move.

> ### Tip
>
> For the purpose of technical analysis, trends are often drawn as straight lines, but this is more a matter of convenience than reality. Trends seldom follow a straight path in real life and are more likely to be curved.

Trend changes

Trends seldom (never?) continue indefinitely, and even the strongest trend usually falters. Detecting changes in a trend is just as important as identifying trends in the first place. For example, if you buy shares in a rising trend and after a while find you're showing good paper profits, you need to be on the alert for a trend change. If the trend falters and changes to a downtrend, all your profit can be eroded. You might even end up with a loss if you don't detect and act promptly in response to the trend change.

There are many ways a trend can change. You might see a smooth transition or a sudden change, such as a gap.

Three possible sudden trend changes are illustrated in figure 9.8.

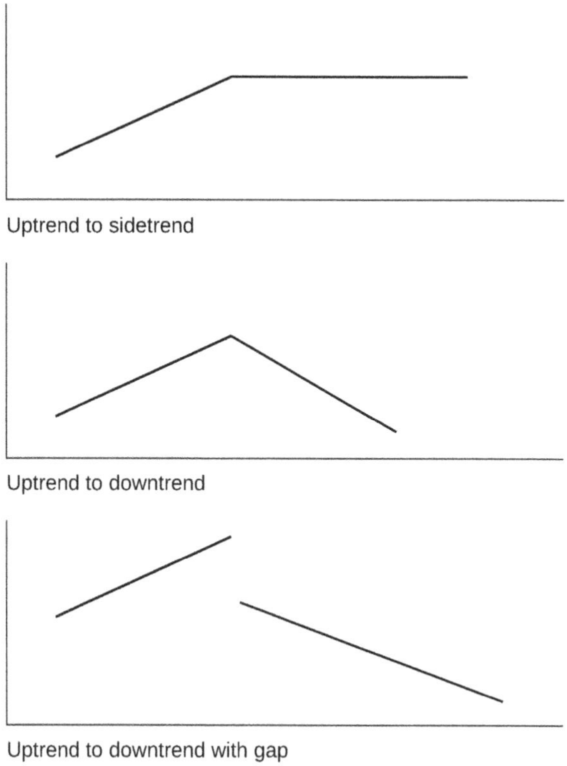

Figure 9.8: Some possible trend changes

Tip

Trend changes aren't necessarily sudden or dramatic (like those illustrated in figure 9.8); often they're gradual and smooth. These types of trend changes can be the most difficult to detect promptly.

Identifying trends and trend changes

There are two basic methods for identifying trends and trend changes, namely:

- visual inspection (eyeball method)
- use of a trend identification tool such as a moving average.

Visual inspection—line chart

The simplest way of detecting trends and trend changes is by visual inspection (the eyeball method) using a line or area chart. Trends and changes in trend can be fairly self-evident, and most charting software allows you to draw trendlines on the chart and possibly save them for future use.

Figure 9.9 shows a line chart in which I have inserted some straight trendlines.

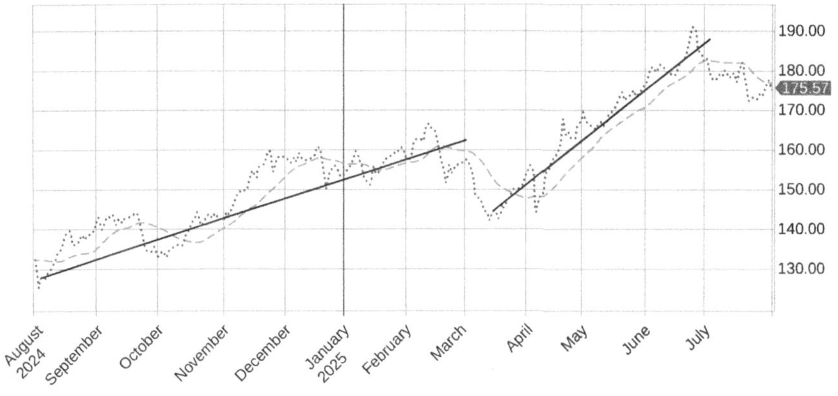

Figure 9.9: Line chart with trendlines
Source: CommSec

You can see two distinct uptrends on this chart. Both faltered and were replaced by downtrends. The first falter was only short term before the second uptrend became established. After that, it is difficult to determine (and too early to tell) whether the faltering of the uptrend will be short term like the first falter or if the falter will change to a sidetrend or remain a downtrend.

Tip

When a trend is clearly shown on a chart, it may not be necessary to add your own trendlines, but you may wish to do so for added clarification and emphasis.

Visual inspection—price range chart

When using a price range chart such as a bar, OHLC or candle chart, trends are defined and identified somewhat differently:

- *Uptrend:* Successive lows trend higher and the trendline is drawn by joining the lower ends of the bars. The trendline slopes upward.
- *Downtrend:* Successive highs trend lower and the trendline is drawn by joining the upper ends of the bars. The trendline slopes downward.
- *Sidetrend:* Both the highs and the lows are approximately level and parallel.

The minimum number of bars you can use to identify a trendline is two, because you need two points to be able to draw a line. Two points aren't really enough, however, and you need at least three or more for reasonable confirmation of the trend.

Tip

The more bars you can draw your trendline through, the more confident you can be about the trend.

The three basic trends on a price range chart are shown in figure 9.10.

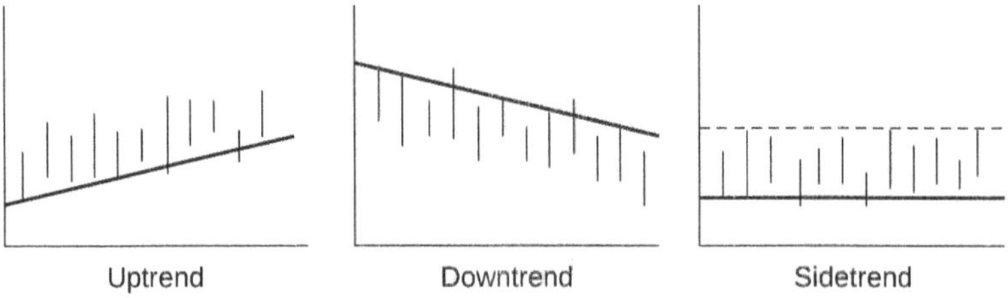

Figure 9.10: Basic trends on a price range chart

Tip

One or two price bars may overlap the trendline, but this doesn't detract from the validity of the line provided sufficient bars touch the line.

Support and resistance levels

If a share price moves up and then later down to the same value a number of times, this price becomes a support level. A support level is a consensus level where buyers support a price because they believe it to be fair, and the buying pressure stops the price from falling below this level. On the other hand, if share prices bounce below a certain level and rise back to it a number of times, this level becomes a resistance level. A resistance level is a consensus level at which sellers exit because they believe the price is a maximum one or else they're taking profits in the expectation of a downturn. The selling pressure prevents the price from rising above the resistance level.

A support or resistance level can't be identified unless it is 'tested' at least twice and preferably three or more times.

Support and resistance levels are illustrated in figure 9.11.

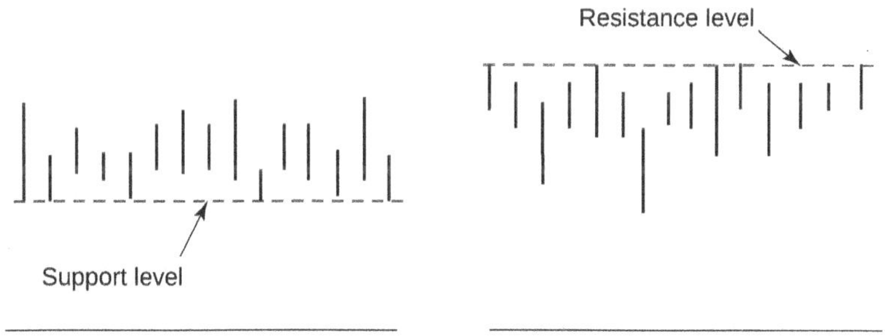

Figure 9.11: Support and resistance levels

Tip

Support and resistance levels are horizontal lines. But if a support level slopes upward, this indicates an uptrend and if a resistance level slopes downward this indicates a downtrend.

Channels

If support and resistance levels are parallel, they're known as channels and they indicate a sideways drift. These channels may continue for some time but eventually there may be a break upward through the resistance level or downward past the support level, heralding a change in investor sentiment. A favourable change in sentiment results in an upward break, whereas an unfavourable one causes a downward break. After these breaks, a new channel is often established. If the break has been upward, the new support level is often the old resistance level. Conversely, if the break has been downward, the new resistance level is often the old support level.

Figure 9.12 shows an upward channel breakout to a new channel.

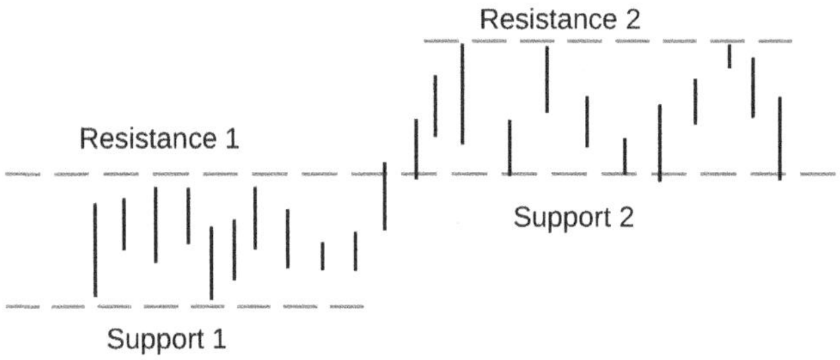

Figure 9.12: Upward channel breakout

> **Tip**
>
> It is not necessarily the case that in an upward break a new support level is the old resistance level or in a downward break that the old support level is the new resistance level, but it occurs frequently enough for it to be worth taking into account when analysing charts.

Sometimes prices move as if they're in a sloping channel, which could be either an uptrend or a downtrend. It's just another variation of a trend, but in this case both the bottoms and tops of the bars form straight lines. For example, in figure 9.13 I show two prominent up-sloping price channels.

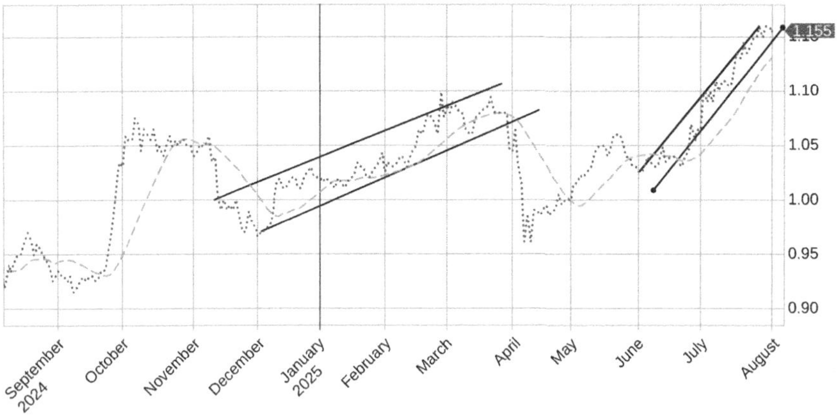

Figure 9.13: Sloping channels
Source: CommSec

Patterns

Often, a number of chart features combine to form a pattern. Commonly identified patterns include double tops and bottoms, head and shoulders, inverted head and shoulders and wave patterns. For further information on these and other patterns, please refer to my book *Charting Made Simple*.

Tip

Identifying the basic trends I've defined will serve you well; you don't need to bother about the more sophisticated patterns unless you really get into technical analysis.

Trend identification tool

The inspection (or eyeball) method is one way you can identify trends, but it's a subjective method. An objective method that doesn't depend on your judgement is to identify trends using a trend identification tool. The most common of these is the moving average, which has two common variants—simple moving average (SMA) and exponential moving average (EMA).

Simple moving average (SMA)

A simple moving average (SMA) is the average of the closing prices over a certain number of trading periods. You can choose the number of trading periods; it can be as short as five days or as long as 250 days.

The method of calculating a simple moving average is best illustrated with an example. To simplify the maths, I've used a very short moving average of only three days (see table 9.1).

Table 9.1: 3-day simple moving average

Day	1	2	3	4	5	6	7
Closing price	1.00	1.20	1.10	1.05	1,12	1.15	1.10
3-day SMA			1.10	1.12	1.09		

The moving average figure in the third column is 1.10 (average of 1.00, 1.20 and 1.10); the figure in the fourth column is 1.12 (average of 1.20, 1.10 and 1.05) and the figure in the fifth column is 1.09 (average of 1.10, 1.05 and 1.12). Now fill in the last two columns yourself to see if you get the idea.

You should have calculated 1.11 for day six and 1.12 for day seven.

When using a charting website, you don't need to perform this calculation as the charting software does it for you. On the CommSec site, a default trend line is added to your charts, as shown in figures 9.1 to 9.6 (in these cases, CommSec uses a 20-day SMA).

Tip

Moving average lines are usually curved lines and differ from support, resistance, uptrend and downtrend lines, which are usually drawn as straight lines.

Exponential moving average (EMA)

With an SMA, all prices are treated equally. For example, in a 31-day moving average, the price 31 days ago influences the average as much as yesterday's price. Many analysts believe that this makes the average respond too slowly to changes, and there's certainly some validity in the argument that what happened 31 days ago isn't as significant for today's investor as yesterday's price move. Also, with the SMA a single price affects it twice (initially, when it's included in the average, and then again when it's taken out of the calculation).

The exponential moving average (EMA) overcomes these difficulties as the values are weighted so the more recent prices have greater weighting than older ones. This makes the average more sensitive to recent market action. As time goes on, older prices decay and their effect on the average fades away.

Tip

While very different formulas are used to calculate the SMA and EMA, I've found that it really doesn't make a significant difference which type of moving average you use. I suggest you experiment for yourself and decide which one you prefer.

Moving average time periods

The advantage of a moving average is that it smooths the volatility and allows you to see a trend more clearly. The disadvantage is that a moving average always lags recent market action, so a trend change isn't reflected in the moving average until sometime after the change occurs. The time period of the moving average affects both the smoothing and the time lag as follows:

- *longer time period:* greater smoothing and greater reliability of the indicated trend or trend change, but the average is slower to respond to changes in market action (increases the time lag)
- *shorter time period:* less smoothing and faster time response (reduces the time lag), but the indicated trend or trend change is less reliable.

When choosing the moving average time period it's a matter of compromise, as summarised in table 9.2 (overleaf).

Table 9.2: Comparison of short-term and long-term moving averages

	Short term	Long term
Smoothing	Little smoothing	Much smoothing
Sensitivity	Trend changes can be detected more rapidly	It takes longer to detect trend changes
Advantage	There's potential to enter or exit more quickly	Greater reliability in the trend or trend change
Disadvantage	Less reliability in the trend and trend change	Values can change significantly before a change is detected

Tip

I suggest that for short-term trend identification you use a moving average in the range 5 to 11 days. For intermediate trend identification use a moving average in the range 13 to 31 days. For longer term trend identification and longer-term investing, use a moving average in the 50- to 250-day range.

You can see the difference between shorter-term and longer-term moving averages in figure 9.14. This chart shows two moving averages: a 9-day EMA and a 50-day EMA.

Figure 9.14: Candle chart with two moving averages

Source: CommSec

On the website, colours distinguish the moving averages and also the up days from the down days. Without colour coding, you can distinguish the moving averages because the 9-day EMA closely follows share price movements, whereas the 50-day EMA smooths out the short-term fluctuations and shows the longer-term trend.

Tip

On the CommSec site, the default moving average is a 20-day SMA but you can change this by clicking the little down arrow next to the share code on the chart. You can change the time period of the moving average and also whether it is an SMA or EMA, and you can also use the colours of your choice to further customise your charts.

Trading signals from multiple moving averages

If you use two moving averages simultaneously—a shorter one (10–20 days) and a longer one (30–50 days)—you can obtain trading signals, as illustrated in figure 9.15. In this figure the lighter line is the shorter moving average and the heavier line is the longer one.

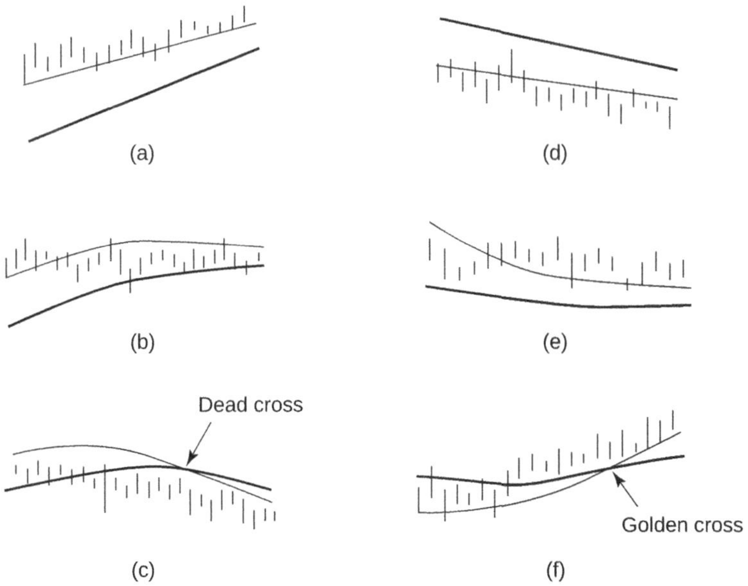

Figure 9.15: Trading signals from moving averages

(a) Strong uptrend—buy

In a strong uptrend, the bars are consistently above the short moving average, which in turn is consistently above the long moving average, and all three are moving upward. The greater the separation between the short- and long-term moving averages, the greater the strength of the uptrend.

(b) Uptrend faltering—caution

Strong uptrends seldom last forever; eventually most uptrends falter and lose momentum. Sometimes this faltering may be only temporary and the price takes off again, but in other cases a sideways drift or a trend reversal may follow. This is a time for caution and close monitoring of market action.

This signal appears on the chart when bars start to drop below the short moving average, which starts to turn down while the long moving average line starts to flatten out.

(c) Uptrend reversal—sell (or stay out)

Should the faltering uptrend develop into a trend reversal, this is the time to sell (or stay out of the trade).

This signal (known as a dead cross) appears on the chart when the short moving average crosses and drops below the long moving average. The price trends down and the long moving average will generally start to move down as well.

(d) Strong downtrend—sell (or stay out)

In a strong downtrend, the price is consistently below the short moving average, which is consistently below the long moving average, and all three are moving downward. The greater the separation between the short- and long-term moving averages, the greater the strength of the downtrend.

(e) Downtrend faltering—monitor closely

Often, a downtrend falters and loses momentum. Sometimes this is a period of consolidation before the price heads down again, but it may also be the end of the downtrend or a precursor to a trend reversal. This is a time to monitor closely.

This signal appears on the chart in a downtrend when the price starts to rise above the short moving average and soon after the short moving average starts to rise upwards. The long moving average line flattens out as downward momentum loses pace.

(f) Downtrend reversal—buy

Should the faltering downtrend develop into a trend reversal and change to an uptrend, this usually presents an excellent buying opportunity because at around the reversal point you can enter at a low price and make maximum profit in the re-established uptrend.

The signal is known as a golden cross. It appears on the chart when the short moving average crosses and rises above the long moving average. The price is trending up and the long moving average may start to move up as well.

You can see examples of both dead crosses and golden crosses in Figure 9.14. In some cases the trend change lasted for some length of time, but in other cases it was fairly short lived. Note that the indicated trend changes lagged the most recent action, so by responding to these trends you wouldn't have entered or exited a trade at the best point for maximum profit.

Tip

You can also obtain trading signals from three moving averages. If you want to check these out, please refer to my book *Charting Made Simple*.

Gaps and spikes

It's very common to see gaps and spikes in OHLC and candle charts. These are sudden jumps in the share price that can go up or down. A downward gap in a share price chart is often due to the shares going ex-dividend and not indicative of any significant change in sentiment. However, all other gaps and spikes are usually significant and well worth investigating. They indicate a major change in investor sentiment, which is most likely due to some significant change in company fortunes that should have been announced. However, many gaps and spikes appear even though there has been no accompanying announcement. In such cases, it's most likely that investors and traders have pre-empted some major change, even though it hasn't been officially announced. Sometimes, despite the gap or spike, a significant change in company fortunes doesn't eventuate, meaning that the gap or spike was purely due to hype and not fact.

Gaps and spikes were also discussed in chapter 7.

Tip

Remember that gaps won't appear on line or area charts.

Whipsaws

Moving averages (like all trading tools) aren't infallible and may produce unproductive trading signals known as 'whipsaws', especially when volatility is high. Whipsaws occur when you get a trading signal but, soon after, you receive a contrary signal indicating the opposite trade. For example, you receive a buy signal, but soon after you receive a sell signal.

Acting on a trading signal

When you detect a trading signal on a chart, you face a quandary:

- If you act immediately, you may be whipsawed unprofitably.
- If you delay acting and wait for confirmation of the signal, much potential profit may be lost.

Before you act on a trading signal, I suggest you obtain confirmation before you act so there's less likelihood of a whipsaw. Two simple types of confirmation are:

- **Time confirmation:** After you detect the signal, delay acting on it for several trading days until the signal is confirmed. For example, if the price rises for several days after a buy signal first appears, this provides confirmation of the signal.

- **Percentage confirmation:** After you detect the signal, delay acting until the share price moves by a certain percentage in the direction indicated by the signal. For example, a 3% rule is common; using this rule, you wait for the share price to move by 3% before you act.

Tip

For a longer-term investor, I feel it's better to forgo some profit by obtaining confirmation of a trading signal, rather than acting immediately and risking being whipsawed.

Additional indicators

The basic chart analysis I've described in this chapter will help you to identify trends and trend changes and improve your likelihood of making good profits from your investments. However, no technical analysis method is infallible, and on some occasions you can be unprofitably whipsawed into or out of trades, even though you may have obtained time or price confirmation. A tactic to help you avoid a whipsaw is to use one or more additional indicators (known also as filters). Fifty or so additional indicators have been devised and are available on many sites that have a charting facility. However, you may have to pay for a subscription to get access to the ones you want to use. The CommSec broking site provides some indicators classed as upper or lower indicators. Upper indicators are those you can superimpose on the main chart, whereas the lower indicators are shown as a separate, smaller chart below the main chart (where volume is normally shown).

If you use an additional indicator, there are two possible outcomes:

- The indicator confirms the signal received from the primary indications and this gives you more confidence in the signal.
- The indicator contradicts the primary signal and this saps your confidence in the signal. This is known as a divergence and suggests that you should exercise caution.

Tip

I suggest you keep it simple and don't try to use too many indicators until you become more adept at charting and technical analysis.

Some of the most commonly used additional indicators or charting tools you can use include RSI (Relative Strength Index), MACD (Moving Average Convergence Divergence), Momentum, Money Flow Index, OBV (On-Balance Volume) and Bollinger Bands. As you might expect, the developer of each indicator or tool claims it to be superior in some way to others, but in my experience none of the ones I've tried is infallible. One of the most widely used indicators is the RSI, which aims to tell you when a security has been overbought or oversold. When overbought, you would be tempted to stay away; when oversold, you would be tempted to jump in.

Tip

It is beyond the scope of this book to try to describe all the indicators available and how to use them. More information can be found in my book *Charting Made Simple*.

The most important charting rule

In this book I've consciously avoided using the terms 'always' or 'never' because with investing there are very few occasions when these absolutes apply. Shares and most other securities have a habit of confounding the best analysis and behaving in unforeseen ways. However, I'm now going to give you the best charting tip I possibly can—and I will use the word 'never'.

Tip

Never buy shares or other securities when the price is downtrending. If you want to buy them, wait until the price bottoms and the trend reverses. You may lose some potential profit, but in the long run you'll avoid disasters. If the downtrend doesn't reverse ... stay away!

Key points

- Analysis of charts (technical analysis) is a useful technique to help you make profitable trading and investment decisions.
- Most online broking sites have a charting and technical analysis facility, and some public-access sites also provide this facility.
- As well as providing basic charts in default format, many sites allow you to customise the chart to suit your preferences.
- The most essential chart is a price chart, and this can be presented in various formats, of which the line (or area) chart and the candle or OHLC chart are the most useful and common.
- Candle charts provide most information but aren't good for longer term charting as the candles tend to merge and become difficult to distinguish.
- Charting helps you to identify trends, which can be short term or long term. Traders use short-term trends, whereas investors look for longer-term trends.
- The three basic trends are uptrends, downtrends and sidetrends. Over a time period, these trends may be combined in many different ways and may form identifiable patterns.
- With a price range chart such as the OHLC or candle chart, trends should be identified by drawing lines through the extremities of the bars.
- When identifying an uptrend or support, the trendline should be drawn through the base of the bars, and to identify a downtrend or resistance the trendline should be drawn through the tops of the bars. Two bars are the minimum required for this purpose, but three or more give better confirmation.
- Parallel horizontal resistance and support levels indicate a sidetrend, where the price bounces between these levels without going anywhere.
- The timeframe over which the chart is drawn can vary from very short (one day) to very long (ten years or more). You need to select a time period appropriate to your planned trade or investment. A good tactic is to select multiple time periods and look at one after another. Start with a longer time period to capture the long-term trends and then shorter time periods to home in on the more recent action.

- Gaps and spikes often appear in charts, and these merit investigation. However, in many cases the reason for them is difficult to ascertain.
- When shares go ex-dividend, a downward gap inevitably occurs, and this gap doesn't signify a trend change.
- One way of identifying trends and changes in trend is by visual inspection—also known as the 'eyeball' method. A more objective method of identifying trend and trend changes is by using moving averages.
- The time period of a moving average should be appropriate to the timeframe of the proposed trade or investment.
- Multiple moving averages using both shorter- and longer-term periods can be used to provide trading signals. When there's a change in trend, the 'golden cross' is usually a relatively reliable buy signal and the 'dead cross' is usually a relatively reliable sell signal.
- A strong trend is usually accompanied by increased volume.
- When a trend is established, it's usually the best strategy to trade with the trend rather than against it; that is, to buy in an uptrend and sell in a downtrend.
- If you act too quickly on a trading signal you can be 'whipsawed' and this is an unprofitable exercise. You can minimise the likelihood of a whipsaw by using a time delay or a percentage delay.
- Another option for minimising the risk of a whipsaw is by using additional indicators or tools in conjunction with the primary ones. There are many of these available, of which some common ones include MACD, RSI, Bollinger Bands, Momentum, Money Flow Index and OBV. I suggest you learn more about them and experiment for yourself before you decide which of them (if any) you might use.
- Above all, remember the KISS principle from chapter 1 ('Keep it simple, stupid!'), especially when you first start out with technical analysis. Additional complexity won't necessarily improve your ability to identify trends and trend changes, or to make more reliable investing decisions.
- And finally, never buy shares when the chart shows they are in a falling trend mode. This is known as 'trying to catch a falling knife'—just don't do it.

Chapter 10
Benefiting from indices

In this chapter I describe the various indices available online and how to benefit from using them.

Bottom-up and top-down approaches

In chapters 8 and 9, I discussed two approaches to making share investing decisions: fundamental analysis and technical analysis (charting), which are known as 'bottom-up' approaches because you start by investigating the 'grass roots' of a business and how the shares have been performing. These approaches help you decide whether the shares are worth buying or whether, if you're holding them, you should consider selling.

A completely different approach is a top-down one, where you start by looking at the economy of a country as a whole and then work through the sectors in that economy before finally considering the companies within each sector. In order to apply a top-down approach you need to use indices, as these allow you to form an impression of the performance and prospects of businesses in similar sectors of the economy.

To give you a better idea of the top-down approach and the value of indices, let's look at investment property. Suppose you wanted to buy an Australian investment property to make capital gains in a rising property market. One approach you could use would be to search properties for sale, find one that looked promising, then investigate this property further to decide whether or not to purchase. This would be a bottom-up approach.

An alternative approach would be to examine the statistics relating to the various states and territories in Australia to determine which ones had the fastest-growing property markets. Having selected a state or territory, you could then search for the suburbs with the fastest-growing property market in that state or territory and finally home in on properties for sale in the suburb that looks to be the most promising. This would be a top-down approach.

The same principles apply to shares. A true top-down approach is a global one, where you start your search by looking at countries with a stock exchange and searching for those that have the fastest-growing sharemarkets.

Although bottom-up and top-down approaches are fundamentally different, you don't need to choose one or the other. Indeed, it's a good idea to use both.

I will focus my discussion on Australian sectors and indices; nowadays, many Australian investors invest globally, but the same principles apply.

Tip

An easy way to invest globally is by purchasing an ETF (exchange-traded fund) that invests in the country or countries you are interested in. Currently, many analysts consider India to be one of the fastest-growing economies in the world, so it could be worthy of your consideration.

Indices

All sharemarkets consist of a diverse range of companies that can be divided into various groups according to the type of business they operate.

These groups are known as sectors. The performance of the market as a whole or of each sector can be measured by a statistic known as an index. An index viewed in isolation has no significance and bears no direct relationship to a dollar value. However, changes in an index are significant, particularly a percentage change in the index and whether it's a rise or fall.

Using an appropriate index you're able to:

- gauge how the sharemarket as a whole is performing
- gauge how a sector within the market is performing
- compare the performance of different sectors and so determine the best performing ones and those with the best investing prospects.

Tip

Australian indices are calculated by an American company—Standard and Poor's—rather than the ASX. This is indicated by the letters 'S&P' at the start of the index name (although this prefix is often omitted).

Market index

A market index gives you an idea of how the market as a whole is performing. In theory, all listed shares would be included in the index but this is impractical, so the index comprises a certain number of shares—usually those with the highest market caps, so the index represents the greatest proportion of dollars invested in the market. A change in the index therefore provides a fairly good indication of the change in value of the broader market.

Sector index

A sector index gives you an idea of the performance of a particular type of business. For example, the financial index is made up of companies in the finance industry (banks and so on), whereas the health care index consists of companies in the health care industry.

Tip

Australian market and sector indices may change from time to time as new indices are added or existing ones removed or changed. Companies included in the index can also change. The Australian indices I quote in this chapter were up to date at the time of writing.

Index codes

Australian market and sector indices are identified by a code in the same way that a code is used as a shorthand way of identifying a stock or other investment instrument. Each index code starts with the letter 'X'. For example, a widely used Australian index—the All Ordinaries—has the code XAO.

Tip

You can use charting and technical analysis with indices in the same way as you would shares by using the appropriate index code instead of the share code.

Price index

A price index is calculated by dividing the dollar value of a hypothetical portfolio of shares by a benchmark value. It's the same principle as is used to calculate the consumer price index (CPI), except this is based on the value of a basket of typical consumer goods and expenses rather than shares. Like the CPI, a share price index is a ratio and doesn't have a dollar value. The benchmark value used isn't significant but was arbitrarily chosen at some time past. From then on, the benchmark value doesn't change, but the value of the index changes as the value of the basket of shares in the index changes.

You might wonder why an index is used rather than the dollar value of the shares. The reason is simply to produce a more easily handled number that's in the thousands rather than in the millions or billions, which would be the case if the raw dollar value of a large share portfolio was used.

Tip

Most indices are price indices. The qualifier 'price' isn't usually stated so when you see an index quoted you can assume it's a price index.

Accumulation (total return) index

The return from longer-term share investing consists of both capital gains and dividends. However, a price index is calculated on price only and therefore reflects capital gains (or losses) only, so it reflects only one aspect of financial performance. This disadvantage can be overcome by calculating an accumulation index (also called a total return index), which is calculated by including the dividends paid on the shares in the basket. An accumulation index therefore provides a better measure of total investor return.

Because dividends are included, an accumulation index will show a higher growth rate than the corresponding price index. While an accumulation index gives a better measure of true share investor return, it still understates the true return because it doesn't take into account the value of imputation credits that are often associated with a dividend.

Tip

Accumulation indices aren't as widely quoted or available as price indices. However, you can convert a price index into a total return index by including the average dividend return. For example, if the price index showed a gain of 8% in a year and the average dividend was 4%, the total return index would show a gain of 12%. In addition, you could add another 1–2% to take into account the value of the imputation credits, but it's difficult to be accurate because the franking level for different shares can vary.

Weighted and unweighted indices

There is a further variation in the possible share mix used to calculate a price or accumulation index: the number of shares in the hypothetical portfolio can be weighted or unweighted. An unweighted index is based on a basket of shares in which there's an equal number of shares in each stock chosen. For example, there might be 100 CBA shares, 100 BHP shares, 100 WPL shares and so on. On the other hand, in a weighted index the number of shares is weighted according to the market cap of the shares included in the index.

This means that in a weighted index, shares with a higher market cap make up a greater proportion of the index than shares with a lower market cap. The justification for this is that the higher the market cap, the more dollars are invested in the shares and the greater the effect a price change in these shares will have on the majority of share portfolios. Therefore, a weighted index provides a more accurate measure of market performance for most investors than an unweighted one.

A disadvantage of a weighted index is that because the market cap changes when the price changes, the mix of shares included in an index isn't constant and can change as share prices fluctuate. This particularly affects shares at the fringes of the index. For example, shares just outside the index may move into the index when their price rises, while other shares just inside the index move out because their price drops.

Tip

All Australian indices are weighted but not all indices outside Australia are weighted. For example, the Dow Jones index, based on a hypothetical portfolio of 30 stocks on the New York Stock Exchange, is an unweighted index; therefore, the shares do not move into or out of the index regardless of changes in their share price. The Dow Jones index is still used and quoted because it's been around for a long time, is well known and—despite its simplicity—has proved to be a good barometer for the US market. However, the S&P 500 index (based on 500 stocks) is really a better measure of US market performance.

Liquidity

There's another variation possible in an index calculation, and that's liquidity. Most Australian indices apply liquidity criteria and this means that to be included in the index, shares need to meet liquidity criteria based on the average number of shares traded per day. This excludes illiquid shares from the index.

Tip

Liquidity criteria apply to all Australian indices other than the All Ordinaries index (XAO). The benchmark value used to calculate this index was set in 1980 at 500 points.

Example 1

To demonstrate how an index is calculated and used, let's compile an index of your share portfolio. Suppose your portfolio had a value at the end of the last financial year of $53 520. You could divide this by a benchmark value of $535.20, so at the end of the last financial year your portfolio had an index value of 100 ($53 520/$535.20).

Suppose that at the present time the value of your portfolio is $58 937. Your portfolio index would now be 110.1 (58 937/535.20). So, if a friend asked you how your portfolio was performing, you could answer, 'My portfolio has increased in value by a little more than 10%'.

In a similar way, you could compile a sector index of your portfolio by dividing your portfolio up according to sectors and performing the same calculation for each sector.

Tip

You don't need to know the initial benchmark value to gauge performance changes in the index.

Australian market indices

The major ASX market indices and their composition are shown in table 10.1 (overleaf). As I've mentioned, Australian indices are compiled by Standard & Poor's, which is why the index is prefaced with the letters 'S&P'. However, when referring to an index in Australia the letters 'S&P' are often omitted and tacitly implied.

Table 10.1: Australian market indices

Index Code	Makeup
XAO	500 largest market cap stocks
XKO	300 largest market cap stocks
XJO	200 largest market cap stocks
XTO	100 largest market cap stocks
XFL	50 largest market cap stocks
XTL	20 largest market cap stocks

Tip

The name 'All Ordinaries' implies that the index measures the movement of all ordinary Australian shares. At the time of writing there are about 2000 ASX-listed entities, so even though the All Ords represents over 90% of the Australian market, it's made up of only about 25% of all listed shares. This is another example of Pareto's Principle (the 80–20 rule) because a small number of shares have a high market cap and there are a large number of shares with a low market cap. In other words, most investor dollars are concentrated in the shares of a relatively small number of large companies. You'll probably find this also applies to your own portfolio—most of its value could well be in shares in a relatively small number of companies.

Using market indices

You can use market indices as an aid to your share investing decisions in the following ways:

- You can gauge the overall performance of a sharemarket. In Australia, the All Ords is often used.
- They provide a benchmark against which the performance of your portfolio can be evaluated. This is a subjective judgement, and you can choose whichever index you think is most appropriate to compare to your portfolio.
- If you have invested in a managed fund or superannuation fund (including your own SMSF), you can use an appropriate index to measure the fund's performance relative to it. Sometimes the fund

manager does this for you by comparing the performance of the fund to the most appropriate index.

- They provide a benchmark against which the performance of a particular share can be measured. For example, you can compare how a share is performing relative to the market as a whole and this helps you to make trading decisions.

Tip

When monitoring the capital gains in my share portfolio and my SMSF, I use the All Ords index as most of my portfolio value is in large-market-cap shares.

Charting market indices

You can chart a market index or a number of indices on the same chart to compare their relative performance. An example of a single index chart is shown in figure 10.1, where the XAO index has been charted over a year with a trendline.

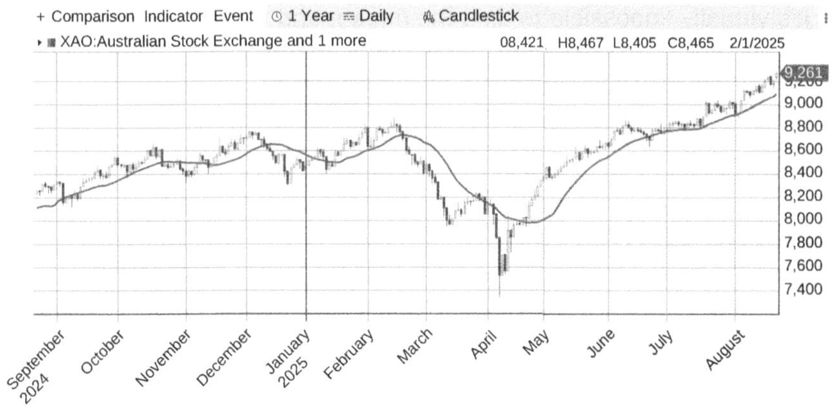

Figure 10.1: XAO index chart
Source: CommSec

You will note that the index was in an uptrend until mid-February 2025, when President Trump's announced tariff policies made markets jittery and investors pessimistic. However, optimism had replaced pessimism by April and the market recovered—in fact, it reached new heights.

Market index makeup

If you want to, you can find out which shares are included in an Australian market index. On the CommSec site, you do this by clicking the 'Constituents' tab after you have called up the index. Naturally, if you choose an index that comprises a large number of shares you will have a very large table!

Investment timing using market indices

An example investment strategy is as follows:

> ***Increase your capital invested when the market is rising and reduce it when the market is falling.***

While this strategy seems logical, it isn't really useful because the majority of the significant market action occurs on a relatively few days (Pareto's Principle). The good days are very hard (impossible) to pick in advance, and if you're out of the market on the good days you miss out. Also, of course, jumping in to or out of the market incurs extra brokerage fees.

> **Tip**
>
> It's virtually impossible to time the market and it's not practical to try and do so. Trying to switch into or out of shares to match the market ups and downs is most often a fruitless exercise.

Sector indices

Sector indices are calculated by breaking the market up into groups of shares according to the primary nature of their businesses. The simplest sector grouping is to classify them into one of two sectors:

- industrials
- resources (mining and oil stocks).

While such a simplistic division is often used in the media, it's really not adequate for investment purposes, so a more complex sector breakdown is used. Australian sectors conform to the Global Industry Classification

Standard (GICS), so they align with global sector groupings. However, some Australian sectors are unique to us and are relevant only in Australia.

The main Australian sector indices—that is, the ones that are frequently quoted and used—are listed in table 10.2. The three-letter code for the index applicable to each sector is shown along with the types of industries included in that sector.

Table 10.2: Australian sector indices

Sector	Code	Index makeup
Energy	XEJ	Exploration, mining, production, transportation of consumable fuels
Materials	XMJ	Manufacture of chemicals, construction and packaging materials, mineral mining and production
Industrials	XNJ	Manufacture of capital goods, provision of commercial services, transport and transportation infrastructure
Consumer discretionary	XDJ	Industries that are more sensitive to economic cycles such as manufacture of household durables, leisure and clothing items. Also provision of consumer services such as hotels, restaurants, media and retailing
Consumer staples	XSJ	Industries that are less sensitive to economic cycles such as manufacture and distribution, retailing of food, beverages, drugs, non-durable household goods and personal products
Healthcare	XHJ	Manufacture, development and provision of pharmaceuticals and healthcare products and providers of healthcare facilities
Financials	XFJ	Banking, finance, insurance and investment advisers and providers
Real estate	XRE	Companies involved in the marketing and development of real estate
Communication services	XTJ	Providers of services for communication and allied industries
Information technology	XIJ	Development of hardware and software for computers and other information services and provision of information services
Utilities	XUJ	Provision of utilities such as electricity, gas and water
Metals and mining	XMM	Producers of industrial metals, minerals and precious metals

Note: Table 10.2 was produced using the ASX website. The description includes only a summary of the index makeup. There is a fuller description of each sector on the ASX website.

Notes:

- This is not a complete list; some of the more obscure sectors have been omitted. A comprehensive list and description is available on both the Market Index and the ASX websites.
- Interestingly, household durables, textiles and apparel are included in the consumer discretionary sector whereas alcohol, tobacco and personal products are included as consumer staples!
- Even though companies included in an index are in the same type of industry, there can be considerable differences between them. For example, in the metals and mining sector or in the energy sector, there's a great deal of difference between established producers and speculative explorers.
- In most cases, the index includes only larger companies; that is, companies included in the ASX 200 or ASX 300 market index and smaller companies are excluded because of their relatively low market cap.
- As you might expect, as share prices and market caps change, the companies at the fringes of a sector index can also change as some come in and some go out.

Evaluating sector performance

You can evaluate the performance of any sector and compare it to another sector or a broader market index using the percent chart (refer to chapter 9 for more on the percent chart). A typical percent chart is shown in figure 10.2, where I have compared the performance of the financial sector (XFJ) to the broader market as measured by the All Ords index (XAO).

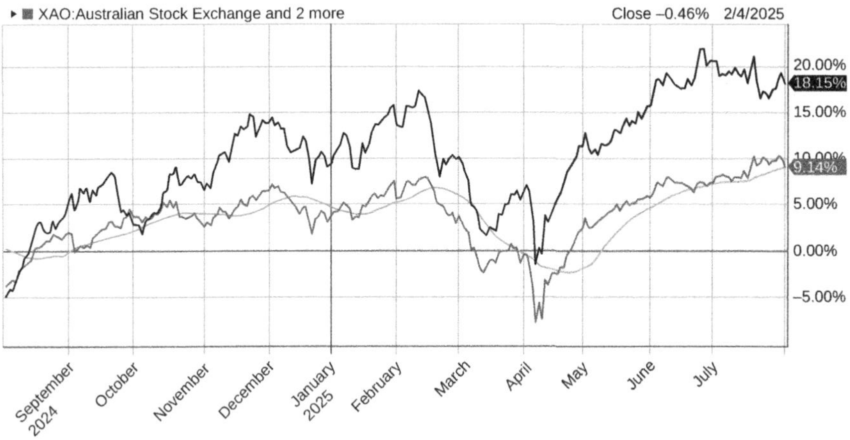

Figure 10.2: Index performance comparison
Source: CommSec

You can see that the financial sector (top line) outperformed the general market. This can primarily be explained by Australians' love of banking shares and particularly those of Commonwealth Bank, which had a stellar run during this period.

Tip

The percent chart provides an 'apples to apples' comparison that's easy to interpret. Once you've set up the parameters for the charts, you can quickly run through all the sectors you're interested in and identify the best performing ones. It's best not to compare too many sectors at the same time because the chart will become too cluttered.

Strategic use of sector indices

You can use sector indices to assist both your trading decisions and your investment decisions. As a general rule, the greatest potential for capital gains is with shares in high-performing sectors, although sometimes a share in a low-performing sector may buck the sector trend (but this is less common). Classifying sector performance is also known as distinguishing between hot sectors and cold sectors.

Tip

In times of uncertainty and increased volatility, the gold sector usually outperforms other sectors because gold is regarded as a safe haven for investment.

Portfolio management using sector analysis

You can use sector indices to assist you when setting up and managing your portfolio. There are essentially two approaches to doing this: a balanced approach and a concentrated approach.

Balanced approach

Using a balanced approach, you set up your portfolio with shares in each of the major sectors so the value of the shares in each sector is approximately the same. Ideally this would suggest a portfolio with shares in about ten different sectors.

Tip

When your shares are a mix from various sectors there'll be times when shares in some sectors will outperform others. In the long run, however, a well-diversified portfolio should track market performance fairly closely and a reasonably balanced portfolio is usually good for long-term investing. As sector performance changes over time, you may need to rejig the sectors in your portfolio or change the relative value of shares in each sector.

Concentrated approach

If you're prepared to take more risks, you could set up a concentrated portfolio. As the name suggests, a concentrated portfolio is one where your capital is concentrated in a relatively small number of sectors, and/or the parcel value of the shares in some sectors is substantially different from the value of those in others. Most likely you would have the most capital invested in the hotter sectors, with less in the colder ones.

While a concentrated portfolio is about the only way your portfolio can outperform the market over the longer term, this strategy does have several downsides:

- There is an increased level of risk; that is, there is a greater risk that your portfolio will underperform the market.
- You may need to switch from one sector to another as the relative performance of the different sectors changes with time, and this could have capital gains tax implications and cost more in brokerage.
- It's dangerous to assume that past performance will continue into the future. Quite often the best performing sectors one year aren't the best performing ones in the following year. Indeed, quite often a reversal occurs from one year to the next and a hot sector goes cold while a cold sector becomes hot.

Therefore, if you're a long-term investor without the time or inclination to constantly monitor sectors and switch and change, your best strategy could well be to maintain a fairly balanced portfolio.

Tip

Remember the saying 'what goes around comes around' or, put another way, 'every dog has its day'. There's no guarantee that the best performing sectors today (or in the past) are necessarily the ones that will perform best in the future. Therefore, you need to monitor sectors fairly regularly so you can detect changes in relative performance in a timely manner.

Sector conformity or divergence

If the fortunes (and share price) of one company within a sector change, the question is: what impact (if any) is this likely to have on other companies in the same sector? Three scenarios are possible:

- similar effect
- neutral effect
- opposite effect.

Similar effect

This effect occurs when shares within the sector react in a similar way; that is, good news causing a share price rise for one company flows on to others in the sector, so their share price also rises. Conversely, bad news and a fall in share price for one company flows on to others within the sector and their price also falls. This is a 'flow-on' effect, because investors perceive that good news affecting one company in a sector is likely to flow on to others in the same type of business. For example, if a retailer's share price rises when they report an increase in profits due to increased levels of consumer spending, this news will most likely lift the shares of other retailers in the sector.

Neutral effect

This effect occurs when the change in the fortunes of one business within a sector is seen to be unique and of no relevance to others in the same sector. For example, a change in major governance at one company could affect its share price, but this change has no relevance to others within the sector so their share price shouldn't change.

Opposite effect

This effect occurs when a change in the fortunes of one company within a sector has the opposite effect on others in the same sector. For example, bad news and a fall in the share price of one company causes a share price rise for others within the sector (or vice versa). For example, if a major manufacturer experiences serious quality control problems with some of its products, necessitating a recall, this will most likely cause a fall in the share price, the severity of which depends on how costly the problems will be to fix (if indeed they can be fixed). However, shares in a major competitor within the sector could well rise because investors perceive that this competitor will be able to increase its market share (and profitability) by stepping in and filling the void.

Tip

When evaluating the effect of a change in fortunes (and share price) of one company on others in the same sector, there's no general guideline and each case needs to be considered as a unique situation.

Sector index makeup

If you want to, you can find out which shares are included in a sector index. On the CommSec site you do this in the same way as for the market index by clicking on the 'Constituents' tab after you have called up the sector index. Table 10.3 (overleaf), taken from the CommSec site, shows the makeup of the XEJ index.

As you can see, the CommSec site shows not just the individual shares included in the index, but also the prices and price movements for the day.

Trading an index

It's possible to trade a market or sector index as you would trade shares. In other words, you can 'buy' or 'sell' an index, depending on whether you think the index will rise or fall. Clearly you can't do so with a conventional online share trading facility because the value of an index isn't expressed in dollars. However, you can trade an index if you trade CFDs (contracts for difference). While the principles of share trading and technical analysis are the same for CFD trading as for shares, detailed discussion of the ins and outs of CFD trading is outside the scope of this book. Nowadays, many online brokers operating in Australia offer a CFD trading facility, and if you want to trade using CFDs you need to set up an account with one that does.

Index tracking funds

If you'd like your share portfolio to match the performance of a sector or market index, you can set up your portfolio with the same shares that are included in the index and in the same proportions. However, this isn't really a practical proposition for the average share investor unless the index consists of only a small number of different stocks.

An alternate approach is to buy shares (units) in an index tracking fund. As the name suggests, index tracking funds are set up with the specific purpose of tracking an index. They do so by setting up a portfolio of shares in all the companies included in the index they're tracking and in the same proportions. Clearly for the All Ords index this would require a portfolio of 500 different stocks, which wouldn't really be feasible. However, it's certainly a feasible proposition to set up an index tracking fund based on only 20 or 50 different stocks.

Table 10.3: Energy sector XEJ index makeup

Index Make Up

Energy

CODE	SECTOR	BID $	OFFER $	LAST $	CHANGE	CHANGE%	OPEN $	HIGH $	LOW $	VOLUME
ALD	Energy	28.530	25.050	27.180	0.000	0	0.000	0.000	0.000	0
BPT	Energy	1.290	1.130	1.230	0.000	0	0.000	0.000	0.000	0
NHC	Energy	4.530	4.120	4.390	0.000	0	0.000	0.000	0.000	0
PDN	Energy	6.720	6.010	6.400	0.000	0	0.000	0.000	0.000	50000
STO	Energy	9.520	7.200	7.940	0.000	0	0.000	0.000	0.000	0
VEA	Energy	2.280	1.980	2.110	0.000	0	0.000	0.000	0.000	0
WDS	Energy	32.280	21.520	26.900	0.000	0	0.000	0.000	0.000	0
WHC	Energy	7.260	6.200	6.720	0.000	0	0.000	0.000	0.000	0

Source: CommSec

The idea of an index tracking fund is that the fund's performance should match the performance of the index, so by buying into the fund you can effectively buy into the index in only one transaction.

Tip

An index tracking fund won't usually perform as well as the index being tracked because of the management fees involved in setting up and running the fund.

Effect of inflation

Inflation is the increase in price (and cost) of goods and services in an economy. It's theoretically possible for an economy to experience periods of deflation (a reduction in prices and costs) but this is far less common. Without going into the economics of inflation and deflation, the important point for an investor is that inflation reduces the purchasing power of money. In other words, if you spend $100 purchasing goods and services this year with cash you have saved, and inflation is running at 3%, then next year you'll be able to buy only $97 worth of goods and services. Therefore, for an investor, it's important to consider the effect of inflation in order to get a true picture of the return on investment in terms of what money will buy, because money itself has no intrinsic value.

The effect of inflation is seldom taken into account in quoted financial statistics. For example, if a managed fund reports that the fund returned an average of 5% per year over the last ten years, you can be sure this doesn't take into account the effect of inflation over this period. Similarly when evaluating market or sector performance using indices as described in this chapter, inflation isn't taken into account.

Tip

The only time inflation is included in performance statistics is when the statistic is described as 'inflation adjusted' and this is seldom quoted. If you want to consider the effect of inflation, you need to determine the inflation rate and deduct this from the calculated or quoted return on capital.

Key points

- Market and sector analysis is a useful 'top-down' approach that attempts to identify markets and sectors that are outperforming (or underperforming) others.
- There's no reason why top-down and bottom-up approaches can't both be used when you're evaluating investments; indeed, it's a good idea to do so.
- You use the top-down approach to maximise the probability of your portfolio outperforming the market by weighting your shares in the best-performing markets and sectors.
- Australian indices comply with the Global Industry Classification System (GICS) and are weighted according to the market cap of the shares in the index.
- Market indices provide a method of evaluating market performance and a useful benchmark for comparing the performance of a fund or portfolio relative to the most relevant market index.
- Sector indices are based on the type of industry involved. Some sectors contain many stocks, while others have relatively few.
- Sector analysis allows you to identify the best performing (or worst performing) sectors within the sharemarket.
- You can use technical analysis (charting) to analyse market and sector performance in the same way as you would analyse share performance.
- If you wish to track sector performance, you can invest in a fund that is designed to do so. However, fund performance won't generally be as good as the index performance because of the management fees involved.

Chapter 11
Strategies to improve profitability

In this chapter I'll look at the various types of risk associated with online investing and suggest strategies for managing those risks. I'll also outline some general investment strategies that take risk into account, so you'll have the foundations you need to improve profitability.

Risk

Risk is the likelihood of an adverse event. With investing, risk is the likelihood of a financial loss or making a profit significantly less than that which might otherwise be attainable.

Understanding and managing risk can help minimise losses and maximise gains on the sharemarket. Avoiding scams and input errors can also save you headaches along the way.

Scamming risk

Online investing has many advantages but also exposes you to some risks you wouldn't encounter if you chose to invest offline. For example, an online cash transfer exposes you to risks you wouldn't get if you went to the bank and arranged the transfer personally. Unfortunately, ever-increasing use of online and app-based banking has resulted in increasing scamming activity as scammers devise more sophisticated ways of separating you from your hard-earned cash.

Financial institutions have recognised this — they have become more adept at scam recognition and methods of combating scams. Often multiple passwords and other safety devices are required. Banks and other financial institutions are often required to compensate people for their losses, so it is in everyone's interests for online financial activity to become more secure.

If you intend to invest online (which I assume you do, as you're reading this book), you need to acquaint yourself with methods of recognising and avoiding scamming activity.

> **Tip**
>
> There are many websites such as Scamwatch that outline common types of financial scams and are well worth the visit. Your bank or financial institution may also have information available and sometimes there are courses in scam recognition and avoidance you can attend. The golden rule is this: 'If you have any doubt, stay out'.

Preventing mistakes

An essential part of any risk management strategy is to minimise the likelihood of trading mistakes. You may wish to revisit chapter 7, where I outline several errors that can occur when you invest online and how to avoid them.

Risk management and risk minimisation

In many people's minds, risk management is synonymous with risk minimisation, because for most activities in life we manage risks by trying to minimise them. For example, when we're in a motor vehicle we fasten our seatbelts because this minimises the risk of personal injury in the event of an accident.

With share investing you need to adopt a different mindset. Risk management isn't the same as risk minimisation. The reason for this hinges on the connection between investing risk and investing return. Simply stated, if you want a higher profit (return on your investment), you need to take more risk. If you're not happy with a higher level of risk, you need to be satisfied with a lower return.

We'd all love to find a really safe haven for our capital that produces high, reliable returns year after year with no risk of ever incurring a loss or a reduction in profit. Unfortunately, this type of investment exists only in cloud cuckoo land; in the real world, the higher the expected return from an investment, the greater the risk involved. When you invest, you're leaping into the future, as you can't profit from past action. Any profits occur in the future, and the future always has an inherent degree of uncertainty and risk.

The very fact that you're reading this book suggests that you recognise these facts and are prepared to take more risk because you want a higher return on your capital than you could expect from a safer haven such as a bank deposit. With investing, the name of the game isn't to minimise risks, but rather to manage them so you don't take unnecessary risks.

Tip

With any investing (and certainly share investing), you need to shift focus from risk minimisation to risk management.

Risk profile

Because risk and return are inextricably linked, the first step in managing investment risk is to decide what level of risk you're comfortable with. This depends on your personality and a host of other factors, including your age, gender and life experiences. For example, risk tolerance usually decreases with age; older people tend to be prepared to take less risks than younger people. Also, men are generally prepared to take more risks than women of a comparable age. Your risk tolerance level may be influenced by your financial and family situation; for example, a married person with children and a sizeable mortgage will tend to have a lower risk tolerance level than a single person with no dependants.

A simplified approach to evaluating your risk tolerance profile is to consider which of the following categories best apply to you:

- *Conservative*—you are most comfortable with a low level of risk and are prepared to accept comparatively low returns.
- *Moderate*—you are prepared to accept a reasonable level of risk in order to get reasonable returns.
- *Aggressive*—you are prepared to accept a high level of risk in order to get high returns.

Tip

If you're unsure of your risk tolerance, you might want to use a more sophisticated risk assessment model to evaluate your risk profile. If you search for 'risk profile questionnaire' online then you'll be able to find a variety of options, such as Equip Super's risk profile questionnaire.

Ideally, your risk profile should reflect in your portfolio makeup. For example, if you're relatively conservative you might decide to have a 60/30/10 share portfolio mix, meaning that 60% of your portfolio will be in blue-chip shares, 30% in medium-risk ones and 10% in speculative ones. A more aggressive investor might decide on a 40/30/30 mix (or another higher-risk combination).

The mix isn't necessarily static, probably as you age and gain more investing experience, your tolerance will change and with it your portfolio mix.

Tip

Aim to align your investment portfolio with your risk tolerance level.

Volatility

As the name suggests, volatility is 'jumpiness'; that is, the extent to which there's a variation up or down from the general trend. Volatility applies to all facets of share investing, but most importantly to share price, company income and earnings. Volatility is the opposite to stability; that is, the greater the stability, the lower the volatility and vice versa.

To illustrate volatility, consider figure 11.1, which shows the performance of two investments: A (solid line) and B (dashed line).

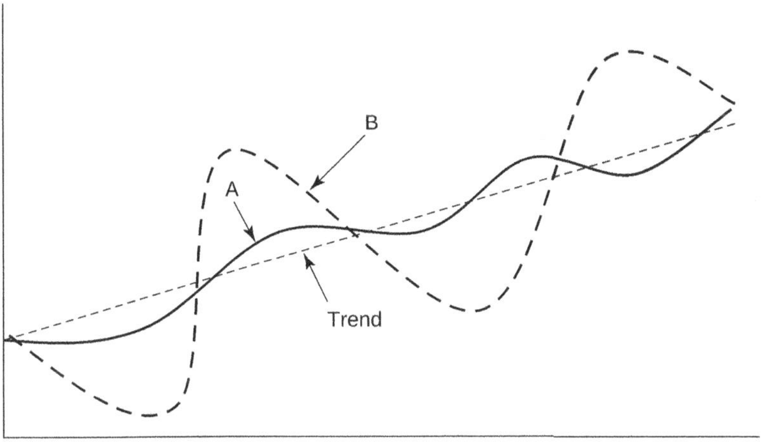

Figure 11.1: Volatility

You can see that both A and B follow the same trendline and start and finish at the same points, but A is far more stable than B.

Price risk is closely related to price volatility; that is, if volatility is high, the price fluctuates significantly in a relatively short time and therefore there's more risk. I discuss price risk in more detail later in this chapter.

> **Tip**
>
> Shares in companies that don't make profits are generally more volatile and therefore riskier. Speculative shares are usually volatile and risky but have the potential for high capital gains.

You can get an estimate of the volatility of shares by a statistic known as beta, which is calculated by a rather complex statistical formula that I won't go into. The bottom line is that the higher the beta, the greater the volatility. A beta value of around 1 indicates volatility that's about the same as in the general market; below 1 the volatility is lower and above 1 it is greater. Clearly, the lower the beta value the lower the price risk, so if you are risk-averse you should choose shares with low beta values. Note that the beta of the All Ords index isn't exactly 1 due to the statistical calculation method used with the selection of shares that comprise the index.

Tip

Most websites that publish shares' financial statistics should include the beta. On the CommSec site, beta can be found in the 'Financials' section under 'Summary'.

Another way of assessing price volatility is from the range in prices—that is, the difference between the highest and lowest prices in a period of time.

The volatility formula shown here gives a volatility percentage score, and the higher the score the greater the volatility:

$$\text{Volatility\%} = \frac{(\text{period high} - \text{period low})}{\text{period low}} \times 100$$

Conventionally, the time period is the most recent 52 weeks, so the formula will calculate the most recent annual volatility. For more volatile investments, it's not unusual for the formula to indicate a volatility of 100% or more.

Tip

You may wish to include volatility as one of your criteria when deriving a 'health test' for share fundamentals (refer to chapter 8 for more on a financial health test for shares).

Example 1

I'll use the volatility formula to calculate the price volatility for shares where the 52-week high is \$29.10 and the 52-week low is \$16.82. Applying the formula:

$$\text{Volatility\%} = \frac{(29.10 - 16.82)}{16.82} \times 100 = 73\%$$

This is a relatively low value and indicates low price volatility.

Now consider a mining share where the 52-week high is \$1.615 and the 52-week low is \$0.565. Applying the formula:

$$\begin{aligned}\text{Volatility\%} &= \frac{(1.615 - 0.565)}{0.565} \times 100 \\ &= 186\%\end{aligned}$$

This is well above 100%, confirming the volatility in the price of these shares.

Earnings risk

Earnings (or profit) is the key driver of share prices. Earnings risk is the risk that there'll be an earnings downgrade; that is, the earnings per share (EPS) will reduce below that of previous periods or below what has been forecast (or anticipated) by the market. Investors love to see a stable and growing EPS, and shares that have a track record of stability and growth in EPS are rated highly. Earnings downgrades are regarded as bad news, and should they occur, the share price is usually punished—often to a greater degree than the downgrade warrants.

Far more important to share prices than past earnings are the projected future earnings, which like anything projected into the future, has a degree of uncertainty. However, there are some factors to consider that can give you an idea of future earnings, such as:

- *Earnings history*—if there is a track record of stable or rising earnings, there is more likelihood of this continuing into the future.

- *Business stability*—if the business is in a stable industry (like banking), future earnings are more stable and predictable. However, a primarily agricultural business is subject to the vagaries of the weather and could suffer greatly during adverse climatic conditions, such as a flood or drought. Similarly, the fortunes of a speculative mining company are dependent on whether or not they make a worthwhile find, which can be highly unpredictable.
- *Growth prospects*—how will the business be able to grow profits in the future? Is the market getting saturated or are new competitors entering the sector? For example, in my view a business in the green energy market has much higher growth prospects than one in the fossil fuel business.
- *Stable and competent board of directors*—how long have the directors been with the company, or have there been many changes in board members?
- *Financial fundamentals*—the most stable businesses have sound financial fundamentals (refer to chapter 8 for more on conducting a financial health test for shares).
- *Analysts' consensus*—financial analysts often form and publish a consensus opinion of future prospects, which can provide a useful guide.

Tip

The preceding list is far from exhaustive; however, by considering these factors you can form an opinion of the stability or riskiness of future earnings and therefore the share price.

Price risk

The factors considered above are fundamental ones. But before you decide to buy into any investment you should also use technical analysis (charting) to minimise the chance that you will invest in the right security at the wrong time. As I have mentioned before, price can be based on speculation or hype and not have a factual basis. You certainly don't want to buy into a stock when the price has been hyped up to an unrealistic level and note with dismay that soon after you jumped in, the price fell significantly below your purchase price.

> **Tip**
>
> It's a good idea to always use technical analysis to check recent price action before trading.

Upside/downside potential

With share investing, it's a good idea to consider the downside potential, which is essentially the worst-case scenario. One way of doing this is to try to identify a realistic price support level. With speculative shares you might decide that a realistic downside level is zero (the shares could become valueless), but can you see this happening with one of the major banks or retailers?

In conjunction with the downside potential, it's a good idea to consider the upside potential; that is, a realistic future price. This enables you to calculate the up/down ratio (reward/risk ratio) by dividing the upside potential by the downside potential. The higher the ratio, the greater the profit potential and the lower the risk.

For example, consider two investments, A and B, with estimated support and resistance levels as shown in table 11.1.

Table 11.1: Upside/downside potential

	A	B
Price	$1.86	$5.34
Support	$1.75	$5.00
Resistance	$2.11	$5.60
Downside potential	$0.11	$0.34
Upside potential	$0.25	$0.26
Ratio up/down	2.27	0.76

By this method of evaluation, it's clear that investment A represents a better and less risky investment than B, because there's a much higher upside to downside ratio. Indeed, this calculation indicates you should avoid B altogether unless you are very confident of a reversal of fortunes in the future.

Tip

It's a good idea to have realistic downside and upside potential estimates before you invest.

Sector risk

Some sectors are inherently more risky than others. A low-risk investor will avoid the risky sectors, whereas a high-risk investor will favour them.

The recognised safer and less volatile share sectors include:

- banking
- alcohol and tobacco
- gambling and gaming
- infrastructure and utilities
- property trusts
- consumer staples.

The riskier and more volatile share sectors include:

- tourism and leisure
- mining and resource exploration
- biotechnology
- telecommunications
- internet and new technology.

Tip

Try to align your risk profile with the sectors you invest in.

General investment strategies

I'll now outline some general investment strategies that you may find useful.

Diversification

A concentrated investment is one where a substantial amount of your investing capital is invested in one or just a few securities. This carries an inherent risk because if there's a downturn in their performance, your entire investment will be a losing one.

The most widely accepted strategy to overcome this risk is to have a diversified investment mix with different types of investments in different sectors. Diversification is based on the principle that 'you don't put all your eggs in one basket'.

Diversification is usually a good investing strategy, but it won't help if the whole market is impacted, such as by a nationwide or global event like a major war or epidemic outbreak. If this happens, there is very little you can do about it because trying to get in or out of the market at such times is usually a counterproductive exercise.

Tip

Diversification spreads the risk and is a widely adopted investment strategy, but it reduces profit compared to the profit you could have made if your investing capital had been concentrated in a few of the best-performing investments.

The impact of tracking error

The stability of a share portfolio compared with the overall market (represented by the All Ords) can be measured by what's known as tracking error. The higher the diversification, the lower the tracking error and vice versa. This effect is shown in figure 11.2 (overleaf).

No. of stocks	Tracking error %
1	40
2	20
4	10
6	7
8	5
10	4
20	2
40	1

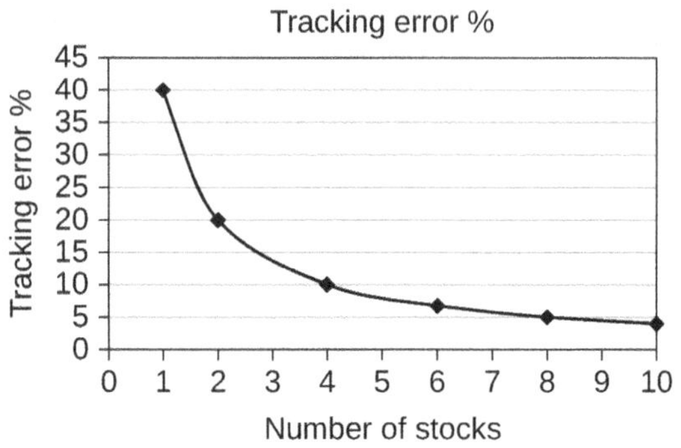

Figure 11.2: Tracking error

The law of diminishing returns kicks in as the number of stocks in your portfolio increases. That is, you significantly reduce tracking error by holding five or six stocks rather than one or two, but there's a further reduction of only 2% by holding 20 stocks rather than 10.

Tip

If you want a well-diversified share portfolio, you should hold at least five and preferably ten stocks in different industries or sectors.

Internal diversification

Many companies have an inbuilt internal diversification with their range of products and the markets they service. History shows that for Australian companies, internal product or market diversification is successful only when the company doesn't diversify into products or markets that don't fit with their established core competencies. As a general rule, Australian conglomerates don't usually perform better than Australian companies that concentrate on specific products or segments of the market they're really familiar with and where they have a competitive edge. Nowadays, there seems to be a move away from conglomeration; for example, Woolworths used to sell liquor and operate poker machines but it shed both of these and now concentrates on groceries and household items. As further examples, BHP hived off its gas and oil energy section to Woodside, while Tabcorp set up a separate lottery company—TLC (The Lottery Corporation).

Tip

Australian companies that have tried to diversify globally have often ended up with burnt fingers. Exporting from Australia is one thing, but setting up and operating internationally is another kettle of fish entirely and often proves to be unsuccessful.

Single-stock diversification

It's possible to diversify by investing in just one stock, such as a diversified managed fund or an investment company. There are a number of Australian listed investment companies (LICs) and exchange-traded funds (ETFs) that invest in a wide variety of different securities in both the Australian market and overseas ones—notably the USA. When the company or fund is listed in Australia, you can trade its shares using the ASX facility in the same way as all other shares.

Tip

I suggest you consider including at least one LIC or ETF in your portfolio. By doing so, you can obtain diversification with just one stock. As a bonus, Australian LICs and ETFs generally have a good track record of profitability.

Avoiding irrational optimism or pessimism

In previous chapters I've pointed out that it's generally safer to follow a trend rather than to go against it. While this is usually the safest and best strategy, there's a heightened risk associated with following the trend when the trend moves into a region of irrational optimism or pessimism. This occurs when traders get 'carried away' and the hype drives prices to unreasonably high or low levels that subsequently prove unsustainable. Irrational optimism or pessimism can occur with specific shares, sectors or the market as a whole.

To understand how this happens, imagine a share price that has been rising for some time. Traders and investors sense the mood of optimism—they want to jump on board and get a slice of the action because of their fear of missing out (FOMO). This drives prices even higher and adds fuel to the fire. Prices rise beyond a sustainable level, because it's a level that can't be justified by a rational analysis of realistic earnings prospects. The opposite effect can occur when prices are driven down for some time in a mood of pessimism, sparking a fear of loss that can end up being almost a panic.

When irrational optimism or pessimism take hold in the market, the inevitable consequence is that eventually someone 'pulls the plug', leading to a sudden reaction in the opposite direction. I've illustrated this in figures 11.3 and 11.4, which are pictorial representations of irrational optimism and the subsequent correction to the long-term trendline.

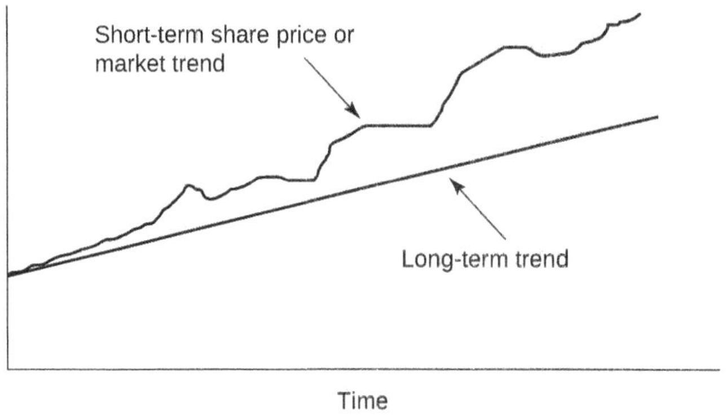

Figure 11.3: Irrational optimism

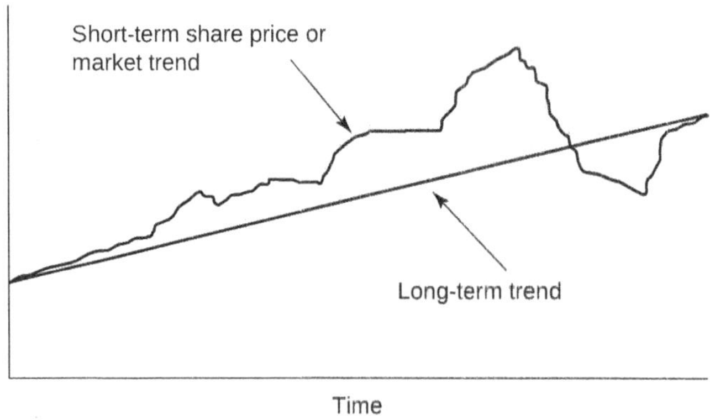

Figure 11.4: Irrational optimism correction

There are two signal markers that help you identify irrational optimism (and the opposite effects for irrational pessimism):

- The price rises to well above the longer-term trendline.
- The P/E ratio (price/earnings ratio) rises to well above the historical sector level to a level that's unsustainable. That's to say, the price can't be justified by realistic earnings expectations.

Tip

When a price climbs high above the long-term trendline or when a P/E ratio rises to a level that can't be justified by earnings (and is much higher than the sector average), beware, as sooner or later a downward correction is likely to occur. On the other hand, a price correction to an irrationally low level, after a fall, can present a good buying opportunity, provided the bounce is sustained and not a 'dead cat' bounce (that is, the bounce is only brief, and the price subsequently continues to decline).

Avoiding personal bias

We all have our unique likes and dislikes, and this applies to investing as much as it does to anything else. Personal bias when investing can result in a 'blinkered' view that disrupts rational decision making. For example, a well-known confirmation bias is that we tend to heed new information that reinforces our own belief system and ignore (or play down) any new information that contradicts it. With investing, this bias causes us to look at investments we like through 'rose-coloured spectacles' and downplay any negative indications. At the same time, we tend to ignore the positive signs that may affect shares we don't like.

As much as you might think you're making rational investing decisions, you can't avoid a certain amount of personal bias. In particular, try to avoid 'falling in love' with favoured investments that in the past have made you good profits and that you feel an attachment to.

> **Tip**
>
> The world is constantly changing, and good investments in the past won't necessarily be good ones going forward, so you need to re-evaluate your investing preferences constantly in the light of changing circumstances.

A good way of preventing personal bias from influencing your investing decisions is to avoid decisions based on 'gut feeling' and instead try to be rational and make decisions based on sound planning using fundamental and technical analysis.

> **Tip**
>
> Be aware of the risk of personal bias affecting your investing decisions; try to make rational and objective decisions rather than subjective ones. It can be most helpful to have a rational plan and *stick to it*. Chapter 6 provides a guide to planning your online share trades.

Investing as a partnership

Rather than 'going it alone', you may be able to participate in an investing partnership. This can be an informal arrangement or a formally set up partnership.

Advantages include:

- There's more capital available; for example, a partnership with ten investors contributing $5000 each has a cash pool of $50 000 to invest.
- You share the risk. Clearly with ten investors, each investor is bearing only 10% of the overall risk.
- You can bounce ideas around with others and obtain fresh insights and viewpoints. This can be an enjoyable experience as well as an opportunity to broaden your horizons. It also helps to prevent you from getting 'into a rut' or succumbing to personal bias.

- You get into a disciplined routine of reviewing the performance of the portfolio regularly.

The disadvantages are:

- If you want to set up a formal investing partnership, it takes time (and some cost) to set up a partnership agreement, open a partnership bank account and obtain a tax file number.
- If the partnership is formally set up, it's necessary to file a separate tax return.
- You'll need to attend meetings that may not always be held at a convenient time or venue for you, although a conference call may be a feasible option.

Tip

Sharing investing ideas with others helps to broaden your perspective and minimise the risk of personal bias.

Avoiding profit erosion

Profit erosion can occur when your investment is showing good 'paper' profit but you don't cash in all or part of the profit. If there's a subsequent downturn in fortune, you could watch in dismay as your profit dwindles or even turns into a loss.

A strategy to avoid this is to set profit stops (profit targets) with your broker. This is a conditional selling order that crystallises your profit when a target price is reached. If your profit stop is activated, the risk of a price fall is eliminated. After your order transacts, it makes no difference to you if the price falls because your profits are already in your account.

Another strategy is to set stop-loss orders with your online broker. This order won't prevent some profit erosion if the price falls, but it should limit the amount of the fall so you still can exit with a profit.

Profit stops and stop-loss orders were outlined in chapter 7 and you may wish to review this discussion before utilising this strategy. The chief disadvantage of profit stops is that they limit your profits when prices are rising. I tend not to use them because they violate my fundamental principle of not selling in a rising market. I prefer to use stop-loss orders, raising the trigger if the price rises but not revising it downward if the price falls. However, this is a personal preference, and many authors and trading systems advocate the use of profit stops. They justify this strategy by quoting the stock market maxim: *You can't go broke by taking profits.* To which I counter, '*You can't become rich by selling too soon*'.

Tip

I feel it's better to let profits run until there's a trend change rather than selling when a pre-set profit-stop price is reached. However, you need to make up your own mind about this, as many analysts advocate the use of profit stops.

Avoiding sequential trading

Sequential trading occurs with share investing when you sell shares in one stock and reinvest all your capital from that sale into the purchase of shares in another stock. This carries an inherent risk because of a mathematical quirk that has nothing to do with the specific shares involved.

For example, consider the following scenario.

You buy a parcel of shares for $1.00 each. The price rises by 50% then falls by 50%. Are you better off or worse off, or do you break even? The surprising answer is that you're worse off. If the price rises by 50%, the share price will rise to $1.50. If the price now falls by 50%, the price will fall to $0.75 and you've made a 25% loss! Strangely, the same effect occurs when the price falls by 50% and then rises by 50%. You still make a loss of 25%!

The risk applies to your share trades when you trade sequentially; that is, you reinvest all proceeds from one sale into another. For example, you buy a $2000 parcel of speculative shares. Subsequently the price rises by 50% and you sell the shares for $3000. If you use the proceeds to buy another parcel of shares you will be trading sequentially. If the price now falls by 50%, you make a loss of 25% on the combined trades because your capital has dwindled to $1500, so you've lost $500!

An obvious strategy to avoid this problem is not to reinvest all your capital from one trade into another; that is, try to maintain a relatively constant value for each trade. This allows you to increase your total investing capital and allows you to re-invest in other securities and thus increase your diversification. In the previous example, after you've sold the first parcel for $3000 you invest only your original parcel value of $2000 on the next trade and keep $1000 in cash. If, on the second trade, the price falls by 50% and you sell the shares, you will receive proceeds of $1000. The net result of the combined two trades is a break even and not a loss, because you still have the $1000 of capital in cash you kept from the original sale and you get $1000 from the second trade sale. So, you still have $2000 of investing capital, which is what you started with.

The general way of applying this strategy is to maintain approximately equal parcel values. Then if the share price of one parcel rises by a certain percentage and the other falls by the same percentage you break even and don't make a loss on the combined trades.

Tip

If you can pick a string of winners, sequential trading can produce large profits. But it's a very risky strategy and one I suggest you avoid unless the market is in a prolonged bull phase (or you're very good at picking a string of winners).

'Getting it wrong'

When you trade in the expectation of future price action, you naturally think you're right. But it's a sobering thought to remember that you can't buy unless someone else sells and you can't sell unless someone else buys. In most cases, therefore, another trader is taking the opposite view to yours. I hope by now you've taken on board my suggestions and are planning your trades using sound fundamental and technical analysis to give yourself the best chance of getting it right. Perhaps you're inclined to think you have an edge on other traders who aren't quite as clever or disciplined as you are. There's no doubt that some people have a natural flair for predicting price movements and get it right most of the time; however, in my experience there aren't many fools investing, so it's not easy to consistently have a run of winning trades or consistently beat other investors. I suggest that a good mindset is for you to think that despite all your good planning or possible cleverness, it may turn out that you're right only half the time.

This might seem like a rather depressing thought, but all is not lost. In fact, even if you're right only half the time, there are three strategies available that enable you to still make a profit. The only time these strategies won't work is when the entire market is in a strong bear phase, in which case 'all boats fall when the tide goes out'.

The three strategies are:

1. multi-parcel trading (cost or price averaging)
2. applying a 1% rule
3. letting profits run but limiting losses.

Strategy 1—Multi-parcel trading

This strategy when applied to purchases is also known as 'cost averaging' and when applied to selling as 'price averaging'. The multi-parcel strategy is a variation of the principle of 'not putting all your eggs in one basket'. Suppose you have $20 000 trading capital that you want to invest in a particular security because you're anticipating a price rise. Rather than buying a single $20 000 parcel, you could buy an initial parcel of $10 000. You then wait to see what happens. If you're right and the price rises, you could buy another $10 000 parcel. If you're wrong and the price falls, you don't buy any more shares and indeed, should the price fall to your stop-loss limit, you sell.

This strategy is sometimes described as 'having an each-way bet', but it really isn't the same type of strategy at all. When you place a wager, you can't change your bet after you've placed it, regardless of how the race progresses. Multi-parcel trading is more like placing an initial bet and then being able to watch how the race progresses before you decide whether to wager more or to cut your losses and get out.

You might wonder about the value of the multi-parcel strategy if you assume you're correct in your judgement only 50% of the time. It seems that half the time you'll make more profit and half the time you'll make less profit. Since there are additional trading costs involved, in the long run it seems you'll make less profit by using a multi-parcel trading strategy. In fact, when applied with sound strategies, multi-parcel trading can improve long-run trading profitability, as the following example will demonstrate.

Tip

Multi-parcel trading is a very good risk management strategy for online trading because the low trading cost doesn't have a significant impact on profits. If the parcel value is high, you can extend multi-parcel trading to three or even more parcels.

Example 2

You have $20000 to invest in shares. After careful analysis, you've selected XYZ shares, currently trading at $10.00. For the purpose of this exercise, I'll assume you can trade online with a parcel value up to $20000 for a cost of $20.

Single-parcel strategy

Buy 2000 shares at $10.00.

If the price rises, hold the shares but set a trailing stop loss of 10% of the market price.

If the price falls to $9.00 after the original purchase, sell.

Multi-parcel strategy

Buy 1000 shares at $10.00.

If the price rises to $10.50, buy another 1000 shares and use a trailing stop loss of 10% for the total shareholding.

If the price falls to $9.00 after the original purchase, sell.

(continued)

I'll now look at 'getting it right and wrong' scenarios and assume they're equally probable:

Scenario A: You get it right and the share price rises to $12.00.

Scenario B: You get it wrong and the share price falls to $8.00.

Single-parcel strategy

Buy cost: 2000 shares @ $10.00 = 20000 + 20 = $20020

Scenario A: Price rises to $12.00

Shares value = 2000 × 12 = $24000

Profit = 24000 – 20020 = $3980

And you continue to hold.

Scenario B: Price falls to $8.00 but you sell at $9.00

Revenue from sale = 2000 × 9.00 – 20 = $17980

Loss 17980 – 20020 = –$2040

Assuming each scenario is equally probable, the combined probable value of the single-parcel strategy is:

3980 – 2040 = $1940

Multi-parcel strategy

Buy cost: Initial parcel: 1000 shares@ $10.00 = 10000 + 20 = $10020

Scenario A: Price rises to $12.00

You bought another 1000 shares when the price reaches $10.50.

Buy cost: 1000 shares @$10.50 = 10500 + 20 = $10520

Total buy cost for both parcels: 10020 + 10520 = $20540

Shares value 2000 × 12 = $24000

Profit = 24 000 – 20 540 = $3460

And you continue to hold.

Scenario B: Price falls to $8.00 but you sell the parcel of 1000 shares@ $9.00

Revenue from sale = 1000 × 9.00 – 20 = $8980

Loss = 8980 – 10 020 = –$1040

Assuming each scenario is equally probable, the combined probable value of the multi-parcel strategy is:

3460 – 1040 = $2420

Conclusion

You can see that if you get it right, the single-parcel trade results in $520 more profit than the multi-parcel trade, but if you get it wrong it results in a $1000 greater loss. This is because if the price rises, both single- and multi-parcel trades produce profit on 2000 shares, but in the multi-parcel trade, if the price falls, the loss is incurred on only 1000 shares and not 2000. So, if you assume that it's just as likely that you could get it wrong as get it right, you swing the odds in your favour by multi-parcel trading.

Note that in this example, when the share price rises, I've assumed you continue to hold, so the profit at this stage is an unrealised one; that is, a paper profit. If you did crystallise profits, the actual profits would be slightly less ($20) due to brokerage.

Strategy 2—The 1% rule

Another strategy you can use to manage the 'getting it wrong' risk is based on the 1% rule. The rule is to limit your loss on any one trade to only a small proportion of your available capital; that is, 1% of it.

As an example of the rule, suppose your total investing capital is $100 000. You buy parcels of maximum value $10 000 and set a maximum 10% stop loss on any one trade. If you get it wrong, your maximum loss on a trade is $1000, which is 1% of your trading capital. With smaller amounts of investing capital, you can still use the 1% rule provided you reduce the parcel value of any one trade. For example, with $20 000 investing capital you would need to limit the parcel value to $2000 in order to apply the 1% rule with a 10% stop loss. By doing so, if you get it wrong you'll still lose no more than 1% of your investing capital.

I've derived the following formula to allow you to calculate the maximum parcel value for any single trade using the 1% rule:

$$\text{Maximum parcel value} = \frac{\text{Total investing capital} \times 0.01\%}{\text{stop loss}\left(\text{expressed as a decimal}\right)}$$

For example, if your share investing capital is $70 000 and you apply a 10% stop loss (0.1 decimal), the maximum parcel value would be:

$$\frac{70\ 000 \times 0.01}{0.1} = \$7000$$

When you set a 10% stop loss on this parcel, if you get it wrong your maximum loss is 10% of $7000, which is $700. This is equal to 1% of your investing capital, because 1% of $70 000 is $700.

Note that for simplicity's sake I don't include trading costs when I use the 1% rule, so if a stop loss is activated, the actual loss will be a little higher than indicated.

Tip

Some investment advisers recommend a 2% rule, but a 1% rule gives a higher margin for safety and is the one I suggest you use. The beauty of the 1% rule is that even if you get it wrong with five trades in a row, you'll lose a little less than 5% of your total investing capital. Assuming there's an equal likelihood of getting it wrong as getting it right, the chances of getting it wrong five times in a row are 1 in 32 or only about 3%—which, I don't need to tell you, is very unlikely.

Strategy 3—Let profits run but limit losses

The single most important investing strategy is to let your profits run but limit your losses. If you apply this strategy in combination with the 1%

rule, you can make a profit even if you're right only half the time, and even if the market is directionless (sideways trend). I'll demonstrate how this works in the following example.

Example 3

Let's say you have $20 000 to invest and you purchase shares in ten different stocks for your portfolio, investing $2000 in each. I'll assume that your choice of shares turns out to be a 50/50 proposition; that is, it turns out that you've chosen as many losers as winners and the up and down movements are equal. The letters A to J have been used to denote these shares.

After one year, the situation is as shown in table 11.2.

Table 11.2: Share price movements

A	up 50%
B	up 20%
C	up 10%
D	up 5%
E	no move
F	no move
G	down 5%
H	down 10%
I	down 20%
J	down 50%

If you adopt a buy-and-hold or 'bottom drawer' strategy, you'll finish the year even—with no capital gains profit or loss on your portfolio.

Let's now see what happens if you use strategy 3 and limit your losses but let your profits run. A simple form of this strategy is as follows: if a share price goes down 10%, sell—otherwise hold.

The profit/loss using this strategy is summarised in table 11.3 (overleaf). Note that for the sake of simplicity in this example I've ignored brokerage.

Table 11.3: Profit/loss using strategy 3

Shares	Invested ($)	Price change over year	Sell ($) or hold (H)	P/L ($)
A	2000	+50%	H	1000
B	2000	+20%	H	400
C	2000	+10%	H	200
D	2000	+5%	H	100
E	2000	0	H	0
F	2000	0	H	0
G	2000	–5%	H	–100
H	2000	–10%	S	–200
I	2000	–20%	Sell at –10%	–200
J	2000	–50%	Sell at –10%	–200
Total	**20 000**		**Total**	**1000**

By using this simple strategy you're showing a $1000 capital gain on your portfolio, as compared with breaking even with a buy-and-hold strategy. Note that, as with the previous example, the profits shown in this table are actual 'paper' profits because you're still holding your winners.

Conclusion

This example illustrates the tremendous importance of the strategy of cutting losses while letting profits run. Even if you select as many losers as winners in a sideways trending market, you can still make a 5% capital gain with your portfolio. If your selected shares pay a reasonable dividend of about 4% fully franked, giving a grossed-up yield of about 6%, your portfolio actually shows a total profit of about 11%—and this in a directionless market and with only 50% winners! Imagine how well you can do if you improve your selection expertise so you select more winners than losers—particularly if the market is in a bull phase where most share prices trend up!

Key points

- Risk and potential return (profit) are linked, and if you want a higher return on your investing capital you need to accept a higher risk.
- Share investing is more risky than safer alternatives, such as bank deposits, but in the long run produces higher profits. These profits can be from dividends or capital growth (or both). In addition, as noted previously, franked dividends receive favourable taxation treatment that boosts your profit further, whereas interest on bank deposits doesn't get this benefit.
- With investing, you need to change your mindset from risk minimisation to risk management.
- It's a good idea to get a feeling for your risk profile; that is, the amount of risk you're comfortable with. Your investments should be compatible with your risk profile.
- Risk is closely related to volatility—the short-term fluctuation above or below the average trend. The greater the volatility, the higher the risk.
- The Australian sharemarket rises and falls over the years, but over many years the overall trend has been upward. In addition to the capital gains potential, many shares pay a good dividend (often fully franked) that provides a steady income stream regardless of price fluctuations. Therefore a simple but effective investing strategy with shares is to be a long-term investor.
- When considering an investment, try to estimate a realistic downside potential (maximum loss) as the worst-case scenario. At the same time try to estimate a realistic upside potential as the best-case scenario. Then calculate the ratio of upside to downside potential and select investments that maximise this ratio.
- You can reduce the downside potential risk by using stop-loss orders (particularly on your more speculative trades).
- Profit stops effectively eliminate the risk of a paper profit turning into a loss should there be a downturn. However, profit stops violate the strategy of letting profits run, so you need to take this into account when considering using profit stops.

- Diversification reduces risk but also reduces the likelihood of substantial above-market gains. A concentrated portfolio is riskier but offers the potential for above-market returns. To diversify effectively with shares, you need at least five and preferably ten stocks in different sectors.
- Another good way of diversifying is by investing in a listed investment company (LIC) or exchange-traded fund (ETF).
- Beware of irrational optimism and pessimism in the market because, usually, a correction will follow.
- Signal markers indicating irrational optimism are when the price rises upward well above an established trendline and the P/E ratio rises to well above the historical sector level to one that's unsustainable—that is, the price can't be justified by a realistic earnings forecast.
- When irrational pessimism corrects and optimism appears, this can be a good buying opportunity.
- Beware of personal bias in your investment decisions and particularly 'falling in love' with investments that have been good performers in the past.
- Sequential trading carries an inbuilt mathematical risk that can be managed by diversifying and keeping the parcel value of each trade approximately the same.
- With each trade you make, you run the risk of 'getting it wrong'. Remember that there's always a trader who is taking the opposite view to yours.
- Even if you get it wrong half the time, there are three strategies you can use that enable you to still make a profit.
- One of these strategies is multi-parcel trading. This strategy is particularly applicable to online trading because of the low brokerage. The strategy will reduce your profits if you get it right but will more than compensate for this over the long run by reducing your losses if you get it wrong.
- Another strategy is the 1% rule, which limits your losses on any single trade so that even if you get it wrong several times in a row the effect on your entire investing capital won't be disastrous.

- The most important investing strategy of all is to cut losses but let profits run. This strategy allows you to make a profit in a directionless market, even if you get it right only as often as you get it wrong.
- If you apply the strategies I've outlined in this book to the planning and management of your share investments, you should be able to make excellent profits from online investing in the Australian sharemarket, especially in the longer term.

Index

Note: Page numbers in **bold** indicate tables and *italics* indicate figures.

Printed and bound by CPI Group (UK) Ltd, Croydon, CR0 4YY
11/08/2026
02193754-0002